Presented to

MILWAUKEE
PUBLIC
LIBRARY

for the
Citizens of Milwaukee
from the

MILWAUKEE
JOURNAL SENTINEL

ENTER
THE PAST TENSE

Other Intelligence Memoirs and Biographies from Potomac Books

American Guerrilla: My War Behind Japanese Lines
by Roger Hilsman

Counterspy: Memoirs of a Counterintelligence Officer in World War II and the Cold War by Richard W. Cutler

Flawed Patriot: The Rise and Fall of CIA Legend Bill Harvey
by Bayard Stockton

Gatekeeper: Memoirs of a CIA Polygraph Examiner
by John F. Sullivan

Hide and Seek: Intelligence, Law Enforcement, and the Stalled War on Terrorist Finance by John A. Cassara

The Meinertzhagen Mystery: The Life and Legend of a Colossal Fraud
by Brian Garfield

The One That Got Away: My SAS Mission Behind Enemy Lines
by Chris Ryan

White Tigers: My Secret War in Korea
by Ben S. Malcom with Ron Martz

ENTER
THE PAST TENSE

MY SECRET LIFE
AS A CIA ASSASSIN

Roland W. Haas

Potomac Books, Inc.
Washington, D.C.

Library of Congress Cataloging-in-Publication Data
Haas, Roland W., 1952–
 Enter the past tense : my secret life as a CIA assassin / Roland W.
Haas.
    p. cm.
 Includes index.
 ISBN 978-1-59797-086-0 (alk. paper)
 1. Haas, Roland W., 1952– 2. Intelligence officers—United
States—Biography. 3. United States. Central Intelligence
Agency—Officials and employees—Biography. I. Title. II. Title:
My secret life as a CIA assassin.
 JK468.I6H377 2007
 327.12730092—dc22
 [B]   2007007591

ISBN-13: 978-1-59797- 086-0
(alk. paper)

Printed in the United States of America on acid-free paper that
meets the American National Standards Institute Z39-48
Standard.

Potomac Books, Inc.
22841 Quicksilver Drive
Dulles, Virginia 20166

First Edition

10 9 8 7 6 5 4 3 2 1

To my wife, Marilyn,
and my children, Annemarie and Damien,
who stuck by me during my darkest hours

and

To Colonel (Ret.) Ben Malcom,
a true American hero
who showed me the way and opened the doors.

CONTENTS

FOREWORD

I met Roland Haas one day in 1998 while working out at Gold's Gym in Peachtree City, Georgia. I am a retired Army Special Forces Colonel while Roland was the Assistant Deputy Chief of Staff for Intelligence for the U.S. Army Reserve Command at Fort McPherson, Georgia. Over the next several months, we had the opportunity to talk at length and soon came to share some of our similar experiences working under cover around the world for the U.S. government.

During 1952, I was inserted 150 miles behind enemy lines in North Korea and was the only American leading an eight-hundred-man North Korean guerrilla unit in support of South Korea. In 1990, this TOP SECRET special forces/CIA joint operation was downgraded to unclassified. By 1994, I started writing a book about this operation in North Korea. My coauthor, Ron Martz, and I wrote to the CIA on February 7, 1994, and requested the release of certain information detailing my joint operations with the CIA. The CIA turned down our request. I then contacted Maj. Gen. John Singlaub who had been the CIA station chief in Seoul during my operations in 1952, and he agreed to write the foreword to my book, verifying my claims. That book, *White Tigers, My Secret War in North Korea*, was published by Brassey's, Inc., in December 1996.

Roland read my book and invited me to give an address to about two hundred key personnel at the Reserve Command headquarters as part of the command's officer professional development seminar series on June 1, 2001. Over the course of the next year, Roland and I continued to meet and discuss our past experiences, going into ever more detail. I was impressed with Roland's background and encouraged him to start writing a book detailing his exploits with the Agency in support of the U.S. government.

In December 2005, Roland advised me that he had completed a draft manuscript and had started looking for a publisher. After reading his work, I sent an e-mail to my editor highly recommending he read the proposed book. To help ensure that Roland was who he claimed to be and had actually done what was described in his book, my editor, knowing that I maintained ties with the Agency and the Army Special Operations School, asked if I could vouch for Roland. I replied that I had absolutely no reservations in vouching for Roland.

Based on the problems I had encountered trying to persuade our government agencies to release information pertaining to my record, I advised Roland to skip that tedious, hopeless step and proceed without Agency approval. I advised him to validate his story through a combination of pictures that he had maintained as he moved from country to country throughout Asia and Communist Eastern Europe, his original passport with the valid stamps and dates showing his presence in these key countries, and whatever official documents, orders, and so on he might be able to acquire. Luckily, he had a lot of this material at hand.

The story of our government's role in using highly trained professionals to do certain unsavory but very necessary types of undercover/clandestine missions is not often pretty but has been in need of telling for some time. I can't think of a more knowledgeable and experienced person to tell that very important story than Roland Haas.

Ben S. Malcom
COL, US Army (Retired)

PREFACE

I was taught that when writing an informative piece, especially in military writing, it is imperative to use the BLUF (Bottom Line Up Front) method. In writing this book, this posed a problem for me in that there are so many "bottom lines."

I have been—in no particular order—a son, brother, husband, father, star gymnast, gym owner, champion weightlifter, black-belt-level martial artist, biker, stellar student, actor, writer, poet, teacher, artist, patriot, aspiring Marine, spy, and senior intelligence officer for a major Army command. I have also been a hypocrite, liar, thief, alcoholic, drug abuser, patient in a substance abuse rehabilitation center, and last, but not least, a killer. I have taken six of the Seven Deadly Sins (leaving out Sloth) and raised them to an art form, happily adding them as character traits rather than defects. I have been beaten, knifed, shot, and tortured. I have arrogantly knocked at death's door often and have been granted brief access a couple of times. Although my motives were always justified, at least from my perspective, I cannot mince words in my defense. I am who I am, and more to the point, I have done what I have done. The blame begins and ends with me.

Among these bottom lines, I suppose the one that matters the most to me is the reason for writing this story in the first place. My family deserves to know, after all of these years, who and what I have been, as well as who and what I am now. How and why did I spiral into such self-destructive be-havior? What is it that drives a highly motivated overachiever to look at his own potential destruction as excitement and as a potential release more than anything else? Moreover, this book is also my attempt at making amends to many whom I can no longer reach.

There is, of course, the danger that in also revealing my-self as a reformed alcohol and drug abuser, I am giving the skeptical reader the opportunity to dismiss my story as fan-tastic and delusional. However, I am not writing this book to convince anybody about anything and have long been sensitive to the fact that there is a lot in the world that one doesn't understand and that one's beliefs or disbeliefs do not change reality.

In writing this book, I have changed the names of many of the people who have had supporting roles in this story. First, it is not my purpose to embarrass or disparage anyone still living. Also, I don't wish to be prosecuted at this late date for anybody's demise, in which I may have played a part, es-pecially in some foreign country. Other people—some fam-ily, some friends, and some celebrities—appear as them-selves in that either their roles have been totally innocu-ous or they are just too well known for me to attempt to mask their identities.

There will also be some gaps in the narrative, intentional on my part, in that I cannot divulge activities that may be classified. I will not put anybody in harm's way by divulging certain sources or methods. Additionally, I also have abso-lutely no interest in being charged with violating any of the regulations, acts, and laws regulating what United States citi-zens involved in intelligence operations can and cannot do. One thing in my favor is that the government will absolutely deny some of what is contained here. Since you cannot clas-sify what you do not acknowledge as ever having happened, I am confident that I am breaking no trust.

I am not a historian; this book is not meant to be an official account of U.S. involvement in the internal affairs of foreign governments. As I have already stated, I am quite certain that the U.S. government, and, perhaps some others, will be very quick to disavow any knowledge of anything in this book in general or of me in particular.

What this book does portend to be is a subjective account of one man's experience of and involvement in what historical perspective might ultimately come to see as meaningful events in Europe and the Middle East. It is, in the final analysis, the story of my headlong march into the past tense.

Roland W. Haas
Atlanta, Georgia

May 2007

CHAPTER 1

THE TRANSITION BEGINS

Roland Walter Haas began his rapid transition into the past tense on March 17, 1971, at the Naval ROTC facility of Purdue University in West Lafayette, Indiana. He did not find out he had an incurable disease or get hit by a truck, or suffer any other life-ending accident. He did, however, cease to exist as he had been known to family and friends, and even to himself. Roland entered the past tense.

I was taught that unless a person is dead or absent, one should not refer to him in the third person. This presents a real problem for me in that I am here and alive. "Roland," however, is quite dead and has been for more than thirty years now. However, to keep the confusion level down as much as possible, I'll just refer to myself in the first person as if who I was before 1971 and who I am now are the same man.

It was a typical March day in Indiana, not yet spring, but winter was slowly and messily trudging its way off of the calendar. I was in my second semester at Purdue University on a full scholarship with Naval ROTC. Although it was Naval ROTC, I had decided that I was going to take the Marine Corps route, an option open to overtly gung-ho midshipmen. Unfortunately, this was an unpopular decision among my friends and family. By 1970, the U.S. involvement in Viet Nam was viewed with great animosity by most of the American public, and those who went to fight were often jeered as baby killers rather than hailed as soldiers. As an ultra-conservative school located in the middle of Indiana, Purdue did not suffer through the virulent antiwar protests that plagued other colleges around the country; as a matter of fact, all of the branches of its ROTC were completely full. Even so, the school and surrounding community failed to support what our military was doing in Southeast Asia, especially since the action in Viet Nam did not seem to be a war with any end in sight. But unpopularity was a position I could tolerate, having grown used to it over the years in my personal life. So becoming one of what I considered to be an elite group of heroes seemed like the right thing to do.

On that day in March, I was ordered to report to the ROTC building by the corps commander for what I was hoping would be routine career counseling, and not something worse. I had already discovered that in the Marine option, anyone could be rebuked for all kinds of mundane reasons. And in my observation, along with those who were gung-ho patriots, the Marine midshipman corps also seemed to attract sadistic sociopaths who had made it into college. I was not sure into which category the corps commander was placing me, or for that matter, which category he was in. With plenty of fear and trembling, I entered the office of my military advisor, a 5′4″ Marine major who reminded me of the little chicken hawk in the Foghorn Leghorn cartoons, since he was always pounding his chest. He also had a reputation for bedding the female midshipmen. Apparently, that was considered a perk, and was one of the reasons I chose the Marine Corps option in the first place, in the hope of exercising it if I came back as an ROTC instructor.

After the obligatory berating from the Major (and the equally obligatory servile groveling from me), he told me to take a seat. Things were looking up; I would not have been ordered to sit if I were in trouble. My military personnel file was on the desk in front of him. I reevaluted; maybe

I was in trouble after all. The Major told me that somebody outside of our chain of command wanted to talk to me.

At that point, a man in civilian clothes whom I did not recognize entered the room, dismissed the Major, and took his place at the desk in front of me. Without introduction, he said that he had been reviewing my records. He pulled another, thicker folder out of his briefcase, which also had my name on it, opened it, and started telling me my own life history. He told me things about myself that I never suspected existed in any files. He reviewed my life from my years as a young boy on into high school. I was growing increasingly uncomfortable. My whole purpose while attending Purdue had been to blend in and not attract any undue attention, good or bad. My performance of the military duties necessary to a midshipman had been mediocre at best and unsuitable to the point of embarrassment for somebody pursuing a commission in the Marine Corps—if that was the reason the man was reviewing my files.

However, then he started on a strange kind of interview.

"So how's your German?"

"I thought you knew all there was to know about me."

"Just answer the question."

"Native. I spoke it before I could speak English."

"Any particular dialect?"

"Bavarian. But you name it, give me a week, and I'll speak it."

"Romance languages?"

"Five years of Latin. I guess I can learn others if I had to."

Then he went on in Russian:

"Вы говорите, что Вы можете говорить на русском языке."

You say you can speak Russian.

"Я не говорил. Но да я могу."

I didn't say that. But yes, I can.

"Где Вы учились говорить на русском языке?"
Where did you learn to speak Russian?

I answered again as we continued our conversation in Russian.

"To this point, I have been pretty much self-taught. I enjoy reading Russian novels and actually enjoy Dostoevsky and Tolstoy."

"Do you think that you could pass as a Russian?"

"Yes, I'm pretty sure that I could."

"And what makes you think that?"

"I also read Russian newspapers and watch Russian movies. They give me a much more contemporary frame of reference. Besides, I am blonde and have some Russian features."

"And what about the favorite Russian pastime, drinking? Do you think you would be able to handle your vodka?"

"I don't see a problem there. Like a champ, actually!" (Although the drinking thing was more boast than reality at that point in my life, it would soon prove to be a very prophetic statement.)

"Russians really love to curse."

"Believe me, I know it!"

"So what would you say if you wanted to curse up a storm and sound like an authentic Russian?"

"I would start with your mother! Russians have a real thing about mothers and sex, and more specifically, mothers with male genitalia."

"OK. That's enough. No need to belabor the point. You also have some Russian relatives, don't you?"

"Yes, that would be my Uncle Mike. Mikhail Tarnawskj —he lives in Buffalo. He is actually Ukranian, served in the Russian army, and then got captured by the Germans. He was smart and stayed in Germany after World War II. He married my Aunt Agnes, or Tante Aja as we kids call her, my father's cousin."

"Did he ever speak Russian to you or did he ever speak about politics?"

"A little Russian now and then, nothing really involved. As far as politics goes, it never really came up."

At this point, he shifted back into English, so I followed suit.

"So virtually your entire family is foreign born?"

"Pretty much. Two uncles have married American girls, but the rest are pretty much all German."

"And one Russian."

"Yes, and one Russian."

"And what about the political leanings of the rest of your immediate family? Wasn't your father a German soldier in the war?"

"If you could call it that. From what I know, my father was just a kid who got drafted near the end of the war when Hitler was left with old men and young boys to carry on the fight for a lost cause. He was one of the lucky ones. Got captured by the Americans in France. At least that's the way I heard the story. It undoubtedly saved his life. When he got back to Germany, he worked for the de-Nazification bureau. As soon as the chance offered itself, he decided to emigrate. He could have gone to Africa and get into the wood industry, but instead he chose to go to America. Soon after landing in the United States, he joined the New York National Guard both as a show of loyalty and as a way to learn English. All of my relatives who came over to the U.S. are, without question, loyal Americans. I don't think any of them would ever move back to Germany. And I know they wouldn't want to change anything here, even if they could. Every one of them always votes a straight Republican ticket. Really conservative."

"Just one more thing. We know that you have corresponded with Radio Moscow and Radio Peking. Radio Peking even sent you a copy of readings from Chairman Mao. What's that all about?"

"Just a short wave radio hobby thing. It's something a lot of my friends were into back in Lakewood. You cruise the radio dial until you hear a program you can understand. Log everything you hear and send a report of that transmission log to the station. After they verify that you did indeed hear their transmission, they send you something called a QSL card. Don't ask me what that's actually supposed to stand for, but it verifies that you did indeed receive their broadcast. It's kind of like a postcard with their call letters or station name on it. They're like baseball cards; you just try to collect as many as you can. I've actually corresponded with over 100 radio stations, including places like Prague and Tirana, Albania. Sometimes they go ahead and send you some other stuff, usually propaganda. Nothing special about Moscow or Peking."

"Nothing except the fact that the U.S. Postal Service notifies certain authorities when it notices that somebody is getting mail from hostile or communist countries. You and your whole family were on a watch list for quite some time because of the stuff they sent you."

"Believe me, it was just the harmless hobby of a high school loner with lots of time on his hands."

He seemed satisfied with what I had said. At least he didn't betray any feelings one way or the other. Then, he visibly relaxed a little bit and smiled as he explained that apparently I had piqued considerable interest somewhere, kind of like a high school football standout who is being watched by college scouts. And now I was being given the chance to opt for a particular discipline, what the military refers to as a Military Occupational Specialty, or MOS. I found this curious since as far as I knew, except for pilots, virtually all Marine officers were infantrymen. I didn't know that a Marine officer could do much of anything else.

The man went on to explain that I was being offered the chance to go into clandestine intelligence. If I chose that path, I would opt out of any career as a Marine, soldier, airman, or any other service having to do with the conventional military forces. Sitting across from me at the desk, the man (who now told me to just call him Phil) revealed that he was a recruiter for one of our "three letter intelligence agencies." Three letter intelligence agency? The ones I knew about flashed through my head: CIA, NSA,

FBI, DIA. Who knew how many more existed?

This was beginning to feel more and more like a flashback to some acid trip. Maybe the "windowpane" the weekend before was too strong and was now making a comeback? Maybe this was still last weekend and I hadn't come down yet! Clandestine intelligence? I had heard of this kind of thing but had never met anybody directly involved. CIA recruitment of college students during the Nixon administration had become somewhat of an urban legend on campuses in the early 1970s. But this was no urban legend, nor was it some drug-induced dream. This was real.

As the gravity of this began to sink in, all I could think was, "Holy Crap! He's really, really and truly, cross my heart and hope to die, asking me if I want to become a spook!"

CHAPTER 2

PREQUEL: THE BIRTH OF A LONER

I was born on April 2, 1952, at Deaconess Hospital in Buffalo, New York. With a birth weight of exactly 7 pounds 11 ounces, and having missed April Fools' Day by barely two hours, it was generally assumed that I was going to be a pretty lucky kid. My parents, Walter and Maria Haas, were German immigrants who had come to this country just prior to my birth with virtually nothing. I was the oldest of what would eventually be a family with four children. My brother Bob came along two and a half years later, followed by my brother Ed, and finally, my sister Sharon. My earliest memories are of a horrendous childhood on Ivanhoe Road, a lower working class neighborhood in Cheektowaga, a suburb of Buffalo.

My life at home was tolerable; besides, I didn't know any better. My mother spoke little English. My father, all 132 pounds of him and armed with his prewar school English, joined the New York State National Guard and worked two jobs so that we could make ends meet. My mother took in washing and ironing. We lived in a tiny upstairs flat of a duplex. My father had managed to buy an 8mm movie projector with which we would watch the same silent Mickey Mouse cartoons over and over.

It was outside of my home where living was treacherous. I was a small, skinny kid who spoke mostly German in a working class neighborhood in the early 1950s.

Most, if not all, of the kids there had fathers who had recently returned from fighting the Nazi Huns in Europe. As these kids looked up to their parents, they naturally wanted to be like them, and in their minds, I was one of the Nazi Huns their fathers had gone away to defeat. As a result, the kids in my neighborhood reveled in making my life miserable.

Leaving the house was risky, but I didn't have much choice in the matter. Being the old-world German that she was, my mother would force me out into the sunshine and fresh air because, as every German mother knows, it was good for my health, never mind that the temperature might be 2°F outside. Little did she know how detrimental to my health going outside really was. I learned at a very young age to keep my mouth shut; maybe if I didn't say anything, the other kids wouldn't persecute me as a "no good Kraut."

The only safe places for me were the numerous cemeteries that were located a few blocks from our flat. If I was careful and lucky, I could slink from car to car, tree to tree, until I reached one of the cemeteries where I would lean up against a tombstone and read or daydream in relative peace. I was an early reader and devoured anything I could find. Ironically, my favorite cemetery was the Jewish one where many of the tombstones had pictures of the deceased. I sat for hours, running my fingers over the strange, Hebrew lettering, and fantasizing about what their lives had been like. I created elaborate families and relationships for my dead acquaintances.

It seems ironic that a kid who was constantly being beaten up just for being German would be drawn to a Jewish cemetery. I did not discover until much later that there was an eerie explanation for this. In 1923, my grandmother, Teresa Emmert, was a young girl who worked as a housekeeper for a Jewish family. Sometime during the course of her employment, she had a sexual affair (willing or not, she never said) with the head of the house that resulted in her becoming pregnant and giving birth to my father, thus giving me 25 percent Jewish blood. Considering what was beginning to happen in Germany with the rise of Adolf Hitler, it's not surprising that the source of her pregnancy was never discussed. It was stigma enough being an illegitimate child, but it would have been much worse to be illegitimate and 50 percent Jewish as well; it could have resulted in a death sentence if that knowledge had ever become public. When my grandmother wed sometime later, her husband Stefan adopted my father legally with the assumption that his paternity was "unknown."

After spending most of the day and evening in the cemetery with my fantasy companions, I skulked back home, again going from car to car and tree to tree, feeling just as empty and alone as when I started the day. If I did not have any luck sneaking out of the neighborhood, which was the case more often than not, I would be spotted, chased down, and beaten. These were not simple, everyday beatings; they were down and dirty ass whoopings. There would be nothing left of me but a heap. That was me—a heap—day after day, week after week, and never quite figuring out what I had done to deserve such violent treatment at the hands of my peers.

One time when my luck was running particularly thin, a group of neighborhood bullies followed me into a cemetery. In an attempt to hide, I ducked into a small mausoleum whose door I noticed was slightly ajar. Entering into the pitch black space from the bright sunshine, I couldn't see a thing. I had no idea what to expect in there, but I knew what would happen to me if I didn't disappear somewhere. What happened next came as a complete shock as I ended up falling some six feet onto a newly deposited but not yet cemented-over casket. There I sat in total terror, absolutely sure in my fertile imagination that any moment the newly deceased occupant of the box below would grab me and pull me inside for disturbing his rest, or worse yet, for a little company. I quickly concocted a horrible, monstrous image of an evil spirit that lurked in the blackness. It was one thing to think about the dead people as they probably were in life and assign them pleasant personalities, but it was quite another to possibly come face to face with an animated corpse. Yet at the same time I figured it would be far less painful to die of fright, which I was precariously close to, than face another beating.

Another time when I was caught by the fearless young Nazi hunters, I was tied up and dragged off to a large empty overgrown field that had a manhole leading down to a sewer in the center of it. After a quick trial, during which I never said a word or uttered any sound at all, I was sentenced to rot to death, literally. I simply sat there with curious detachment, letting my mind fly off to more pleasant places to avoid the pain. The fact that I never cried or even whimpered during the whole episode seemed to enrage my captors even more. After all, what good is terrorizing somebody if they don't show any fear and beg for mercy? It's not that I wasn't afraid; I was scared to death. I just didn't express it. They pried off the cover to the manhole and unceremoniously threw me, still tied up, down into the sewer and then replaced the heavy iron cover. Sitting down there in the darkness I could hear the rats and feel the bugs on me. And the smell was horrendous. The only thing that saved me that time was that one of the assailants got cold feet later that night. Afraid of being caught, he told his parents what they had done. His father fished me out of the sewer, untied me, and told me that I had better not tell anybody what had happened or he would personally send me back into the sewers. It was clear that his actions were motivated more by fear of what might happen to his son than any sense of decency toward some worthless immigrant kid.

One beating in particular was so bad that it sent me to the hospital at the age of eight with a ruptured appendix. My crime that day was riding my bike out in the open where I could be seen. I was chased down, knocked off my bike, and kicked senseless. I was convinced, as I am to this day, that the only thing that kept me from being killed was my ability to play dead, or nearly dead, which made them stop kicking me.

I had a strict Catholic upbringing but had early given up on receiving any relief from the God of that religion. As a matter of fact, I was pretty sure that he was in on the "kill the Kraut" campaign. Although I prayed for help, the beatings only seemed to worsen and happen with more frequency. And then it seemed that God would compound my suffering by keeping me frail and sickly. Not only did I contract all of the normal childhood diseases such as measles, mumps, and chicken pox, but a bout with a rare case of scarlet fever left me quarantined in the house with only my mother for company. There were times where I thought that I would eventually contract every disease known to man, including ones I didn't realize people couldn't catch, such as potato famine and hoof in mouth. The one advantage of being sickly was that I didn't have to go outside for a few weeks at a time while I convalesced.

I had long before become convinced that it would be better to die than to endure any more of these stompings. Since my tormenters had consistently proven themselves either incapable or unwilling to kill me on their own, I decided that it would be best if I just killed myself to end the whole thing. Along with being an early reader, I was also an early pragmatist. At the age of nine, I swallowed a full bottle of aspirin, left instructions on where I was to be buried (I didn't think my choice of the Jewish cemetery would be acceptable to my parents, but it was worth a try), and laid down, ready to die. The problem was that what I swallowed was a bottle of mild-dose aspirin for children, leaving me fairly sick, but very much alive.

A ray of hope did present itself shortly thereafter when my parents had managed to put aside enough money to buy a house slightly higher up the food chain than our flat on Ivanhoe. Moving to the new house at 360 Pine Ridge Road meant a new school, a new beginning, a chance finally to make some friends. Unfortunately, after years of not speaking at all, I found that I had no capacity for conversation. I didn't know what to say, so I continued to stay mute. This, in turn, led to the same situation I had been in before—an outsider who was considered too weird to befriend.

I did manage to make one friend, a neighbor named Frankie C., whose parents were Italian. For a while, Frankie would come over and play kickball or shoot a game of horse under our basketball hoop. Frankie was somewhat mentally impaired, but he was a friend, and that meant a lot to me at the time. There was another advantage to this friendship in that Frankie happened to have an older sister named Linda.

Frankie's sister, Linda, although a bit overweight, was pretty. Although Frankie was not very bright, next to Linda, he seemed like a genius. Linda was slow on thought of any kind. Frankie created all kinds of games for us to play, most of which involved Linda taking all of her clothes off. I had seen copies of *Playboy* magazine (a few copies of which I had procured during the course of a paper drive and which were now safely hidden in my garage), but the photos didn't have the same effect as having a real live naked Playmate. It never seemed strange to her, or maybe she didn't mind that she was the only one playing everything from kickball to hula hoop totally naked. Frankie and I would be playing some one-on-one dodge ball when Linda would want to join us. Frankie would say, "You're older than us and heavier, it wouldn't be fair if we got hit by a ball thrown by a heavier person. We could get seriously hurt." Linda would protest that that just wasn't fair, and that she wasn't that much heavier than us. After mulling over several options it was eventually decided that if she took her clothes off she would be lighter and thus the game would be fair again (I can't remember what argument was used for hula hoop, but it must have been a good one). However, sensing that something might not be right with the situation, she also never told her parents.

One thing I learned from that experience is that one person can never make another person do something he or she opposes, but most people are willing to do a lot more than they will admit if relieved of the consequences of a guilty conscience. Using a person's phobias and taboos and twisting them to seem totally natural, or conversely, that no other choice of action is possible, often meant "anything goes."

Then one winter day some of the other popular kids came over to Frankie's house and saw me there. They started to ride him about hanging out with "the weirdo" and took it to the point that Frankie was faced with a dilemma. Was he going to risk his status as one of the cooler kids at Pine Hill Elementary School, or would he put me in my place?

My answer came when Frankie cleared his throat before slowly and ceremoniously spitting a huge, sloppy gob of mucus squarely into my right eye. I guess all of those years of abuse coupled with this new humiliation at the hands of the only kid I ever thought of as a friend took its toll. I saw red and snapped. Grabbing a large ice pick, the kind that had a large big flat (and sharp-edged) piece of metal at the end of a pole, I swung with all of my skinny might and buried it deep into Frankie's side. A look of shock came over his face as he fell down while everybody else ran away screaming. I (as well as all of the other kids present) was convinced that I had killed him and, curiously, at that point I didn't really care; he was dead to me anyway as of that point.

As it was winter and Buffalo, the heavy snowsuit Frankie was wearing kept my blow from doing him any serious injury, but my outburst did have a couple of positive effects. First, although the other kids still thought I was weird, they now also believed that I was a homicidal maniac. Nobody wanted to risk me exploding and seriously harming or even killing them. Second, I realized that I could take control of a situation as long as I didn't try to play by any rules of fair play. After all, where was the fair play when they ganged up on me? From that time forward, I was essentially left alone. And that suited me fine, except for the fact that I didn't have Linda to play with anymore. It would be a long time before I would see a real live naked girl again, and that was probably the thing I found saddest about the whole situation.

CHAPTER 3

DIFFERENT TOWN, SAME STORY

The summer of 1965 offered another chance for me to break out of the lonely existence I had come to embrace. My father, who had risen in one of his jobs from stock boy to store manager—for an East Coast retail chain called Neisners—was offered a larger store in Lakewood, Ohio, a suburb of Cleveland. We were going to move again, this time not just a couple neighborhoods away, but out of town, out of state. I felt no sadness at the prospect of leaving Buffalo forever.

Spending so much time alone reading and thinking had served to sharpen my mind. In a new environment with no reputation for weirdness, I believed that I would have a chance to fit in. Add to that the fact that I would be starting seventh grade—middle school—where everybody is new to the environment. I felt bolstered and ready for the challenge.

But I was also determined that I would never again stand for being pushed around and beaten to a pulp. I joined the YMCA, which was a block from where we lived, and participated in archery, swimming, diving, judo, gymnastics, ice skating, tennis, and weightlifting. My sole purpose was to be better than anybody in any sport I took on. Still shackled with a loner mentality, I pursued individual rather than team sports. The one exception was ice hockey, where I became an all-star goalie. But even though the goalie is a member of the team, he generally stands alone, separate from the other players.

I worked my way through all levels of the Red Cross's water safety and life guarding courses rapidly and became one of the youngest ever to earn the Water Safety Instructor (WSI) badge. I had the same success with judo. Whereas the other students often held back for fear of injury, I had long been accustomed to enduring pain. With no regard for my own well being, I tore through everything the instructors could throw at me, earning belt after belt. Sometimes my aggression with the other students brought on warnings from the instructors not to be so rough in class.

The same disregard for personal safety helped me in gymnastics. Specializing in the long horse vault and floor exercise, I ran as hard as I could and hit the spring board, launching myself, twisting and turning, where I would imagine myself flying through the air like Superman. The freedom I felt was exhilarating. I would have pursued an Olympic gymnast level were it not for the fact that one boy I knew very well at the YMCA broke his neck on a dismount from the rings. Although my self-regard was low and my capacity for risk was high, I did not want his fate.

The cold, dark weight room of the YMCA also became a refuge for me. Back in 1965, few people regularly worked out with weights. Even professional football players still looked at weightlifting somewhat suspiciously. I usually had the room to myself. I had no idea what I was doing, but I would experiment endlessly, relishing the feeling in my newly discovered muscles. Grabbing the weight, I would copy things I would see in some of the early muscle magazines. Rather than dreading the pain that inevitably followed a day after heavy lifting, I relished it; it made me feel more alive. Trial and error taught me how to work my muscles. All things considered, I was lucky that I avoided doing any lasting harm to myself.

Free time was usually spent doing odd jobs to earn money. Spring and summer I cut lawns. In the fall I raked leaves. During the winters—and they are as long in Cleveland as they were in Buffalo—I would shovel snow. The money I earned went to buying protein, whether in the form of hamburgers at the local *Big Boy* restaurant or Joe Weider protein tablets, which I bought from the owner of a health food store who had been a champion competitive body builder. Protein pills in the 1960s tasted awful, but I was willing to go to any lengths to add muscle and strength. Money that was left I spent on sports equipment such as medicine balls, javelins, weight lifting items, and hockey gear.

All of this extra athletic work also led to something I had really never experienced before—recognition. Along with the belts in judo as well as the ribbons, medals, and trophies in other sports, at Harding Junior High I became a "gold striper" (somebody who aced all of the physical fitness tests in gym class) and won the coveted Amos Alonzo Stagg award as the YMCA's athlete of the year. Unfortunately, the recognition came from outside sources only.

At home I sought but didn't receive acknowledgment from my parents, who never attended a single athletic event in which I competed. When I came home with a ribbon, medal, or trophy representing nothing short of an Olympic win in my mind, my parents gave it not a second glance or mention. I didn't know whether it was that they didn't care or if their lack of expression was benign neglect. And to be fair, both of them worked so much that they were terribly tired all of the time. I was to find out later that something much worse was happening.

I looked forward to school as never before. I had made a few close friends—Fritz, Jim, Steve—and finally had people with whom I could talk. Unfortunately, there were still the bullies—greasers as they were called back then. Dressed in plain white T-shirts, jeans, and black leather jackets, they modeled themselves after the Jets in *West Side Story*, right down to the cigarette stuck behind the ear.

One boy in particular terrorized Harding Junior High, and that was Jim K. A small, greasy punk who had failed whole grades countless times, K. picked a student at random in the halls about once a week and ordered him to meet him after school at a certain place for a fight. If he showed up, he was beaten and defeated. If he didn't show up, K. hunted him down and beat him even worse.

As I feared, one day K. focused his sights on me. Not so long before I had suffered regular beatings and psychological abuse in Buffalo and I had determined never to endure that again. However, I was not fool enough to think I could stand up to Jim K. in a one-on-one fight. I did okay in judo but realized that the class space was more of a choreographed environment where I could, for instance, hit a speed bag that didn't hit back. K. had a reputation for fighting dirty, using brass knuckles, and carrying a switchblade. He was also older and much more experienced in the delivery end of street fighting. I, unfortunately, had only mastered the receiving end. And even more unfortunately, I had mastered that part of fighting very well.

But I had to show up. With a heavy feeling brought on by the not-too-distant memories of Buffalo, I cut the last two classes of the day and, without letting my few friends know where I was going, headed to the appointed spot early to await my fate.

When I reached the field, I noticed among all of the junk a two by four about four feet long. I picked up the piece of wood and headed toward K.'s house. It was common knowledge that he cut school almost every afternoon, especially on days he had a fight. Apparently, he was planning on making a career out of the seventh grade. Before I arrived, I ducked behind a bush that I knew K. would have to pass. Sure enough, before too long he approached with the usual cigarette hanging out of the corner of his mouth and a look on his face that radiated hate. As he passed, I stepped out behind him and clubbed him in the back of the head as hard as I could, which opened up a nasty gash and knocked him cold.

Now what? I wasn't sure what to do next but soon decided that none of this would have a lasting effect if he did not know who had hit him. So, rolling him over onto his back, I stood at his feet and nervously waited for him to regain consciousness. After about twenty minutes, he groaned a couple of times and opened his eyes. Although I was terrified by now, as he looked up at me I simply said, "You know why I did that, don't you?" Whether he understood me or not was not clear, but he did seem to nod, which was good enough for me. At that, I pulled my foot back and kicked him squarely in the testicles. As he loudly sucked in his breath and all the color left his face, I pulled the switchblade out of his pocket and unzipped his pants. A push of a button and the blade was out of the knife. I could not believe what I was doing—as a matter of fact, I had no idea what I was going to do with the knife at all. It was as if I were watching the whole scene on a movie screen. But I placed the blade up to his battered testicles and told him to kiss the boys good-bye. At that, with a look of sheer terror and a squeaky little groan, he let loose with a stream of urine as his eyes rolled back into his head and he passed out again.

So far, so good. But again, I had to face that nagging question, "Now what?" I knew that K. would eventually wake up, probably enraged. I had to buy myself some time. Even though it would have solved my immediate problem, I realized that I couldn't really kill him. Instead, rolling him onto his stomach, I stood on his right arm just above the elbow. Grabbing his hand, I gave a hard pull until I heard an audible crack. I then did the same to his left arm. The sound of it was almost enough to make me vomit. It would be a long time before he did anything meaningful with either arm—at least that was what I was hoping.

After that, I returned to where the fight was supposed to take place. As always, a fairly large group of kids had

gathered in anticipation of the usual display of sadomas-
ochism, with K. playing the role of sadist. Most were surprised to see that I had actually shown up. They were
even more surprised as it became evident that K. would
not. I waited a good hour, showing no real external emo-
tion even though my heart was threatening to burst
through my chest. I then announced in an as matter of
fact a voice as I could muster that I had better things to
do than to wait for some chicken-shit greaser.

I only saw Jim K. one more time after that. He was
standing on a street corner after a couple of weeks with
both arms in casts and his head heavily bandaged. The
word at school (put out by K. himself) was that he had
fought with a rival gang of greasers and although he put
up a hard fight, being outnumbered he eventually was
overcome. There was no advantage in me saying anything
to counter that; I still knew when to keep my mouth shut
and had not mentioned to my friends what had happened. As I passed him, he glared at me with obvious
hate. I simply stared back and said, "We can always do
that dance again when you're feeling better. I have absolutely nothing to lose and I'm sure as hell not afraid of
you. By the way, how are the boys?"

Although the look of hate in his eyes grew even stronger, I noticed something else there—a combination of fear
and surprise—and I have to admit that I kind of liked it.

CHAPTER 4

Booze and Drugs

Growing up, I don't remember when I first became aware of alcohol as anything other than what everybody consumed in varying amounts depending on their age, and that included babies. We didn't spend money for things such as orange juice—the closest thing at our house being water with just enough *Tang* orange powder to color it. There was, however, plenty of beer and wine.

I remember being at the Oktoberfest some years later soon after the birth of my daughter, Annemarie. Something was obviously bothering her, probably a problem with teething, and she wouldn't stop crying. My grandmother, an old Bavarian from the country, took the baby's pacifier and dipped it into a stein of beer; that's Oktoberfest beer, at about 18 proof! A couple of sucks on that pacifier and Annemarie not only stopped crying but even managed to smile a little before she went to sleep.

My family was, after all, pure German as far back as it was possible to trace. At that time, asking a German if he drank alcohol was like asking other human beings if they breathed air. Posing that question more than likely would be met with a stare of incredulity. Countless generations of my ancestors had taken an addictive, destructive habit and transformed it into a time-honored tradition. The first German beer was brewed by Catholic monks. Thus, as monks worked directly for God, the logic follows that beer was sanctioned by God. Not drinking beer was tantamount to conduct which was unchristian, even ungodly.

My father hailed from the beer-drinking Munich area where almost as much time was devoted to celebrating Oktoberfest as to Christmas. My mother, however, came from Wuerzburg, where the liquid object of worship was wine. *Fasching*, the German equivalent of Mardi Gras, starts at 11 A.M. on November 11, and lasts until the beginning of Lent in February. Drinking and partying were encouraged throughout. Once the liquor caused someone to feel sick to his stomach, he took a shot of *Jaegermeister* to settle it. For those who wanted something a little stronger, there was always *Korn*, a distilled grain alcohol much like American moonshine. The stereotypical picture of a Bavarian man generally shows a rotund figure in *Lederhosen* (leather shorts) with a large red nose and a glazed yet happy red face. The women, equally stout, were shown hefting three or four steins of beer while being slapped on the bottom by their singing, drunken men. No German would ever admit having a problem with alcohol unless the problem was that he didn't have any.

Every day my father returned home from work and drank a couple of beers. This was considered normal and expected. After all, he had earned some peace and relaxation after a hard day, and this was how he got it. My mother kept a gallon jug of cheap Gallo wine sitting on the floor of the kitchen closet. Although I don't recall seeing her pour any wine during my early years, the level in the jug was constantly lowering and new jugs were always ready to replace the vanquished predecessors. By early evening, at my house, any semblance or hope of coherent conversation was gone. Yet, I thought this was typical of all families.

Any deviation from this picture meant something

was wrong. Saturdays, and Sundays after church, the German families drove to the local *Fussballplatz*, or soccer field. The athletically inclined played to uphold the honor of their national pride; all others cheered on the locals. At the end of the game, attention turned to the soccer club bar where the families went with the express purpose of drinking to excess. The kids played in the bar area and sneaked sips from their fathers' beers (not that any sneaking was necessary). Looking at 8mm home movies from my childhood, all of the adults were drunk and happy. Happy equaled drunk. This was life as I knew it.

Later, when I was in junior high, I realized this was not what everybody else in America did. And only later did I understand that the reason my parents did not attend any of my school events was because they were, quite frankly, too drunk and too tired. They did not pass out in public or engage in behaviors that would embarrass us kids. Yet they were alcoholics—functional alcoholics who never missed a day of work because of booze. They were able to hold their own in a conversation, but then again, most of the people with whom they socialized were just like them.

By the time I left for college, I had come to understand that as far back as I could remember my mother had not gone to bed sober. And that same statement was true until she died at the age of 73. She started with wine at about 5 P.M. and moved on to Black Russians, scotch, martinis, or other hard liquor as the evening wore on. A few hours later she would be snoring on the couch in front of the television. She never admitted to me or anybody else that she had passed out and swore that she was actively following the television show's plot. Although I loved my mother with all of my heart—she worked hard and always had a meal on the table for us— I have had to admit that she was a full-blown alcoholic.

I never had much use for booze before college, content with the few beers I might have on a Saturday night.

But all of that changed at Purdue. My first night in the dorm I drank an entire bottle of Bacardi 151 rum. After I took the first drink from that bottle, I knew that I had to finish it, even long past the point of complete drunkenness. I guess it was the alcoholic background I had been soaked in for so long. What followed that night was a horrible bout of alcohol poisoning that left me with my head buried in a toilet bowl for three days. To this day, I can't stand even the smell of rum, and if any manages to find its way into my mouth, I immediately begin to vomit. I quickly figured out that hard liquor and I did not get along, and I put it aside for many years after that.

However, what I lacked in booze consumption, I made up in illegal drug experimentation. Three guys on my floor—all named Rick—introduced me to marijuana. These three, with whom I would later rent a house near campus, took it upon themselves to make sure I got high on that first joint. It took a concerted effort at first, but I was always a very determined person. After that, even the smoke from other people's joints gave me a contact high. I would never consider putting a lit cigarette in my mouth, but somehow, marijuana was okay.

Following that I tried psychedelics such as mescaline, peyote, and acid; sedatives such as Quaaludes (methaqualone); and stimulants such as white cross (methamphetamine). I became adept at dropping a tab of windowpane (LSD) or some other type of hallucinogen and then going about my day attending classes. Rarely did my drug use cause me trouble. Once, however, I attended Russian class while hallucinating. I somehow became convinced that the United States had been invaded by the Soviet Union, and I ran from the class in a panic. I "saw" MiGs in the sky overhead strafing the campus, so all the way back to the dorm I jumped behind bushes for cover. It became my mission to warn everybody at the dorm about what dire straits we were in, and I went door to door babbling my story incoherently.

Later that evening, my brain still wired, I took my manual transmission Opel Kadett and headed for a carnival off campus in West Lafayette. About a mile down the road I became convinced that I had pushed the clutch pedal through the floor of the car. I pulled off the road and crawled under the car to find it. A police car pulled up next to me and the police officer asked me what the problem was. I explained my dilemma, at which point the officer looked inside of my car and told me that the clutch pedal was right where it was supposed to be. After thanking him for his valuable assistance in locating the errant clutch and praising him for his wisdom, he left, and I was allowed to proceed on my way. In that era, with no smell of pot or alcohol, he probably assumed my behavior was the result of mental incapacity, not street drugs.

The carnival itself presented its own challenges to my electrified mind. I cried when I saw somebody break a balloon with a dart, grieving at the loss of this beautiful, translucent blue orb. The hall of mirrors looked like fun, but I became hopelessly lost somewhere deep inside. It was clear to me that what I needed was a map or a guide. As I had neither, I simply sat on the floor and waited for rescue. Soon, a child of about five or six found me and fearlessly led me out of the horrible maze.

Actually, I feel lucky that I did not become a full-blown alcoholic or become addicted to drugs back then. I knew no fear and enjoyed the mind altering effects. I accepted and subsequently ingested almost anything anybody offered me. Luckily, nothing like heroin or cocaine was available on that Midwestern campus in the early 1970s.

All of these events were flashing through my mind as I pondered the offer being made by Phil from Washington, who had sat across from me in the NROTC building that day in March. He had to be kidding! He was considering me, a stoner from a long line of alcoholics? Was I someone my government wanted to have working in "intelligence"? I found the idea preposterous. Like

Groucho Marx said, "I don't care to belong to any club that accepts people like me as members," I had doubts that a U.S. intelligence agency that was purposely recruiting me had any credibility. But what the hell. As I said, I knew no fear and was willing to try almost anything once. It sounded good to me. Why not?

CHAPTER 5

A Life-Changing Decision

"So what do I have to do? Where do I sign? When do I start? How does this change anything that I am doing now?"

Phil from D.C. looked at me for a few moments before he answered. "First of all, not so quick on the draw. We still have a lot to talk about. But if you do decide to go ahead and do this, for now, you don't have to do anything different from your current routine. You continue on with the ROTC training. Knowing a little bit about how the military works can be a good thing, especially when you have to deal with some of those idiots. Change your course of study from pre-med to the humanities and put more emphasis on formal language training, especially Russian. Get more familiar with the cultures of the Soviet Union and East Germany. Immerse yourself in Middle Eastern cultures, too, including Israel and its relationships and problems with the Palestinians. Don't go Navy on us and get any tattoos or other distinguishing marks; you need to look as normal as you possibly can. And most important of all—now listen to me and hear what I'm saying here—keep your mouth shut. This conversation never happened. If you can't do that, you become useless to me. If you have the need to brag, stick with the Marines, because as far as I am concerned then I might as well end this conversation now."

I figured the last part of his comment was for effect only. With as much as he already knew about me and the results of my psychological tests, which he probably also possessed, he knew that bragging was the last thing on my mind. There was nobody I cared to impress any-more. My parents were continuing their benign neglect position. As long as I wasn't arrested or brought shame on them in any way, they were content enough. Image was everything, especially to my mother.

"But what about the major outside this door?" I asked Phil. "Doesn't he have some idea of what's hap-pening in here? You had to tell him something to set this thing up, didn't you?"

"As far as he's concerned, I'm just a civilian with the Office of the Chief of Naval Operations who is scouting out potential candidates to join Naval intelligence. I will let him know that you did not pass muster. You just didn't have what it takes. He'll be more than willing to believe that. He was enlisted before getting his commission; those guys don't put much stock in you college boys. They also don't have much use for 'civilians' like me. For that mat-ter, they don't have much use for the intelligence branch. The only people they trust are grunts. The only way that you could be any lower in his eyes would be if you were in the Academy. Officers who don't start out enlisted never know what true leadership is, as far as his kind is concerned. However he might act toward you in class or on campus, it's all an act; he has nothing but contempt for you. And that's not likely to change."

"So I go on with my life as if all of this never hap-pened—don't call you, you'll call me?"

"In essence, that's it, but there is a lot more to it, too. I'll check in with you now and then when necessary. I'll follow your progress with classes and your military training. Occasionally, I'll send you some stuff to read and study. You're going to have to do your normal sum-mer midshipman training cruise, but I'll supplement that with some extra training of our own—probably jump training this summer for starters."

"Out of airplanes?" I asked, unsure if Phil was serious.

"Yeah, out of airplanes. You'll also have to learn land navigation and basic survival skills. For now, just think of it as an opportunity to get closer to nature. You're going to discover a whole new world of food possibilities, a lot of which you're probably not going to like very much. You're also going to need some small arms training and familiarity with a load of other potential weapons. And, oh yeah, keep going to the gym. And see if you can advance to something more physical than judo—boxing or karate. Don't get me wrong, judo is a good workout, but you need something with a little more finality to it."

"Finality?" I wondered what he was implying.

"When you hit somebody, you are not going to want him to get back up for a long time—if ever. There is no such thing as a good live witness, especially an angry witness with a grudge to settle. And that brings up another question, and I am pretty sure I know the answer or we wouldn't be having this conversation, but I still want you to think real hard about this before, during, and after every phase of your training. Could you, if your life depended on it, kill another human being? And forget about your life depending on it—could you kill just because it's what you have been told to do, what you have to do, for your country or some higher good?"

I didn't have to think too long or hard about that one. I had been in a couple of situations where I would have had no qualms about killing somebody—Jim K. and Frankie C. in particular. Funny, I could not bring myself to hurt a defenseless animal (unless I had to eat). But people? Killing them caused me little possibility of regret, especially if my own life depended on it. I was ready to join the Marines and go off to war, wasn't I? Soldiers kill strangers. They know nothing about those people or their families or friends. Soldiers act because they are ordered to do so. They kill "the enemy." If they thought about it too much, I suppose they would go crazy. But war death was not what I considered as killing in the same terms as murder in peacetime society. It was a soldier's duty.

"And I don't have to sign anything?" I asked Phil. "There's no secret handshake, decoder ring, T-shirt, hat, or even an ID? I don't get to be 'one of the guys'?"

Phil set me straight. "Look, once anything is put on paper, it becomes exploitable; if it's in a file somewhere, somebody can find it and possibly use it for any number of reasons. If you get an ID, then you've also been ID'd for people who watch out for that kind of thing. The only people the Agency has who are on an official payroll and who carry IDs are office people who work at Langley or field offices. They have their purposes as researchers, planners, linguists, and analysts, but they're worthless as far as serious, meaningful clandestine work is concerned. Think of them as decoys; they attract attention while other folks are doing the covert work. And if you have been listening, you hear me keep saying that 'I' will take care of this or that, 'I' will arrange for training, 'I' will check in with you. That's very important. For you, there is no Agency, there is no group, there is no club. The terms the Agency has for people like you are 'nonofficial cover,' or 'contractor.' Your only contact, as far as anything we have discussed, will be with me. I'm your boss. I'm your family, I'm your priest, I'm your shrink. And I'm the closest thing you will ever have to a friend from this point on."

Phil's statements failed to discourage me from considering his job possibility. But I had more questions. "And if I'm not 'official,' not on your books or your payroll, how do I make a living, or explain to people what it is that I do for a living?"

"You'll always have a 'regular' job, your 'cover.' I'll see to that. For now, you are a student. Later on, you'll be something else. Whatever it ends up being, your cover will give you the flexibility you need to do what we need you to do when we need it done so that you don't raise any suspicions. Nobody will ever know who you really are and what you do when you aren't where you're supposed to be. Sometimes, that will be very frustrating for you. You'll probably have to put up with a lot of crap from some real asses who are only impressed with the visible signs of rank or wealth; that's just the way it is—just one of the costs of doing business."

"And what if anything happens to me? What do you tell my parents? What if I'm killed in the line of duty? If I'm captured, do you come rescue me or negotiate for my release, or am I on my own?"

As he had before, Phil stared at me for a while without saying anything, a little longer than was comfortable. Then, looking me straight in the eye, he said, "You haven't been listening. If anything happens to you, we say nothing, because you don't officially exist as far as any official government agency is concerned. And besides, you don't plan for what to do in case of mission failure. Planning for failure invites failure; if you do fail, things will happen by themselves, with or without your plan. You go in, you do your job, you get out. Life is good. If you don't complete your job, chances are that life as you know it is over. That life is not good. There is no in-between. You do, or you do not. If, for some reason, you don't make it back, you fall off the face of the planet. As far as your family and friends are concerned, you become someone who dropped out and ran off somewhere and was killed or lost. So are you still interested?"

I did not get up and walk out. I sat and thought about what he had said. Let's see: I have to jump out of airplanes, I have to do stuff that could get me killed (and as far as I could discern, might involve me killing somebody else), I do get paid but probably not much, I don't get credit for anything I do (but plenty of blame if I don't come through), and if I am captured or killed, my family will be led to believe that I ran off because life was too tough to deal with. When I thought about it that way, the whole deal sounded very much like a no-win situation.

Yet, if I was honest with myself, what alternatives did I consider better? I was already bored with college life; in fact, I was bored with life in general. Getting high as much as I did was losing its appeal. And did I really want to become a Marine? Short hair, being yelled at all of the time, and grim assignments before retiring after twenty years with unknown prospects for a future beyond the military?

Besides, keeping my mouth shut would be no different than what I was accustomed to doing already. Ever since my broken English got me beaten up as a kid, I had been the champ at keeping my mouth shut, so much so that I didn't have much use for anybody else because I did not want to talk to anybody. What relationships I had developed over the years were superficial, at least on my part. Mastering languages and the complexities of other cultures came easily to me. Interacting, conversing, getting to know somebody, and sharing my life just wasn't me. In addition, I enjoyed pushing myself physically. The prospect of pain didn't bother me; I had experienced pain and learned how to live with it—actually more than live with it. I had come to view pain as a reminder of how alive I really was.

On the plus side, there was the whole "cloak and dagger" intrigue of it all. Just thinking about the possibilities raised my adrenaline. But what about the distinct reality that I might have to kill somebody? Ever since I was first dropped into the sewer back in Buffalo, I lost the sense of life's sanctity. I couldn't remember anybody actually caring whether I was dead or alive. So why worry about anybody else, especially somebody I didn't know? Could I actually go through with it? I guess I wouldn't really know until I got into that situation.

The longer I sat and thought about it, even with the little I understood, the more it seemed like the right thing to do. Besides, I acted impulsively back then. Going on instinct and spur of the moment was a character defect that played a major part in who and what I was. And considering consequences was never a long suit of mine. "Just do it!!" was a catch phrase that I considered my personal motto long before Nike adopted it.

As these and a million other thoughts raced through my brain, Phil sat quietly looking at me, waiting. The next words I heard myself say were, "I'm in." As quick, as simple, and as impulsive as that, I changed the entire direction of my life without knowing where this new direction would take me. All I could think was, "Just do it!!"

CHAPTER 6

INITIAL TRAINING

The rest of the semester passed without hearing anything further from Phil. I received my official assignment for my summer NROTC cruise when the semester ended, and I was ordered to report to the USS *Guadalupe*, the AO 32. USS *Guadalupe* was the oldest oiler in the U.S. Naval fleet, which I would board at her home dock in Long Beach, California. Within a couple of days of receiving my assignment, Phil called. He informed me that as soon as my training aboard the *Guadalupe* ended, I would begin jump training. I was supposed to tell my parents and friends that the naval cruise would last a few weeks longer than it would to cover this side trip.

The month or so that I spent on the *Guadalupe* was uneventful. Admiral Elmo R. Zumwalt Jr. was Chief of Naval Operations (CNO) in 1971. He had become the youngest man to serve as the Navy's top-ranking officer, and under his leadership, the Navy assumed a much more casual environment. Zumwalt issued 121 directives over a four-year period known as Z-Grams, which sought to change the way the Navy had conducted business for the previous two centuries. Many of them, like the ones designed to reduce racial tensions by irradicating institutional discrimination, were not popular with the majority. One directive that was somewhat better received relaxed grooming standards so that longer hair and facial hair were allowed. I was unaware of the new policy before reporting, and so trimmed my hair to a close buzz cut, which once again made me noticeable in the crowd.

The *Guadalupe*, a Cimarron Class oiler more than 550 feet long and with a beam of 75 feet, cruised the West Coast at a speed of 18 knots from her home in Long Beach to San Francisco, Vancouver, then San Diego. As an NROTC midshipman, which was considered as the lowest status onboard, I was required to work in all sections of the ship, from boiler room to the signal and command bridges. The *Guadalupe* was powered by four 450-pound CE K-type boilers running geared turbine engines, which made for some excruciatingly hot duty time.

During my short time onboard I was able to observe that the real power of most military organizations was not held by commissioned officers but by the warrant officer and noncommissioned officer corps, contrary to what I was taught in my NROTC classes. On the *Guadalupe*, the seat of power laid with the chief boatswains mate, known simply as the Chief. While the commissioned officers issued nominal orders from the bridge, the Chief manned his chair on a lower deck from where he would dispense his orders. Enlisted personnel who evaded commands from the ensigns through commanders generally received light consequences, but crossing the Chief could result in unofficial but serious physical discipline.

The captain of the *Guadalupe* either ignored or was oblivious to some of the less than legal events on his ship. For instance, one of the nicknames the *Guadalupe* sported was "Tijuana Taxi" owing to the easy availability of drugs and alcohol, which were sold by the guys on the signal bridge. It was common knowledge, or at least rumored that the Chief knew about these deals, but presumably he took a cut of the action. Unspoken, different rules applied to those who commanded and those who served. I learned this in action when one idealistic midshipman found out about the illicit drug trade and threatened to report the whole operation to the captain. Some of the NCOs took him aside. I don't know what was said, but the cadet returned to duty with a broken arm, saying that he had tripped on deck. Nothing was reported about the illegal dealings; life went on as before, and the midshipman, his spirit and fervor for the service now broken, said very little to anybody for the rest of the cruise.

The *Guadalupe* carried a number of fuels, including naval special fuel oil (NSFO), diesel (ND), AV gas, and JP5 (a highly volatile jet fuel). And even though she was an oiler, she carried armaments in the form of four 4 x 2 40-mm and 4 x 2 20-mm guns that were each five inches per 38DP. I was amazed that we didn't blow ourselves up, considering much of the crew's diminished capacity owing to constantly being high. During one exercise we went through, a crewman was designated as injured. He was then strapped to a stretcher to be hauled off to the dispensary. The guys carrying the stretcher were stoned and giggling so hard that they dropped the stretcher a number of times, causing it to flip over so that the poor "victim"—rendered immobile and defenseless by the straps—hit the steel deck, face down. By the time they transported him to the dispensary, he had a broken nose and two broken ribs.

As had been my habit for a number of years, I kept quiet and took a lot of mental notes. This attitude also secured me some acceptance with the crew on the signal bridge, who consequently requested that I be assigned with them, citing my "aptitude" for what they did. Smoking dope on the signal bridge was considerably more pleasant than sweating shirtless in the boiler room.

The cruise ended, and it was time for part two of my summer education. I caught a plane to Colorado and met Phil, who initiated my jump training. We started with classroom work so that I understood the history, science, and technology of jumping out of airplanes. I enjoyed the theoretical aspect of the training and quickly committed everything I learned to memory.

A number of forces— lift, drag, weight, and thrust— act on objects that travel through the air. In an airplane, lift provided by the wings keeps the plane up. The engine provides the thrust, which propels the plane forward. Drag is the air resistance that holds the plane back. The weight of the plane pulls it toward the ground. Older types of simple parachutes have only two of these forces acting on them, namely drag and weight (without an engine there is no thrust, and without wings there is no lift). The weight of the jumper pulls the parachute down while the drag acts in the opposite direction of his downward path. It is necessary to know all of this in calculating the rate of speed at which a jumper will hit the ground.

Once a person leaves the aircraft, gravity will immediately begin to pull him down until he reaches what is called terminal velocity. Terminal velocity is dependent on two opposing forces: gravity and aerodynamic drag. During a skydive, the force of gravity causes a person to accelerate, to fall faster and faster toward the ground. His speed increases by 32 feet per second for each second he falls (32Ft/sec2). Aerodynamic drag will first act to slow and eventually stop this acceleration. This is not to say the person will stop falling, only that the speed at which he is falling will become constant. Terminal velocity, then, is the speed attained when this balance of forces is reached. The typical terminal velocity reached during free fall is around 120 m.p.h. During the free fall, a jumper will reach his terminal velocity within about 12 seconds after jumping. Ideally, deploying the parachute will provide the drag to slow the jumper to the point where he lands at a speed of about 14 miles per hour. Now I knew what was supposed to happen.

Phase two consisted of jumps from a 34-foot training tower. Although the tower was considered a simulation of jumping, it was more realistic in that it added a bit of fear to the training. At the top of the tower was a mock-up of an aircraft door constructed to resemble the

Air Force's AeroCommander aircraft. I sat rigged up in this "door" and waited to hear the command to exit. I then jumped and pretended to free fall as I was suspended about 6 feet below the door I had just exited. Next I had to go through the count to the 'pull' as well as the appropriate body motions. When I finally pulled the rip cord, I dropped another 15 feet as the instructors released the center point suspension, simulating opening shock. Next the instructors released the trolley that swung me into an upright position until I did a parachute-landing fall (PLF) as I hit the ground. In all, I went through this simulation five times before the instructors decided it was time to jump out of the real thing.

The next day as the C141 ascended, the reality of the situation and the uncertainty of the outcome hit me. It's one thing to read about what is supposed to happen when you jump out of an airplane, or what happens when you jump from a tower hooked to a safety harness, but it's quite another thing to get into an airplane and do the real thing. I stared out the door of the plane until the instructor told me to go. And I went. The whole jump was over almost as fast as it started. After a free fall of about 35 seconds, only another minute or so passed before I hit the ground.

My first jumps were done using the old round parachutes on static lines that have a constant rate of descent (no lift), so the ground appeared to come up and meet me. The illusion of the ground rising was more reassuring to me than the reality of rapid falling. With these chutes, an error in PLF could and often did result in broken ankles, if not something worse. After a few days in my accelerated one-on-one course, it was time for me to transition from low level jumps to High Altitude Low Opening (HALO) and High Altitude High Opening (HAHO) jumps. These jumps are what are performed by special operations forces as a primary means of infiltration. HALO jumps, also known as Military Freefall (MFF) are used for free falling in a tactical grouping. They are done from altitudes of 10,000 to 35,000 feet. The jumper deploys his chute after a long free fall of about 2,500 feet, hence the term "low opening." HAHO jumps are done from altitudes of more than 35,000 feet with the jumper deploying his chute fairly quickly, about 10 to 15 seconds after exiting the aircraft (high opening), and then using a compass to guide himself, gliding for distances as far as 30 miles to the designated landing point. Along the way, he has to correct course for changes in wind speed and direction, making this a complicated maneuver. This technique is particularly useful for insertion into enemy territory since the aircraft flies high enough to avoid detection and the jumper exits over friendly airspace before gliding over a border to his objective.

The rigs used for these kinds of jumps are called High Altitude Precision Parachute Systems (HAPPS) and are nothing like the round, static line-type chutes I had jumped with before. HAPPS are also known as stealth parachute systems in that they are hard to see from the ground. Back in the classroom Phil taught me the technology behind these special chutes, the various methods used to control them, and the specialized equipment needed to complete these jumps safely. I learned that for any jumps higher than 12,000 feet I would be wearing an oxygen mask. Otherwise, at that height the air is so rarified that jumpers would suffer the effects of hypoxia (lack of oxygen), lose consciousness, and crash into the ground before they could deploy their chutes. The military euphemism for this occurrence is "deceleration trauma," which, in my language translates to "death on impact."

I also needed special clothing because at that altitude the temperatures are at subzero, which causes normal goggles to shatter and eyeballs to freeze. However, the most important piece of equipment to me was the FF2, the automatic pressure-activated rip cord–pulling device designed to activate the chute if for any reason the jumper falls past a predetermined altitude.

HAHO chutes are maneuverable, much like having wings, meaning the chutes can be manipulated to allow air to rush in and provide lift, which aids in the deceleration process. This becomes critical because of both the high altitude and the fact that to achieve some sort of military objective the jumper generally carried up to 200 pounds of added weight in what was known as an All Purpose Lightweight Individual Carrying Equipment (ALICE) packet. In remote or hostile areas, the ALICE contained your food, water, weapons (special knife and M1911 pistol), survival gear, oxygen equipment (bottle and mask), and any number of other items necessary for successful completion of the mission. Using a regular round chute at that height and carrying that much weight would probably ensure that your ankles would be driven up into your hips, making you look like a character from *South Park.*

The transition to HALO/HAHO began in Dayton, Ohio, where I was taught body stabilization while "flying" in a vertical wind tunnel that had been developed by Wright Laboratories. A vertical wind tunnel is a machine that produces a vertical stream or column of air. If the air stream is moving at a sufficient rate, a person entering the tunnel can be lifted up and suspended in midair. The speed of the vertical air stream generated is equal to a person's terminal velocity, enabling that person to hover from 6 feet to 12 feet off the ground. The aerodynamic drag could be increased or decreased through the use of controlled body positioning. If the speed of the air stream remains constant the "flyer" hovered, soared up (climbed), or dropped down (descended)—all by changing the position of his arms, legs, and body. When I was not enjoying the wind tunnel, I studied altitude physiology and other MFF tactics.

After completing my training in Colorado, I was off to Arizona for the real thing. All of my HALO/HAHO jumps were done at the U.S. Army Yuma Proving Ground near the Arizona-California border on the Colorado River.

Consisting of 1,300 square miles in the center of the Sonoran Desert, Yuma Proving Ground (which is the site for the annual winter training of the U.S. Army "Golden Knights" Parachute Team, as well as the British Royal Air Force "Falcons" precision parachute team) provides an extremely harsh environment, designed to tax people and systems.

My first HALO jump, which was planned for 12,000 feet, was a tandem jump but still managed to pump up my fear factor yet again, something I didn't think was possible. On the one hand, 12,000 feet is a long way up with many opportunities for problems. On the other hand, if something does go wrong with the rig when jumping from 12,000 feet, I wouldn't know I hit the ground. The jump itself was a tremendous rush, considering that I dropped through the sky at about 120 miles per hour for more than 20 seconds (the instructor referred to this activity as "consciously committing suicide until you pull the rip cord"). At that speed of free fall, 20 seconds can seem like minutes.

But just when I considered HALO jumping to be as exciting as jumping could get, I moved to higher heights. HAHO jumping is an intense and difficult form of insertion into a hostile environment. In my HAHO jumps I exited the aircraft at around 30,000 feet and deployed the chute in 10 to 15 seconds, which put me at about 27,000 feet. Then I maneuvered my rectangular chute with a canopy size of about 360 square feet, gliding 25 miles cross-country as I fell toward the earth. After the adrenaline rush of the free fall and the shock of deploying the chute, there was nothing but a feeling of complete freedom. I did a HAHO jump once a day for the next week at ever increasing altitudes, moving up to jumps from 35,000 feet, until I became proficient at landing mere yards away from my target area. The rest of the time on the ground I spent practicing packing my rigging and becoming more familiar with the various pieces of equipment—such as the sophisticated altimeters of 12,000 feet per revolution complete with nightlight that were essential to this kind of jumping.

My last HAHO jump was conducted at night, during a full moon. After being briefed on where I was supposed to land and, more importantly, where I was supposed to get to after landing, and with my ALICE packed to sustain me for a couple of days in case something went wrong (like my getting lost, which seemed likely at the time), I was dropped from 34,000 feet. The jump went off without a hitch, and 10 hours after landing, I reached my assigned destination.

Along with jumping from aircraft, another aspect of my training took place during this time. For a couple of hours every day, I learned about edged weapons (knives) to build and improve my offensive and defensive combat skills. Again, this was an accelerated course of study to introduce me to the lethality of knives. It included close and confined quarters tactics, anatomy study for disabling targets, compounded violent strike execution, how to handle a determined attacker who himself has a knife, measures to counter injuries, and how to neutralize multiple attackers (or defenders). This was scary stuff, but my previous exposure to martial arts helped quite a bit.

With that, my first summer of military training came to an end. I had traveled from a Navy ship to an Air Force simulation center and finished at the Army's premier desert environment training area, thereby covering our three major services. In the process I accomplished the equivalent of qualifying for the jump portion of Special Forces training. I was nineteen years old.

As it turned out, there would be no more summer cruises or Department of Defense–sanctioned military training of any kind. I was about to begin my first mission.

CHAPTER 7

BUSTED

August 1971 found me back at Purdue University for the fall semester. Instead of living in the dorm, this year I rented a house with the three Ricks. We no longer had to worry about the smell of marijuana leaking out into the dorm hall thus inspiring a rule-conscious classmate to report us to the police. Living in the house, we also bypassed the middle man in drug buys and grew our own. With rural Indiana outside our back door it was easy to find a fairly large tract of unused land to cultivate. Only once were we in danger of being caught; after a good harvest our garage was packed with freshly cut marijuana plants. We rented a large drier, plugged it in, and went out for the evening. By the time we returned a few hours later, the entire neighborhood smelled like strong sweet tea. A few neighbors were out sniffing the air and commenting on the strange aroma. Luckily for us the smell by that time was so pervasive, no one could possibly track it to our garage.

The days fell into a predictable routine for me: get up by noon, play some Frisbee, read the books that Phil gave me as well as texts for my classes, work out at the university gym, play pinochle until 3 or 4 A.M., go to sleep. I missed most of my classes but since they were mostly large lecture types, my absence wasn't noticed. I always appeared for tests, and given the fact that I easily remembered everything I read, I generally performed well.

Not only did classes cause me minimal concern, but money also was never a problem. My NROTC scholarship paid for tuition, room and board, and books, and provided me with a few hundred bucks extra each month. In addition, I worked part-time delivering pizzas and received a $500 per month stipend from Phil. I had no bills and plenty of money. Anything I needed or wanted I easily bought. I had a good car, a motorcycle, a new stereo system with a few hundred records, and a color television when black and white sets were what most people owned. I ate well and took a number of short trips to places such as New Orleans for Mardi Gras, Fort Lauderdale for spring break, Churchill Downs for the Kentucky Derby, New York City for the National Invitation Tournament (NIT) to watch the Purdue basketball team play, Chicago for concerts, among others. Life was good.

Then on October 5, Phil called. He told me he wanted to meet with me at the Great Lakes Naval base in Chicago. I was to drive my Opel Kadett Rally Sport and meet him at Fort Sheridan in two days. I felt like I did before my first HALO jump, nervous and at the same time excited at the prospect of what it was that I might be doing. Those feelings of anticipation grew and were almost unbearable by the time I reached Chicago.

Phil met me in a small office in a Navy building and got down to business. Fun and games were over for now; it was time for me to earn my keep. Phil explained that I would go on an extended assignment. It required me to leave school for now and leave my ambitions of being a Marine behind for good. In a few weeks he planned to travel to Purdue to explain further. I was shocked. Fun and games were exactly how I had viewed all that I had done until then—the traveling, the training, the secret meetings and phone calls. Although it shouldn't have come as a surprise, the fact that Phil now expected me to use what I had learned was a revelation. And what did he mean by leaving school for now? That was never part of my own plan. Phil continued.

"I need you to go to Europe and eventually to the Middle East and Asia next fall. Since we don't want to arouse any suspicion, there are a few things you are going to have to do. First, you must be expelled from the NROTC program and Purdue."

He had to be kidding. Except for my first semester when too much partying resulted in grades of mainly Cs, I was a good student with no blemishes on my record. Expelled?

"What will my parents say?" I asked him. "How do I go about getting expelled? Why can't I simply quit school for a while until I finish whatever assignment I am about to do?"

"You can't just quit school out of the blue," Phil countered, "That would seem suspicious. You have no reason to quit temporarily. And you don't take a leave of absence from an ROTC scholarship. You took an oath when you started college and you are, in essence, in the Navy. In order to position you where we need you, the split must be definite and final. Same with Purdue. You may or may not be able to return after this assignment, but for the time being, you have to be out of school."

I definitely did not like the sound of any of this. I had worked long and hard for acceptance and a modicum of recognition and now my identity would include words such as "expelled" and "quitter."

Phil pressed on.

"This is the timeline. You will finish this semester and register for the next one. You will make yourself available for one week of training during the Thanksgiving break and two weeks during Christmas break. You will start classes next semester. On order, you will get yourself arrested. Don't worry, I'll handle those details. The arrest will result in your termination from the NROTC program and expulsion from Purdue. With seemingly nothing left to do here, with your family ashamed of you and you yourself not wanting to face your friends out of your own shame and humiliation, you will leave the country and go to live in Germany. I need you to be based in Europe at first, and Germany makes sense. Since you have relatives there, nobody should ask too many questions. Is all of this sinking in?"

Sinking in?! So far this whole thing has been like trying to get a drink from a fire hose. I was drowning in information that made no sense to me at all.

"Well, that's about it for now. Go back to school. I'll see you over Thanksgiving and we'll talk some more. In the meantime, read everything you can about the people, customs, geography, and politics of East Germany, Turkey, Iran, Pakistan, and India. You'll want to be as smart as you can about these places."

The drive back to Purdue was excruciatingly slow, but my mind was functioning as if I was stimulated on speed while at the same time depressed on Quaaludes. But whether I dwelled on what Phil had told me or not, I had my instructions and all I could do was wait for the next step.

As Thanksgiving break approached I received my orders to report to Camp Pendleton, California. I left for Pendleton a few days before break officially started in that I was told that I would need about ten days for this next phase of my training. Camp Pendleton was the home of the 1st Marine Force Reconnaissance Company. Marine Force Recon units are special purpose units akin to Army Special Forces, Navy SEALs, and Air Force Air Commandos. Force Recon operators are generally used for highly specialized, small scale, high risk operations.

My training focused on special weapons training, specifically the modified and improved M1911A1 .45 pistol, designated as such because it was first adopted for military use in March 1911 (at least that's what I was told). The Marines sent original M1911 frames to their Precision Weapons Section at Quantico, Virginia, where Marine gunsmiths used a variety of pistol parts, (such as improved high visibility sights and improved magazines) from various high-end weapons manufacturers to modify the weapons. Because of this individual, hand-manufactured approach, no two Force Recon M1911s are exactly the same. The extra care and precision that goes into each of these weapons also makes them some of the most reliable pistols in the world. Every part of the pistol is changeable except for the frames, since the government no longer manufactures them.

I shot hundreds of rounds through the M1911 in my relatively short time at Camp Pendleton. I also learned how to break the weapon down, clean it, and reassemble it. One reason the M1911 was the weapon of choice for Force Recon operators was its stopping power. Yet I learned that the whole purpose of firing this weapon in a real life situation was not to stop but to kill the target. Along that line of thought, when I was not training with the M1911, I practiced hand-to-hand combat using knives, sticks, and an assortment of objects that could be used to stop a man—stop and kill a man. By the time I left Pendleton to return to Purdue, I doubt that there was an area of my body that was not covered with ugly, painful bruises.

As it turned out, I did not train over the Christmas holidays, for which I was grateful as I was still sore from my ordeal at Camp Pendleton. But the bruises and hard training did not compare with what I was facing as winter semester commenced. Phil had made it clear that I was expected to sever my ties with both Purdue and my NROTC program. Now, back at Purdue for the time being Phil handed me a Mamiya double lens reflex medium format camera.

"This is your public affairs officer's camera for NROTC official functions. I want you to take this camera and drive to the pawnshop in Indianapolis I have listed here. Pawn the camera and then come back and wait. You will be arrested by the Purdue police in a couple of days when your commandant reports the camera missing. We left enough clues pointing to you. At that point, you should be suspended from school, and the NROTC scholarship will be history as well. Questions?"

Hell yes! Of course I had questions! How did an arrest become a part of the scenario? Would I be sent to jail, or worse, to prison? Would I end up with a permanent police record? My contract with the Navy specified that if I did not complete my degree for any reason, I would be subject to immediate enlistment. What about that? Among the thoughts that crossed my mind, these were the immediate problems I could foresee enough to ask of Phil.

"Relax," Phil consoled me. "To make your departure from Purdue credible, the arrest is necessary. It also will give you credibility with some of the people you will encounter down the road. An official arrest on the books will make them less suspicious of your motives. I promise you that there is no chance of jail time and you won't be saddled with a lasting record of any kind; we'll take care of that. As for your NROTC scholarship, forget about your contract. You won't be enlisted in the Navy. And although you will be discharged from the service, we will see to it that you receive an honorable discharge. The idea here is that you appear as a good prospect gone bad. And for your future, you cannot have any ties at all left with the Navy."

Relaxing was out of the question, but I knew I had to do what I was told. I had gone too far down this path already and there was only one way forward. I drove to Indianapolis and easily found the pawnshop. As instructed, I gave the clerk a bogus story about photography being a lifelong hobby and how I really loved this camera, which had been a Christmas gift from my parents, but I needed the money for a pregnant girlfriend. I acted as nervous as I actually felt to place suspicions in the clerk's mind as to whether the camera was mine to sell. Then I took the money he offered and drove back to Purdue to wait.

I waited, and I waited, and I waited some more. After a couple of weeks, during which the personnel in the

NROTC unit did not notice that the camera was missing, Phil told me to go to the police station, confess, and turn myself in. "Tell them you made a dumb mistake," he said, "and can't live with yourself without setting things right."

Again following instructions, I went to the police station. After telling the desk sergeant my story and giving him a written statement, I was told I could leave. I couldn't believe what I was hearing and wondered what would it take to get arrested around here? I returned to my apartment and continued to attend classes as if nothing had happened.

Finally, on March 1, 1972, the hammer fell, and I was taken out of my apartment in handcuffs, charged with arson, grand larceny, and conspiracy against the government—not at all the charges I was expecting! How did the simple theft of a camera grow into a triple felony? It seems that there had been an unsolved fire at a bookstore as well as in the ROTC armory on campus. In addition, books and various other items were missing from both places. The police, in an attempt to clean up their unsolved case lists, and seeing that I had access to both facilities, concluded that I was the arsonist and thief. Then, since the armory was a DoD facility, they added the conspiracy charge to wrap it all up. Later, a lengthy article appeared in the pages of the local newspaper praising the police for "cracking the case" and getting "a dangerous person" off the streets. If I weren't so wrapped up in the middle of the whole mess, I would have laughed.

With my head reeling from the charges, I was taken to the West Lafayette jail with an escort of police cruisers, booked, and allowed my one phone call, which I used to call my parents.

"Hi, mom."

"Roland, how are you?"

"Been better, mom. I'm in jail."

"Jail! *Mein lieber Gott!* What did you do?'

"Nothing, really, mom. Most of it is a mistake."

"Mistake? What do you mean, mistake? The police

don't make mistakes! What did you do? Why are you in jail? What are people going to say about us?"

My mother was a firm believer in the infallibility of the state, perhaps owing to her traditional German background. If the authorities proclaimed it, it must be true. As for me, out of the dozen or so of her rapid-fire questions, not one of them had to do with how I was doing. Her panic stemmed from how my actions might affect my family, and as it turned out, the effect on my parents was devastating, although my parents never mentioned the incident in public (probably devising some cover story as to why I was no longer in school). After I told my mother the charges and endured the resulting recriminations from her, I was finally able to tell her that I was okay (not that she asked) and needed her to post the $10,000 bond to the court so that I could come home.

A number of years later, while visiting relatives in New York City, I brought up my arrest and expulsion from school. My aunt and uncle had no idea what I was talking about. Yet my mother never let me forget in private what I had done to her and to the rest of my immediate family.

Well, I had completed the first stage of a plan I still knew very little about. As expected, I was expelled from Purdue and dismissed with an honorable discharge from the Navy. Phil followed through with his part of the deal. Through the efforts of my attorney, the charges were reduced to simple theft. I say "my attorney" although I had never met the man and had no idea how he came to work for me; I was starting to get used to the fact that things "happened," and only if I needed to know why would I be told. The judge of my case entered a finding of "reserved judgment," which meant that if I didn't appear in his court on another charge, I would escape any kind of punishment for this one and my record would be sealed. So much for the first (and only) time I would ever be locked up in an American jail. Unfortunately, a much more intense and considerably seedier incarceration was still awaiting me in the Middle East. Had I known that, I might have quit this whole scenario, but ignorance being bliss (and me being quite ignorant at the time) I figured what is done is done. I chose to continue down the path to whatever it was that was waiting for me.

CHAPTER 8

GERMANY

Phil had told me that I needed to situate myself in Germany by fall, so it was time to figure out a good way to do this. Convincing my parents that I needed to leave the United States was no problem. Because my having been expelled from Purdue and the Navy was a great source of shame to them, my leaving the house and better yet the country would forestall their need to answer a lot of questions from family and friends, as well as alleviate their shame every time they looked at me. I spoke fluent German and had a large number of relatives who lived in Germany. Being that they did not know that I had been disgraced, they would, presumably, welcome me. However, I needed a good reason to go live there.

The solution was simple and served my own purposes of continuing my education. I decided that I would apply to several German universities and see what came up. I applied to Heidelberg, Munich, Hamburg, and Berlin. The process was an easy one. Fill out an application, get my transcripts, get recommendations from my German professors at Purdue, demonstrate proficiency in the language by composing a written narrative of my life (*Lebenslauf*) in German, and procure a letter from the police stating that I had never been arrested or in trouble. Oops! A potential stumbling block. To circumvent this problem my father simply went to the police chief (a good friend of his) of my home town,

Lakewood, Ohio, and had him certify that to his knowl-edge, "Roland Haas has never been arrested or suspected of any crime." What he did not include were the words "in Lakewood, Ohio." For all intents and purposes, it looked as if he had certified my innocence for the entire country.

I sent my materials in and waited patiently. A few weeks later, I received acceptance letters from all four universities. I settled on Ludwig-Maximillians Universi-taet in Munich for a number of reasons. First, I had fam-ily on my father's side there. They had been going through guilt trips for years, ever since he had left Germany for the United States, because of how they treated him as a child, being illegitimate and all. Taking me in made them feel like they were making amends for their past trans-gressions. Second, the university in Munich does not test. What I mean by this is, as incredible as it might sound, they do not administer tests during or at the conclusion of each individual course. An all-encompassing series of tests is administered prior to graduation. Along with not testing, they also do not take attendance. The student registers for classes which are then entered into his aca-demic record (*Studium Buch*).With no tests and no atten-dance requirements to worry about, I had all the free-dom I would ever need to come and go as I pleased, all the while looking like a full-time student.

With that decision made, I sent Munich my letter of intent to matriculate and set about taking care of all the details necessary to complete the process. I applied for and received my passport, got my shots and then set about arranging transportation. My parents had made it clear that since I had gotten myself into this mess, I would have to cover all of the costs myself. The Agency was not going to cover costs as a sudden influx of unearned money would raise red flags. Although I did have some savings left after settling my attorney and court fees, I settled on the cheapest flight I could find. Icelandic Airlines had an extremely low fare to Luxembourg via Keflavik Airport in

Iceland. From Luxembourg I could catch a train to Munich, and from the Munich train station, I planned to catch the local S-Bahn (Munich rapid transit system) to my uncle's house at 191 Kerschensteinerstrasse in Unterpfaffenhofen, a suburb of Munich.

I boarded an Icelandic Airlines DC-8 in mid-October, 1972, and after a short layover in Reykjavik, touched down in Luxembourg. International travel, especially alone, was new to me, but everything, like money exchanges, directions, and train connections went smoothly. Of course, being fluent in German helped quite a bit. Arriving in Munich by train, I was surprised to see that my Uncle Franz was there to meet me. Franz was a big beer drinker; he had a beer every morning for breakfast and continued drinking throughout the day. Considering all of the alcohol he consumed, I was amazed at how lean and tremendously muscular he was. Franz's favorite activity, after beer drinking, was fighting. More often than not he combined the two, starting quite a few barroom brawls. Unfortunately, this also led to Franz serving time in local jails as well as one stint in prison. It also resulted in him being permanently barred from many of the bars in and around Munich.

After greeting me he told me that we would be dropping my luggage off at my Uncle Reimund's house, where I would be staying, and then immediately head over to the *Teresien Wiese* where Oktoberfest was in full swing. Unfortunately, I will never remember much else of what happened that day since I ended up drinking 12 liters of Oktoberfest beer (I guess I had to do my part to contribute to the more than 5,000,000 liters of high-proof beer consumed over this two-week period). I still don't know how I managed to drink so much beer, as even 12 liters of water should have been enough to drown me, or at the least, to make me burst.

While waiting for more information about what I would be doing for Phil, I decided that for now I would concentrate on life as a student at Ludwig-Maximillians Universitaet. After recovering from my week-long Oktober-fest beer binge, I set out to explore Munich, the third largest city in Germany and the capital of Bavaria, lo-cated approximately 40 miles from the Alps. The city dates back to 1156 when Friederich Barbarossa, the Holy Ro-man Emperor, gave a small piece of land to Henry the Lion, the Duke of Brunswick. Since the area consisted mainly of a monastery, it was known as *Bei den Moenichen*, or, "where the monks live." It is widely accepted to be the city most Germans would choose to live in if given the opportunity.

Along with acquainting myself with the city, I set out to complete all of the bureaucratic requirements that go along with being a foreigner in Germany—student visa, work permit, mass transit pass, health insurance, registration with the local police station, and so on. I then went to the university, completed my registration, and took part in a number of orientation events designed for foreign students. The group of new students I was a part of were all declared Germanistik majors, (German studies) and consisted of two girls each from Italy and France, one girl and guy from America, and another girl and guy from England.

The faculty of Ludwig-Maximillians—which enjoyed a reputation as one of the finest universities in the world—was exceptional in welcoming new foreign stu-dents and devoted time and attention to orienting them to German university life and requirements. First, they sent the nine of us to a hotel in the Bavarian Alps in the city of Garmisch for two weeks. We met for a few hours each day to discuss the topic *du jour*; the rest of the time was ours to do with as we pleased. For the most part that meant splitting our time between bars and the coed sauna (everything seemed to be coed in Germany, including the locker rooms and showers, which is one of the hardest things for Americans to get used to). That was followed by a week in both East and West Berlin. The agenda was the same as it was in Garmisch; work during the day and enjoy lots of free time at night. The big difference with the Berlin trip was that I used every minute of my spare time exploring the city and getting used to crossing the border into the walled off part of the city administered by the Soviet Union and the communist Deutsche Demokratische Republik (DDR).

Listening to East Berliners in bars and restaurants provided a great opportunity to learn the Prussian dialect and to observe the peculiarities of living behind the Iron Curtain, both of which would become useful to me later on. Being in East Berlin also made it possible for me to meet and carry on lengthy conversations with a number of Russians, many of whom either visited East Berlin from the Soviet Union on vacation (for the most part, Soviets were permitted to visit other East Bloc countries only) or they were stationed there as soldiers. My Russian was pretty good, but for the most part, it was book Russian, and in need of a more conversational grasp.

One of my favorite places to hang out was at the Soviet War Memorial near the Brandenburg Gate, which is the resting place of more than 2,500 Soviet soldiers who died during World War II fighting against the Nazis. The monument is constructed out of artifacts from the war and is flanked by two T34 tanks, supposedly the first to have entered Berlin in 1945. The focal point of the monument is a Soviet soldier in bronze holding a child in one hand while his other hand, holding a broadsword, smashes a swastika. It was guarded around the clock by the Soviet army and was a favorite with vacationing Red Army veterans. Another good spot was the 62-foot-high statue of Lenin which loomed over what was then called Lenin Square (now United Nations Square). The statue was first unveiled in 1970 by DDR leader Walter Ulbricht, whose other claim to fame was the construction of the Berlin Wall. I would hang out at these places, sketching the monuments (at least what I called sketching), and strike up casual conversations whenever I could. I would tell people that I was a German university student from Munich who was there studying Socialism. As far as I could tell, nobody ever figured out that I was American. Nothing beats contact with native speakers for perfecting the nuances of language.

My primary concern during these "visits" to East Berlin was with any potential problems from agents from the *Ministerium fuer Staatssicherheit* (Ministry for State Security), commonly known as the *Stasi*. The *Stasi* had what was believed to be the most comprehensive internal security organization of the entire East Bloc. Conservative estimates held that more than 400,000 people (out of a population of 16 million) actively cooperated with the *Stasi*. After reunification, it was discovered that the *Stasi* kept active files on more than 6 million East Germans, more than a third of the entire population. Every phone call and every piece of mail from the West was monitored. Because of this the East Germans were a paranoid population. Starting a conversation with a Russian was easier than with a German as the general presumption was that any stranger was probably connected to the *Stasi*.

It is hard for somebody who has not experienced life under Ulbricht's and his successor Eric Honecker's control to imagine how thoroughly pervasive the *Stasi* were. Presumably, *every person* who entered East Berlin from the West was thoroughly checked out and followed. On more than one occasion I found myself being photographed by people who looked like tourists. Knowing what I do now about the *Stasi*, any information they gathered including fingerprints taken from a beer glass somewhere, also became part of a *Stasi* file. But since I engaged in nothing illegal or subversive in the East during that time, I never experienced an overt confrontation.

The university picked up all of the cost for these trips. Add to that the fact that the total tuition for attending the university was merely 30 Deutsch Marks (about $10 at that time), with the federal government subsidizing the rest, studying in Germany was an exceptional deal. Aside from the DM 30 tuition, students' expenses included books and room and board. Since I was living with relatives, my costs couldn't have gotten any lower.

The fall semester in Munich started late in 1972 because the city had been hosting the XX Olympic Games. The tragic murder of members of the Israeli Olympic team happened in the Olympic village and, as it turned out, in some of the living quarters that were converted to university student housing after the games. One thing that I had discovered was that although not officially sanctioned, anti-Semitism remained very much a part of the German national mentality decades after the fall of Naziism. Despite the outcry against the slaughter of the Jewish delegation which appeared in the German press, in private many Germans, if not a majority of them, were of the opinion that the Jews somehow had it coming. My own family routinely blamed all manner of social ills plaguing Germany on the existence of Jews. I remember coming back to my uncle's house one day after class with a Dan Fogelberg record. After referring to Fogelberg as *"eine verdammte Jude,"* (a damned Jew), he refused to let me play the album on his stereo system. I sometimes wonder if he ever thought about the fact that his own half-brother was half Jewish and that his mother had had an affair with a Jewish man.

A couple of weeks later I was headed to my French class when out of the blue, Phil fell in step next to me. By now, things like this no longer surprised me. He told me that we needed to talk right away and with that we changed direction and headed across town to the *Matthaeser*, a beer hall where we could talk in private without arousing anybody's attention. There are six major breweries based in Munich—Hofbrau, Augustinerbrau, Loewenbrau, Hacker Pschorrbrau, Matthaeserbrau, and

Paulanerbrau—which combined brew more than 110,000,000 gallons of beer a year. The Hofbrauhaus alone serves more than 10,000 liters of beer *per day*. There was no better place to blend in and not be seen or noticed than in one of these six massive beer halls in Munich. Thanks to their tourist appeal, if you listened closely you could hear literally dozens of languages at any given time. In addition, most of the patrons were too buzzed by the alcohol to hear or understand anything going on around them.

After the obligatory exchange of pleasantries, Phil got down to business.

"It's time for you to take a little trip."

"But I haven't even settled into school yet."

"That's not why you're over here. Remember?"

He was right. With such sporadic contact between us, it was sometimes easy to forget why I was here in the first place.

"We need you to do some things in Turkey, Iran, Afghanistan, and Pakistan. Your cover is simple; you will travel overland through Europe and Asia with a declared goal of going to India, where you will supposedly seek 'enlightenment' from an Indian guru in Premnagar, in the foothills of the Himalayas. Lots of people are doing that these days so your trip should not raise any eyebrows."

Phil was right. Ever since the Beatles had popularized Hindu mysticism by their association with the Maharishi Mahesh Yogi, going to India was a popular thing to do. Of course most, if not all, Americans who did this had the luxury of flying into Delhi. I had to go overland?

"First, you have to get to Istanbul in Turkey. After some preliminary research and work there, you will hit the road, literally, and hitchhike to Tehran. When you get what you need from Tehran, you'll be off to Herat, Kandehar and Kabul in Afghanistan. Then, crossing the Khyber Pass, you will hitch to Pakistan and then on into

India. For the most part, you will do nothing along the way except to lay the groundwork for your final actions which you will accomplish on your return to Germany, using the same route. One exception is in Kabul, where you will act before you head for Pakistan. The trip back will be messier, and I won't bullshit you, the whole thing will be dangerous. If anything goes wrong you will end up dead, or worse, locked up forever in some shithole prison cell. You'll be totally on your own. I won't communicate with you directly and vice versa. As a matter of fact, as far as anybody is concerned, we never met. When I do need to get word to you, you will get a message left at the local American Express office, presumably from your parents."

Jumping out of an aircraft at 35,000 feet was beginning to look like a walk in the park compared to what I was listening to. I was twenty years old and setting off to parts of the world about which most people had no knowledge. I had no knowledge of the languages or people I would meet along the way. And let's not forget the fact that I might not be coming back! I had no information about what my activities might involve, other than they could be "messy." Phil was probably right again; he never tried to bullshit me. If he was telling me this was going to be dangerous, I was pretty sure that he meant exactly that.

"So who do I have to kill?" I said jokingly. When he didn't laugh, or even smile, I suddenly understood the gravity of the situation.

"There is a major heroin smuggling ring with its starting point in Afghanistan. From there, the junk is packed off to Pakistan, Iran, and Turkey. Istanbul is the point at which it moves into Europe and the United States. You are going to be traveling as a potentially high dollar buyer looking to set up a distribution network. After setting up your contacts along the route, and handling one thing in Afghanistan, you will spend some time in India to let the whole thing gel. Coming back, you will cause some major shit at a couple of operational cells along the way. You will also ensure that the people we have targeted for action in this arena will not be able to do anything like this again. Your solution has to have a high degree of finality."

"But if we are so sure that certain known people in certain known areas are processing known narcotics, why can't we wait for the local or national police forces to shut them down?"

"Mainly because the local and national police forces are part of the operations in the first place. There is no way to legally shut them down. No matter what you do, you're not going to shut down the production of heroin and its eventual shipment to Europe and the United States. And, to tell you the truth, we don't particularly want to see them shut down. The heroin trade plays an important role in the way things run, in more ways than one. What you are going to do is remove the current "management" and, in doing so, deliver an important message to whoever follows."

"And what message is that?"

"That there are rules for everything. When you break the rules, you get broken, and you stay broken."

"You're making it sound like 'we' are part of that distribution cycle and that somehow 'we' have been shafted."

"Actually, that's none of your or my business. We do as we're told. You will be told everything you need to know, and not a bit more; and that won't be much. Believe me, it's better that way."

With that, he passed me a large manila envelope with names, addresses, pictures, background information, maps, and a large amount of German Marks and Turkish Lira. "Study this, commit it all to memory, and then get it back to me one week from today, right here. In the meantime, get all the visas and shots you will need for this trip. Whenever you're asked about the reason for your trip, you will reply simply that you are a student."

There was one more item he handed to me—a Gerber

Mark II black bladed knife. I had been introduced to the Gerber as well as the Ka-bar, a knife popular with the Marines, and a number of other blades when I went through my edged weapons training. The MK II he gave me had a seven-inch blade and was a sterile weapon in that it had no markings, making it impossible to trace back to the manufacturer in case I had to leave it behind. But believe me, leaving the MK II behind was not an option as far as I was concerned.

CHAPTER 9

THE ROAD TO ISTANBUL

During the next couple of weeks, I visited the embassies of Bulgaria, Turkey, Iran, Afghanistan, Pakistan, and India, and applied for the necessary visas. I also obtained pertinent information about requirements for travel through those countries. Next, I received cholera and typhus inoculations in order to preempt the prospect of some disease doing me in.

Then I had to tell my aunt and uncle that I would be gone for a while. This turned out to be easier than I had anticipated. Although they had agreed to my living with them, no doubt based on a sense of guilt for how the family had rejected my illegitimate father decades earlier, the longer I stayed the more of a burden I seemed to become to them. My aunt, in particular, had been growing colder and colder toward me. I told them that I was going on a trip to India as part of my studies in philosophy and religion. Although a far-fetched story, they were more than willing to accept it.

The route through Asia had been laid out for me by Phil and was based on where I had to be at any given time to fulfill my mission. How I reached Istanbul was left up to me. I was facing quite a bit of time hitchhiking, so I decided that I would take the train to Turkey. I went to the Munich *Bahnhof*, or train station, and found that the most expedient way through Austria and Bulgaria and then into Turkey would be by taking the Orient Express.

The Orient Express was the name of the long-distance passenger train originally owned and operated by the *Compaigne Internationale des Wagons-Lits*. The train's original route, starting in 1883, went from Paris to Giurgiu, Romania, by way of Munich and Vienna. In 1889 the route was extended to Istanbul. Throughout the years, a number of routes and companies have used the name Orient Express; the line I bought my ticket on was called the Direct Orient Express and the trip cost me DM 180 ($64 USD).

Before leaving, I bought myself a lightweight backpack and sleeping bag. The only clothes I planned to take were two pairs of jeans, a few shirts, underwear and socks, one sweater, and a mohair-looking jacket. I also packed a small combination cooking kit, a small Brownie camera, and my Gerber Mark II knife. Any information given me concerning the who, what, and where of my mission had been returned to Phil; I could not afford a customs official discovering it and linking me to what they were currently doing or to what was, if all went according to plan, going to happen to them. When I look back today on my preparations for that trip, I am amazed at how naïve I was to think that I could survive for months on what little I packed. However, I suppose that naiveté added a good bit of credibility to my story of being a hippy/student once I reached the respective border crossings. I'm sure that the average person did not discern a sinister or even serious purpose to the ridiculous figure I presented.

And with that, I calmly boarded the train and headed east. The train had little in common with the Orient Express in movies or in Agatha Christie's novel, *Murder on the Orient Express.* As a poor student I did not have anything to do with, or even see, the comfortable sleeping cars and luxurious restaurant cars normally associated with the cinematic or fictional versions. I traveled in a second class coach where six to eight people sat in one small compartment. I was, however, pleasantly surprised when a major in the Red Army joined my compartment in Bulgaria. I was able to practice my Russian, and he read my copy of *Playboy*, which I just happened to have with me. According to him, men could not buy anything like *Playboy* anywhere in the East Bloc. He made a point of emphasizing that having that copy would make him something of a celebrity back in his home town. I understood why he said what he did and gladly gave him the magazine before he left the train. He warmly reciprocated by giving me a bag of walnuts.

For me, arriving in Germany from the United States had been a culture shock. Now, going from Europe to Istanbul provided a jump back in time. Each stop along my route seemed to take me back another step in the way of life, eating, and even public manners. Turkey in general, and Istanbul in particular, was a gateway to India or Nepal for Western hippies in the late 1960s and early 1970s, a route often called the Hippie Trail.

Istanbul, the first stop on that trail, was a beautiful, bustling city recognized as a cultural and ethnic melting pot with contrasting European and Western flavors in the many historical palaces, mosques, churches, and synagogues. Adjacent to two of the most imposing structures, the Hagia Sofia and the Sultan Ahmed Mosque, also known as the Blue Mosque, was the Hippodrome, built by the Romans around AD 200 as a venue for chariot races. Very little of the original Hippodrome survived, and by the 1970s, the area had become a place for hippies to park their vans before continuing on the journey toward Nepal.

But the whole reason for my presence was the drug scene. Although it had declined somewhat since 1968, it was enjoying a resurgence of sorts with literally tons of cheap, home-produced hashish and opium available. Anyone also could buy any kind of pharmaceutical known at any drug store, all without a prescription. As Phil explained, the drugs entered Istanbul without difficulty because the governmental intelligence organizations (including those of the United States) and numerous federal and local police organizations sanctioned the roles that Istanbul, Turkey, and Afghanistan played in the process. Afghanistan was the original source of most of the opiates reaching Turkey. Afghani opiates and hashish were stockpiled at storage and distribution areas in Pakistan from where quantities by the ton were smuggled overland to Turkey via Iran. Much larger quantities of opiates and hashish were also moved to coastal areas of Pakistan and Iran where they were loaded onto ships and smuggled to points in Turkey along the Mediterranean, Aegean, and Marmara seas. Turkish-based traffickers and brokers operated directly with narcotic suppliers, smugglers, transporters, lab operators, distributors, sellers, and money launderers inside and outside Turkey. Heroin labs in Turkey illegally acquired acetic anhydride, which was used in the production of heroin, from sources in Western Europe, the Balkans, and Russia. In the early 1970s, about 75 percent of the heroin seized in Europe was either produced in or had as its distribution point Turkey, with four to six tons of heroin arriving from Turkey every month, heading for Western Europe.

Some of the opium was actually grown in Turkey. Turkish farmers grew a lot of opium and had done so for centuries. Their pastoral life was built on the cultivation of the opium poppy. They ate the young leaves of the opium plant in their salads. They fed the harvested plants, minus the coveted opium gum, to their cattle. The only part of the plant the farmers didn't use was the drug-producing gum, which they sold to the government—as they were required to do by law—for use in making legal pharmaceuticals. However, within this process was a flaw, and that was that illegal drug traffickers paid more for the gum than the government did. The farmers, far from being the simple, ignorant hicks their government believed them to be sold a small part of their crop to the government and the rest to the traffickers.

After getting off of the train, I asked for directions to the drug, or hippie, section of Istanbul, which was located in the Sultan Ahmet part of the city, close to the two mosques I have already described. There were plenty of cheap hotels with rooms to be had that ran less than 14 Turkish Lire (about $1 USD) per night. The one I had been instructed to go to was probably the most notorious for drug dealing, the Gulhane Hotel. On the roof of the Gulhane, the owner had constructed a large canvas structure, which was called "The Tent" by the drug users who hung out there. For less than the cost of a room, I could sleep on the straw floor of The Tent. Strangers arriving for the first time would be offered a hit on a chillum—a hashish smoking pipe popular in Afghanistan and India. The hash was so cheap that small pieces that fell to the ground were left, a wasteful oversight which would have been unthinkable in America.

In The Tent, people were passed out all along the floor, and drugs were bought and sold with no regard for any law—although there was a slim chance of being arrested. Because of pressure from the American government and an unfortunate shootout with an American drug dealer named Ralph Gary Bouldin in December 1968, the Turkish police occasionally were ordered to reduce the drug trade by arresting drug smugglers. Foreign traffickers were the easiest to arrest because they didn't know the territory as well as the locals. Most of the foreign dealers were amateurs who were easy to identify, pick up, charge, and convict. However, once a foreigner was convicted, the Turkish government was obligated to lock him up. Because foreigners were held in separate prisons that were more modern and comfortable than the traditional grungy Turkish facilities, the costs for their incarceration was higher than for Turkey's own prisoners. The Turks were cautious of damaging any political relationships with the governments and media overseas, which in turn would hurt the tourist trade.

To accommodate all parties, the Turkish authorities

devised a workable plan. Although they would continue to arrest and try drug smugglers, confiscating their passports to keep them from leaving the country, after conviction the convicted smugglers were released pending appeal. That eliminated the immediate costs associated with their incarceration.

After the convict was released, albeit without his passport, a court official would let it slip that a train ran from Istanbul to Edirne (also in Turkey) in the middle of the night—a very slow train. And while the start and stop points were both in Turkey, because of the geography involved, the train actually passed through a portion of Greece. Since the train did not officially stop anywhere outside of Turkish territory, passengers did not need a passport to ride it. It did not take very long before most of the convicted drug smugglers figured out that they could take this train, with no need for a passport, and jump off while it was slowly plodding through Greek territory. From there they could travel to an American embassy in Greece and, claiming they had lost their passport, apply for a new one. To the best of my knowledge, this is where the term "Midnight Express," as used in the movie of the same name, originated.

I saw my first real live heroin junkie in The Tent. Without saying a word, he unpacked a candle, a bent spoon, a piece of rubber hosing and a hypodermic needle. I watched in fascination as he cooked up his heroin and then injected it. Immediately, he went from surly to really mellow, and then just kind of fell back in a stupor. As it turned out, cooking up heroin was an everyday practice. And freaky as it was, The Tent was also the meeting place for anything drug related, so I was clearly in the right place to get connected.

After a few small buys, I hinted that I was interested in something bigger and on a more permanent basis. This kind of prospect attracted Turkish traffickers because it was an easy way to double their profits. Generally, if an individual bought a large quantity of any drug, the dealer alerted the Turkish authorities regarding how much and of what drug the individual had bought. The authorities would be waiting either at the airport or at the border to make the arrest. After arresting, prosecuting, and releasing the convict (who would most likely leave the country at the first opportunity) the authorities returned the contraband to the dealer who could then sell it to somebody else, thereby continuing the cycle. With any luck at all, one batch of hashish could result in a large number of repeat sales and convictions.

I was hoping to interest a specific dealer, Akhun Berk al Zarqa, as per my instructions. Again, Agency personnel did not have a problem with the drug traffic in general and had no interest in disrupting it. They were looking to remove this specific person and, if possible, any of his lieutenants—all of whom had become rogues. This would send a clear message to other major traffickers, many of them with wider networks, that they too were subject to being "disciplined" if the need arose.

To ask to meet with al Zarqa would raise too much suspicion. Any meeting needed to be his decision. Consequently, over the space of the next few weeks, I made contact with four different sources, always finding some reason why I could not do business with them, before finally connecting with the right guy. My first meeting with al Zarqa was at an eatery called Lale Pastahanesi, or, as it was known to westerners, The Pudding Shop, located at Number 6 Sultanahmet Divanyolu, adjacent to the Hippodrome between the Hagia Sofia and the Blue Mosque. The Pudding Shop soon became the definitive and indispensable meeting place, message center, and travel bureau on the Hippy Trail to Katmandu. Hippies traveling east, driving mostly old run-down cars or Volkswagen vans, parked their vehicles at the Hippodrome and walked to The Pudding Shop to find other travelers to help share expenses. The Çolpan brothers, who owned The Pudding Shop, managed a bulletin board to handle all the messages from people offering or hitching rides home to

Europe or heading to the Far East, as well as to share stories, advice, and tips about the trip ahead.

At that first meeting with al Zarqa, we both proceeded slowly and cautiously. We kept the conversation light, although I made sure that I told him enough about myself that he would be able to go back to his police contacts and check on me to ensure that I was not a narcotics agent sent to entrap him. When we met again a week later, he seemed ready to talk business. I told him how much heroin I was prepared to move, at which point his interest was peaked. Next I told him the bad news, that I would not be dealing right then and there but when I returned from other business I had to complete elsewhere. He argued hard to persuade me to change my mind, probably afraid that I would pursue a better deal somewhere else. But I stood fast, explaining how traveling with $100,000 USD on my person was unwise, especially without having a firm commitment lined up first. He wasn't happy, but he was also not willing to alienate whatever future business he might have with me. He gave me his phone number and address and made me promise that I would get in touch with him as soon as I was ready.

With that, my purpose for this initial stop in Istanbul had been achieved. I had met the target, gained his trust, been given his address, and made certain that he would be anxious to meet with me when the time was right upon my return. For a few days I observed his residence for any potential hazards that would stop me from a quick getaway when the time came. After that I returned to The Pudding Shop to arrange transportation to Tehran, the next planned stop on my agenda.

CHAPTER 10

TURKEY AND IRAN

Before returning to The Pudding Shop, I took a bus to the Istanbul American Express office. Phil had arranged for me to stop at every available American Express office along the route, where a sum of money in the local currency waited for me. This served numerous purposes: I did not carry large amounts of cash at any one time, which would have targeted me for robbery and possibly murder. Also, it alleviated the need to exchange money. There were many black-market currency exchanges along the route, and although one could find some competitive rates, more often than not the black-market currency was old currency no longer recognized by the government and therefore useless. Those unaware of this trick were sure to be cheated. But perhaps the most important reason for going to the American Express offices was that they served as communication centers for Phil, who left messages for me under the guise that he was a family member.

Back at The Pudding Shop, I met with a Swiss tourist named Jakob Valaer. Jakob was in his late thirties and yearly traveled the Hippie Trail to India. A simple farmer from a small village in Switzerland, Jakob was short and slightly stout with a beard that grew down to his chest; he looked like a garden gnome. He neither indulged in drugs nor looked prone to indulgence. In that respect, Jakob was a perfect traveling companion for cover. He was also highly personable and had already secured a ride with some French folks who were traveling in an old Volkswagen van, literally hundreds of which were on the road.

As soon as everybody and everything was stowed in and on top of the van, we were off for the ferry, which was the way to cross the Bosporus and officially enter into the Asian part of Turkey. Next, we drove to Kantel to catch another ferry to Yalova. From Yalova, we drove to the town of Ordu. The weather was cold and wet, the ground a mass of mud, and the scenery looked dreary and impoverished. Every time we stopped and left the van, we were surrounded by hordes of Turkish children begging for money, despite the fact that they never seemed to obtain any money and, speaking only Turkish, could not communicate with the travelers. The most I could offer them was chewing gum, which didn't seem to thrill them, but which they also never turned down. From there, we headed for Ankara, the capital of Turkey and the country's second largest city after Istanbul.

Ankara, like many Middle Eastern metropolises, was made up of two sections, an ancient as well as a modern one. Before it was made Turkey's capital in 1923, Ankara was called Angora, known for its production of the soft goat's wool that bore the town's name. The new Ankara had become a modern city mostly built around its function as the capital and was trying to compete with other European capitals. We agreed that there was nothing to warrant an extended stay and decided to spend only one night.

In the morning, we started our ascent into the Pontus Mountains, straining the van's engine so badly I was convinced we were going to have to help push it. As I happened to have an international driver's license, I helped out by driving part of this leg of the journey. Driving in Asia and the Middle East was an experience unlike any other. It seemed as if nobody used headlights when driving at night. This made for a large number of near head-on collisions and excessive horn honking. With a great deal of luck, we plowed onward through Samsun and Trabzon, finally arriving in Erzerum, the easternmost city in Turkey. Erzerum was Turkey's fourth largest city and was located near the Irani border. We stopped early and camped for the night to make a fresh start the next day.

I had a terrible time falling asleep that night because I was dwelling on what lay ahead of me. Doubt took over my thoughts. What made me think that I could put this grand scheme together? I had no plan yet and couldn't devise one until I saw exactly what I would be facing. Would I be able to complete my mission, or would I lose my nerve? And assuming I was successful, how would I possibly escape without being caught? Although I hated to admit it to myself, my reflection in the mirror revealed me to look like little more than a scared kid. I was twenty years old, but since I had little, if any, facial hair, I looked more like a fifteen-year-old. Most people who looked at me would not believe that I could be capable of doing much more than playing Frisbee and getting stoned. But I soon accepted the fact that my innocent looks could only act in my favor. Once I came to this realization, my doubts dissipated. Besides, I wasn't here to think; I was here to act. I had a purpose.

After starting the day with some strong Turkish tea, we drove straight for the Irani border. There we could see Mount Ararat (Agri Dagi in Turkish) off to the North. Mount Ararat has an elevation of almost 17,000 feet and is the largest volcano in Turkey (although its last major volcanic activity was back around 1840) and lies 10 miles west of Iran and 20 miles south of Armenia. I was fascinated by the fact that The Book of Genesis indirectly identifies Ararat as the place where Noah's ark came to rest after the great flood described in the Bible. There have even been a number of explorers who have claimed to have found pieces of the ark there, and the locals, enjoying the influx of money from expeditionary teams, have taken the story on as tradition.

Iran in the early 1970s was probably the strictest country in regard to trafficking narcotics on the Hippie Trail. To understand the situation fully, a little background information is necessary. Early in World War II (1941), Germany broke the Nazi-Soviet non-aggression pact and invaded its former ally, the Soviet Union, which then quickly formed an alliance with England. Although Iran officially declared neutrality, the British and the Soviets, not wanting to leave anything to chance, occupied Iran and forced the current Shah to abdicate in favor of his son, Mohammad Reza Pahlavi. He ruled as the Shah of Iran from 1941 to 1979, except for a short break in 1953 when Prime Minister Muhammed Mosaddeq overthrew him. To gain control over the Iranian oil industry the CIA and the British funded and led a covert operation, named Operation Ajax (TP-AJAX), to overthrow the prime minister, with the help of the military forces loyal to the Shah. The coup failed during its first attempt, and the Shah had to flee Iran. After a short exile in Italy, the Shah was able to assume power again via a successful, second coup.

Under the Shah, Iran managed to stop poppy cultivation in certain regions in the country. More than 76,944 kilos of opium were discovered and burned between the years 1958–1965. Two years later, Iran's anti-drug effort was rated as the top drug eradication program in the world. Iran had detained 58 percent of the heroin dealers in the world and its heroin seizure amounted to 14 percent of the world's narcotics cache. Iran may have ranked as number one in drug interdiction in 1967 but it suddenly made an about-face in its policies and authorized the cultivation of poppy plants and strictly monitored and rationed the resulting opium consumption.

As rationale for this move, they cited a UN permit in 1945 for poppy cultivation in Iran for medical purposes only. The reality, however, was that cultivating poppy was just too lucrative to stop and for the small landowners doing the growing, it was the only crop that could provide any measurable income at all.

So what you have is a system where you become hard line on foreign drug traders/users to appease your two best allies, the United States and Great Britain, while you look the other way in respect to internal drug production and use. This made crossing the borders into Iran a very dangerous proposition. Signs posted on roads leading up to the border clearly stated that anybody caught with illegal narcotics would be tried (generally on the spot) and executed.

However, a solution soon presented itself to the travelers on the Hippie Trail, both coming and going. People approaching the border would simply pass any drugs they had to those who were leaving Iran. Therefore, the only dry time suffered by a traveler was at the border itself, since once he or she was inside the country, there was plenty of hashish or opium to buy so long as discretion was used.

The border crossing site was actually a compound. The first stop was on the Turkish side where travelers completed the requirements for exiting the country. Apparently, my dealings in Istanbul had alerted some authorities and had been reported to the border facility, identifying me as a potential drug exporter, so I was searched thoroughly, much more so than Jakob and our French traveling companions. The Turkish border guards seemed disappointed that they did not find drugs in my possession. When we were through with the Turks, we drove the van up to a chain-link fence in the center of the compound where a soldier checked that we had valid entry visas. Once again, we were thoroughly searched to ensure we were not carrying any drugs with us. Passing that inspection, we were allowed to enter into Iran.

About four hours later, we made our first stop in Tabriz, which was around 190 miles from the Turkish border. Tabriz was the second largest city in Iran until the early 1970s, was the provincial capital of Eastern Azarbaaijaan, and had been the capital city of Iran numerous times throughout its history. Jakob and the French were in favor of spending time sight seeing, but I needed to pick up my money, so we agreed to meet later before we continued on to Tehran. I immediately made my way to the American Express office on the east side of Shohada Square, opposite Bank Melli Iran. Along with a decent amount of Irani rials, there was also a message from Phil simply stating, "Business dealings with Khalilpour in Tehran resolved favorably. No need to pursue Iranian portion."

Although I was resolved in my purpose for being in the country and on this mission in general, I did not relish doing what I was supposed to do in a country as tightly regulated as Iran was. The Shah had authorized the creation of a secret police force called the *Sazeman-e Ettelaat va Amniyat-e Keshvar*, or SAVAK for short, which was Persian Farsi for the Organization for Intelligence and National Security, reputed to be as thorough as the East German *Stasi* and was well known for its ruthless handling of dissidents and foreign agitators. Leaving Iran after killing a well-known narcotics supplier was going to be the trickiest part of the entire mission. Now that it had been eliminated, I had more time to prepare myself mentally for what was inevitable in Afghanistan.

Feeling that I had dodged a bullet, I registered with the local police (tourists had to register with the local police authorities in every town they stayed in. This was another reason I had not relished pulling anything in Iran—there was too tight a paper trail on everywhere you had been and exactly when you came and went) and I got myself a hotel room for 70 rials for the night. I was looking forward not to have to sleep in or be bounced around in the VW van for a few days. I also enjoyed the peace and quiet of not being tied to Jakob and the French for however short a period of time. The French were friendly enough, but they smoked cigarettes called *Galois*, which were possibly the world's smelliest cigarettes (the French describe *Galois* as "aromatic," which is like describing an Air Wick as cologne). On top of that, they didn't believe in brushing their teeth or washing at all. The combination made the air inside of the van almost unbearable.

Next, I went to a local teahouse for what later became my normal meal while in Iran, tea and bread. I enjoyed the strong tea and the way it was served. Most people in the Middle East liked their tea sweet but did not put sugar in it. Rather, they put a chunk of sugar in their mouths and sucked the tea through the sugar. I loved consuming sugar chunks this way.

After a few days of sightseeing, I rejoined my group and we headed off toward Tehran. The ride (a stretch of about 375 miles) was not memorable but Tehran was another story altogether. The only way to describe traffic in Tehran is chaotic. Horns are constantly honking and laws or rules governing right of way, speed, stopping, and so forth were systematically ignored. It was not unusual to go into a bar, order some beer, and watch television while talking to some young, jeans-clad Iranian ladies. But that wasn't why I was there. I wanted to spend the least amount of time possible there and would have preferred heading off toward Afghanistan the next morning, but it was not my vehicle, and so it was decreed that we would hang there for about a week.

Before heading out of Tehran, I asked to stop at the American Express office in the Park Hotel. I wasn't expecting money, but I had made a habit of checking for messages from Phil. I received no word at all from him.

Our next planned stop was to be Mashad, the capital of Khorasan province. This part of the ride was about 525 miles and would take us through Bojnurd and Quchan.

Finally, after two days of sightseeing, everyone was ready to go to Afghanistan. Having spoken to a group of Australians coming back from Afghanistan, we found out that there was a trick to crossing the border. It seems that the official Irani immigration checkpoint was in a tent in a town some 12 miles before the border itself. Travelers were required to present their passports for stamping and to clear customs at this site before proceeding to the border and crossing into Afghanistan. We did this and headed east. Driving along, all of a sudden we came upon a lone Iranian in uniform waving his arms for us to stop. This desolate guard stand, without a single building, was the official border between the two countries. Without glancing at our passports, he informed us that we would have to backtrack the 12 miles to the immigration station and clear our passports before he could let us cross. When we showed him that we had already done that, he was visibly upset that the little trick for messing with foreigners had not worked in our case. And with that we crossed the border into Afghanistan.

CHAPTER 11

FIRST KILL:
AFGHANISTAN AND THE LOSS OF INNOCENCE

Afghanistan was a 180–degree turnaround from Iran. Iran was fairly well developed (for a Middle Eastern country), but Afghanistan was undeveloped, a fact that was immediately evident in the condition of the road. I say "road," singular, because there was one road leading across the entire country, which is slightly smaller than Texas. At its widest, from east to west, it measures about 770 miles and from north to south it is 630 miles. The northwestern, western, and southern border areas are made up mainly of desert plains and rocky ranges, whereas in the northeast it borders the glacier-covered peaks of the Hindu Kush mountain range, which is an extension of the Himalayas.

Eight regions made up Afghanistan. A circular road to link these regions was planned and constructed during the 1960s with assistance from the United States, the Soviet Union, and West Germany. This road connected Afghanistan's four major cities with the country's primary border crossings: from Herat to Iran in the west; from Kandahar to Pakistan in the south; from Kabul through Jalalabad to Pakistan in the east; and from Balkh to Uzbekistan in the north. This is the only proper road running through Afghanistan. Any other so-called roads were unpaved, unlit, and for the most part impassable to all but the bravest (or dumbest) travelers, as they led into parts of the country that were not especially friendly to outsiders. I had researched Afghanistan and my knowledge was now beginning to be of benefit as I developed a plan for my mission. Afghanistan had an extremely weak central government with little influence or control outside of Kabul. In addition, there was no cohesive or strong national police or military network. This meant that there was no office or group monitoring an individual's every move as there was in East Germany and Iran. I would have much more freedom to act and blend into the background without drawing any suspicion to myself. The real seats of power in the country were based on complex ethnic relationships. Every ethnic group used what is called *qaum*, a word that means "nation," to determine their network of affiliations. Every individual belonged to a *qaum* that provided protection as well as support, security, and assistance, when needed. *Qaum* also referred to a connection between family and ethnic group. In tribal areas *qaum* refers to a common genealogy from extended family, or clan, to tribal ties.

A common male ancestor, after whom the tribe was named, served as the unifying element in Afghani tribal identity and ethnicity. Splits in the family tree, branching from the original tribal founder, caused internal divisions within the tribe. An entire tribe may have sprung from a single man a dozen generations ago and smaller units composed of great-grandsons and grandsons formed subtribes with strong personal loyalty between members.

The Pashtun represent the largest tribal entity in Afghanistan. Pashtun leadership is based on a more or less democratic system of councils called *jirgah*, at which individual members have the right to express themselves freely without fear of reprisal and to deal with tribal business, one of the most important issues being revenge. Revenge, a revered and accepted tradition, could be taken against any member of an offending tribe. This frequently wholesale and continuous cycle of revenge, more often than not consisting of murder, offered a perfect cover for my activities. Barring any eyewitnesses, there would be a whole host of suspects for any killing committed in Afghanistan. And any homicide was not likely to be reported to any central law enforcement authority, because the victim's tribe would assume the responsibility for exacting justice (revenge).

Soon after leaving the Irani side of the border, my travel companions and I came across a uniformed guard. He checked our passports without a word and then let us through. A couple of miles further down the road we arrived at the Islam Qala frontier station. First, a passport official wrote details about us in a large ledger-type notebook. Although officials in Afghanistan did not maintain as thorough a record on travelers as did Iranian officials, they did ask questions. However, the traveler can answer with any lie and it is accepted as truth and copied down. Among the ridiculous questions the guard asked was, "What is the name of your father?" None of us answered the question truthfully, but still he carefully registered our answers and stamped our passports. I imagine the questioning was a rather pathetic attempt to persuade us that we were being thoroughly investigated. Next we moved on to a customs officer who wrote down the details of things we were bringing into the country. He was impressed by my knife and tried to buy it from me. When I declined, he offered to trade a block of hashish for it, which I obviously also refused. Had I accepted his offer, I would probably have been arrested, losing both hashish and knife in the process. I suppose he could have confiscated it, but he handed it back with a disappointed look and let us pass into the country.

Nobody had any plans for sightseeing before getting to Kabul, so we drove on to Herat, our first stop. Three hours after the border checkpoint we arrived in Herat. We stopped for tea and a meal of rice with a fatty, greasy piece of lamb and continued toward our destination for the day, the city of Kandahar. The road led through the desert and there was not much to be seen along the way, except for the occasional truck or a bus. The trucks were all brightly painted and decorated, many telling a story from the Koran. We arrived in Kandahar after dark and shared a cheap hotel room for the night and planned to make an early start to Kabul the next morning.

The following afternoon we arrived in Kabul and I said my good-byes to Jakob and the French. They were anxious to continue to India and Nepal, but my business would keep me in Kabul for several days, if not weeks. They were going to stay at a place called Friends Hotel, near the Indian embassy; I had been instructed to get a room near the fur market at the Najib Hotel, the cost of which I negotiated down to twenty afghanis, or about thirty cents a night. The Najib, reputed to be the drug center of Kabul, if not all of Afghanistan, was built around a small grove of trees, which was a favorite hang-out for hippies either reveling in the 'enlightenment' they had gotten in India, or playing Cat Stevens songs on the guitar, reading poetry, and getting stoned on hash. The evenings were spent eating kebabs and drinking red wine. After the kebabs, joints and chillums sprang out every-where, and everybody got stoned all over again.

Afghanistan was without doubt the number one opium producer in the world, accounting for the major-ity of the world's poppy output. Poppy plants were the most profitable crop in Afghanistan by far, with Afghani farmers making forty times as much from opium as they could from legal crops like wheat. Although poppy culti-vation was officially outlawed, nobody feared any reper-cussions of defying the national law if they enjoyed local tribal protection. Local tribal leaders, warlords, and crimi-nal groups controlled the industry while provincial bu-reaucrats and military commanders took a share of the profits as the product moved through the various prov-inces to points outside of the country.

I was supposed to eliminate one of those local

strongmen in a way that would make a strong statement. I never was fully briefed on why he was my target, but it was not my business to know the why; that was the domain of others much higher placed than I was. I was merely the "action officer." Abdunabi, my target, was a member of the Tajik tribe, the second largest ethnic group in Afghanistan after the Pashtuns. The Tajiks are mostly Sunni Muslims and speak Farsi, the language of the Persians. Because many of the Tajiks have settled in the urban areas (such as they are in Afghanistan) like Kabul and Herat, they developed into an educated elite, amassing significant wealth and political influence. It was that wealth and influence that allowed Abdunabi and his family to rise as narcotics dealers. But Abdunabi had one major character flaw that made it possible for me to get close to him—he was extremely greedy. Normally, a man in his position would not meet personally with a potential business partner; that would be left to others further down the chain of command. But Abdunabi was always trying to increase his personal fortunes, and if he could do so by cutting out others in his organization, he was willing to take that risk

However, I could not directly approach him, introduce myself, and work out a major drug deal. That would be too suspicious. I had to bide my time and let him come to me. I started by hanging out where westerners would congregate. The Najib Hotel was a good start. Another good place to develop contacts was Sigis, a bar run by an enormous German named, of course, Siegfried. Sigis was always crowded with hippies playing chess and listening to music. Although Sigi spoke fluent English, I used my German to get to know him better, gain his confidence, and drop hints that I was there for more than a hashish holiday. I also frequented the Karmozan Cafe, a favorite with the poetry crowd, and Chicken Street (yes, the street sign actually said Chicken Street), a row of hotels and restaurants teeming with hippies. The area looked like a mini Haight-Ashbury, with people wearing tie-died clothes, beads, and yes, even flowers in their hair. Westerners were constantly accosted by what was known as the baksheesh kids, baksheesh being the Dari word for alms, or handouts. These kids would surround you crying out, "Baksheesh, baksheesh," with their hands held out. I learned that many of them had been purposely maimed by their own parents to make them more effective beggars.

While on Chicken Street, whenever I grew to know somebody (which was not too difficult, considering I was sharing generous portions of hashish) I hinted that I had high aspirations for my time in Afghanistan. Within one week I was approached in Sigis by an Afghani who said his boss wanted to meet me. Westerners were not typically invited into Afghani homes (which was fine with me, considering what I had to do), so he told me to go to a room at the Hotel Kabul the next day at 12:00 P.M. The time worked well because I could take a bus to Peshawar, Pakistan, at 2:00 P.M. I bought a ticket for the bus and went back to the Najib to rest for the next day.

The next morning, I had tea and breakfast at a restaurant called the Steak House, where I could get a steak for 30 afghanis (about $.43). Although I was too nervous to eat, I felt I should get a good meal under my belt. Then I rolled up my sleeping bag, packed my backpack, and waited until 11:30 A.M. before departing for the hotel. The Hotel Kabul was an old, large, Soviet-style hotel built in the early 1950s that had become a cosmopolitan, jet-setter hangout in Kabul, in stark contrast to the shabby hippie hotels to which I was becoming accustomed. I knocked on the door and a burly Afghani let me in. Inside were two other Afghanis, making for a total of four of us in the room. I became nervous; I had not planned on meeting three men.

Sitting at a desk in the corner of the room was a medium-built Afghani with reddish hair who introduced himself to me as Abdunabi. The other two he introduced as his brothers. He spoke very decent English and I could tell from his watch, his clothes, and, more importantly, his smell, that he was well-to-do for an Afghani. He asked if I would like some refreshments—tea and pastries—to which I replied yes. He then said something to the others and both men left, I presume, to procure the food and drink.

When they left, Abdunabi stood up and approached me as he spoke. I had no idea how long his brothers would be gone and I needed to act quickly. I stood up to meet him. As he stretched out his hand, I pulled his arm across my chest, slammed my other arm into his neck, pushed my leg behind him, and put him into a reverse headlock. Reaching my arm upward as I stepped back, his own body weight broke his neck as he dropped. There was absolutely no thought in my head as all of this occurred—it was all a matter of instinct, as it had been with Jim K. in Lakewood, Ohio, years before. By coming to this meeting, I forced myself to complete my mission. These men would not have let me leave the hotel alive when they realized I had no money. It was fight or flight, and I chose fight.

I did not know when the brothers would return, but I could not let them discover the body and raise an alarm. I sat Abdunabi in the chair by the desk, facing away from the door and waited. A few minutes later there was a knock. I opened the door with my left hand and was immediately relieved to see one, not both, of his brothers holding a silver teapot and some cups. As he stepped into the room, and while I still had the element of surprise to throw him off his guard, I pulled him behind the open door and, with my knife in my right hand, sliced across his neck from the left ear down to the Adam's apple, making sure that the wound faced toward the wall behind the door. A slit throat is different from most other wounds, in that it results in a tremendous flow of blood immediately that continues for a few seconds. Before death, the blood flow is propelled by the beating heart to cause a pulsating hemorrhage of anywhere from a pint to a quart of blood, which can spray up to 7 feet before the blood pressure stabilizes. After death, blood continues to flow, but at a slower pace, by hydrostatic draining. I did not need that kind of mess in full sight of the next person who would enter the room.

A few minutes later there was another knock on the door. I opened the door smiling but quickly saw that the last brother was not doing the same. Something was wrong. He was either suspicious, in a bad mood, or he simply didn't like Westerners. Before I could grab his arm, he pushed past me into the room. A look of shock came across his face as he saw the blood all over the wall and floor. He spun around to face me at which point I pushed my knife deep into his stomach directly below the navel. As he stood there with his mouth wide open but with no sound coming out, I pulled the knife straight up to the sternum and twisted it to the side. With a gurgle in his throat, he crumpled to the ground and died.

I was told to leave a strong message. Looking around the room, I felt sure that I had. In a normal, healthy adult, 1/11 of his or her body weight is blood. I estimated that each of Abdunabi's brothers weighed 200 pounds, meaning both had about 18 pounds of blood in their bodies before they died. Blood has a density of 1.105 pounds per pint, so I figured each brother had 16 pints of blood in them before they started bleeding. Most of that was now splattered around the room.

It was 12:30 P.M. Only thirty minutes had elapsed since I first entered the room. I had an hour and a half to catch the bus to Pakistan. The whole operation went better than I expected, especially after my initial shock of having to deal with three men. I doubted I would be caught or even implicated in these deaths for many reasons. First, Abdunabi had probably not told anybody where he was going or with whom he was meeting. He saw this as an opportunity to enrich himself, and the fewer he let in on the details, the more there would be for him and his brothers. Second, Afghani men did not answer to the women in their lives and were often gone for days at a time; Abdunabi and his brothers would probably not be missed until I was in Pakistan. Third, there was nothing to tie me to Abdunabi because I had been careful never to ask for him by name. I had not mentioned his name at all. Fourth, I found a large quantity of opium and cash in Abdunabi's pockets, but did not take either, making his death look like a retribution killing. Fifth, because they had a great distrust of the central government, I knew Abdunabi's people would not report this crime to the police. It was something they would handle themselves, one way or another.

I cleaned off my knife and made sure there was no blood on my clothes. I had been careful not to be in the direct stream of blood of either brother. As I surveyed the room and thought about what I had done, it occurred to me that my extensive training alone had not enabled me to do what I had done. I had made a *conscious decision* to commit those acts. My physical training was irrelevant if I was not prepared *mentally* to accept the consequences of my actions. It also occurred to me how irrevocably changed I was. There are few things in life that, once done, cannot be undone. A wrong can be righted, a lie taken back, and stolen goods returned. A life, however, cannot be restored once it has been taken; the carnage in front of me drove that message home with a vengeance. And with that thought in mind, I slipped out of the hotel and made my way to the bus.

CHAPTER 12

PAKISTAN AND INDIA

I was apprehensive during the trip from Kabul to the border of Pakistan. Although I was sure that I was not implicated in the affair at the Hotel Kabul, I had a nagging feeling that something might go wrong while crossing the border. It was 96 miles from Kabul to Jalalabad and the road was incredibly winding, so much so that more than one passenger experienced motion sickness on the bus. And although it was only 96 miles, the temperature became noticeably warmer as we progressed, because Kabul was at a much higher elevation than Jalalabad. Shortly after passing Jalalabad we reached the Afghani side of the border. My pucker factor was elevated and I was almost unable to breathe as I handed my passport to the Afghani border official. He looked at the passport and then at me for what seemed like an eternity. When he stamped it and waved me through I almost couldn't contain my relief.

I quickly reboarded the bus with the others, and we made the short drive to the Pakistani side of the border. It took about three hours to get the busload of people through Pakistani immigration and customs. There I had to fill out a declaration form stating how much money I was carrying into Pakistan. This was tricky because if I carried a substantial amount of money, I would arouse suspicion of being drug dealer. If I didn't have enough, the Pakistani immigration officials could think that I was vagrant and would deny me entry into the country. At that point I saw the wisdom of having money waiting for me at the American Express offices along my route so that I could cross borders without raising suspicions.

After the bureaucratic requirements were handled, it was time to tackle the Khyber Pass. The Khyber Pass is a 33-mile route through the Hindu Kush mountain range connecting the northern frontier of Pakistan, which controls the pass, to Afghanistan. Villages lie on both sides of the Khyber Pass, populated primarily by Pashtuns. The pass varies in width from a meager 3 meters to 137 meters. The mountains on either side are so sheer, ranging from 175 to more than 300 meters in height, that they are impossible to climb except in a few places. The highest point of the pass is precisely on the border between the two countries. It was awe inspiring to pass across the same route that was used by countless armies as the entry point for their invasions. Marco Polo and other traders also used the Khyber Pass as a major trade route for centuries. By 1972 two highways, one for motor vehicles and the other for caravans and foot traffic, paved their way through the Khyber Pass.

An hour and a half after we left the border we rolled into Peshawar, which was as far as my bus was going. I grabbed my backpack and planned to hitch a ride to my next destination, Gujranwala. One evening at the Steak House in Kabul I met a Pakistani named Inam Rasul Butt, from Gujranwala, who was coming back from a business trip in Europe. He extended an invitation to visit him and his family if I were ever in Gujranwala, and I thought this was the perfect way to relax in a place where I could feel safe. I began walking down the road known as the Grand Trunk Highway, which runs from Peshawar to Lahore on the border with India. Before long, I was picked up by a Pakistani heading to Rawalpindi, the capital of Pakistan, who seemed glad to have the company and conversation.

I got out of the car at the local American Express

office on Bank Road. As I expected, there was two hundred dollars worth of Pakistani rupees, about twenty-one hundred rupees, which was quite a bit of money in Pakistan. There was also a letter from Phil, "If you're reading this, I can only assume your business went as well as hoped. Business in Pakistan suspended for now. Should have more news for you upon arrival in Delhi. Enjoy the break."

The fact that he wrote nothing more about the mission in Afghanistan confirmed my suspicions that the brothers had not been discovered at the Hotel Kabul yet. Furthermore, learning that I did not have to work in Pakistan was a relief. I was antsy to move through this Muslim country and get to India as quickly as possible, but I also wanted the rest that Mr. Butt's offer promised. I called him to tell him I was in Pakistan and asked again if I could stop by within the next day or two. He seemed overjoyed at the prospect of having an American visitor stay with him and told me to come.

After walking through Rawalpindi, I was offered a ride to Gujranwala from a Pakistani on his way to Lahore. Gujranwala is the fifth largest city of Pakistan. The locals speak Punjab, English, and Urdu (the only languages allowed in schools and government offices in Pakistan), so I had no difficulty asking for directions to Butt's home.

Inam Rasul Butt was a study in contrasts. He was well-to-do for a rural Pakistani owing to his bus business. Although he seemed to be well traveled, he was firmly anchored in his Pakistani and Muslim traditions. He introduced me to his family, properly shy and demur women who quickly faded into the background. I seldom saw his daughters over the next few days. I arrived a few hours before dinner, so Butt gave me a tour of Gujranwala.

First we picked up one of his brothers who was, according to Butt, a well-known wrestler in Pakistan. Gujranwala's main claim to fame is as the "City of Wrestlers" or "*Pehlwana da shehur.*" The city has hundreds of enthusiastic *Pehlwan* who take part in friendly but fiercely competitive matches (*Dungal*), which are held both within Pakistan and internationally. The locals take these matches seriously and it is not unusual for a match to be attended by thousands of fans. After visiting his brother's training facility, it was time to return to Butt's home for dinner.

Gujranwala is also famous throughout Pakistan for its food, especially meat dishes. The Koran is explicit in its prohibitions against eating pork; therefore lamb, beef, chicken, and fish are basic foods of the middle and upper classes. Butt considered it a badge of honor to have an American stay at his house, and it showed in the dinner his wife prepared. That evening I experienced my first decent meal since leaving Germany. The dinner consisted of Beef Tikka, lean cubes of beef marinated for a few hours in unripened ground papaya, yogurt, and a ginger and garlic paste, then coated with chili powder, and barbecued over charcoal. Along with the beef, we had Green Pulao, a basmati rice dish with onions, peas, cloves, cinnamon, and bay leaves, which is first sautéed in oil and then boiled. To drink, we had Lhassi, milk from which curds and butterfat have been removed.

After dinner, a large number of his friends and neighbors visited Butt's house. Apparently the word had spread that he had an authentic American hippie staying with him, and I was displayed with pride. Tea was served and then it was time to go to sleep. I was given a private place to sleep, although I had told Butt I only needed a warm place, like the kitchen floor, to unroll my sleeping bag. He said he would consider that to be an insult. Besides, the kitchen was where his wife and daughters slept.

As I lay down to sleep, I reflected on the events of the past few days. I had killed three men but I was not bothered by my actions. I was so unconcerned, I was asking for Pakistani recipes from Butt. Was I so cold and callous that I was able to kill with no feeling of dread or remorse? Obviously, the Agency had seen something in me that they felt could be nurtured, trusted, and used. Was that a good or a bad thing? What had those men done to warrant death? Who made that decision? What if the target had been a woman? A child? Could I have done it? What about the next time? I had to get away from thoughts like that. I was told that the "why" was none of my business. I was not a judge; I was an action officer, an executioner.

I woke the next morning ready to continue to India, but Butt implored me to stay for one more day. Apparently, he had more people to whom he wanted to show me. We had tea and Lhassi for breakfast and then went out to explore more of the city. He took me to a brick-making facility owned by another of his brothers, where bricks were made by hand, formed in clay and mud in blocks of wood and then set out to bake in the sun. We also visited a group of Gypsies who had set up camp outside of Gujranwala. The smell of the camp hit me long before we even got close to it.

After a full day of seeing and being seen we returned to another sumptuous dinner. Butt's wife had prepared *Murgh Choolay*, white chickpeas boiled in water and bi-carbonate of soda, then mixed with chicken, and sautéed in onion, turmeric, coriander, chili powder, chopped green chilies, and ginger and garlic paste. I was sure that the Butts did not eat like this every day, but I understood that it was important to him to show me that he was a man of means and it was equally important that his friends and neighbors saw that he had American connections. During the course of the evening's conversation, he asked if, when I returned to America, I would consider sponsoring his brother's immigration so that they could set up an import/export business. I assured him that I would look into it, and with that it was time for bed.

The next morning I packed my few belongings and prepared to hitchhike my way to Lahore. However, Butt insisted that I allow him to drive me, and I did not argue;

there would be plenty of hitchhiking to come. Gujranwala was about 42 miles from Lahore, and we made the trip in less than an hour. Imploring me to remember my promise to help his brother immigrate to the United States, Butt dropped me off at the Nedous Hotel, a place rumored to have housed both Rudyard Kipling and Lawrence of Arabia. It had occurred to me that, unlike Turkey and Afghanistan, I did not need to buy drugs in Pakistan to establish a cover. And since I stayed with the Butts and ate their food, I had no reason to spend my twenty-one hundred Pakistani rupees. So I decided that treating myself to a night in a decent hotel was the best way to spend the money. Unfortunately, I could not convince any of the better hotels to rent me a room, although I offered to pay cash in advance. It seemed that American hippies were not as popular, or trusted, in Lahore as they were in Gujranwala

I finally gave up and went to the youth hostel near the Firdaus Market. After registering, I took a small walking tour of the city. Lahore, the second largest city in Pakistan, was truly a beautiful city, with thousands of years of history behind it. It had been a capital of the Mughal empire, and at one time was the capital of Pakistan, but not for long because its close proximity to the Indian border posed too many dangers. I knew from other travelers in The Pudding Shop in Istanbul that buses left Lahore to cross the border into India every hour, so I did not rush getting up the next morning. After drinking Lhassi with banana in it for breakfast I went to catch the bus.

The bus trip was short because the Indian border was at the city limits of Lahore. Clearing the border was easy, as I had anticipated. I wondered why the guards wrote down so many details when travelers entered the country. It was obvious that that data they collected was not checked when the travelers left. Visitors leaving the country simply walked from station to station to check off exit requirements in assembly-line style. Finally, passports were stamped with an exit visa and travelers were waved through to the Indian side.

After crossing the border into Hussainiwala travelers pass through a symbolic black iron gate. By now, I was pretty accustomed to the border-crossing routine. I declared how much money I had on me and in what national currencies. I also listed my valuables, which consisted of one cheap Kodak camera. Within an hour, I cleared Indian border requirements and was ready to move on to Delhi.

I hitchhiked to Delhi and arrived by late afternoon. In Istanbul a traveler recommended that I stay at the Kesri Hotel in Delhi, so I rode a rickshaw-like vehicle attached to a bicycle to the Main Bazaar, the *Pahar Ganj*, where the hotel was located. To call the Kesri a hotel was a real stretch. For five Indian rupees a night (about fifty U.S. cents) I secured a bed with a bare mattress in a room with three other travelers from England. Bathing consisted of sponging off with a bucket of cold water. But it was a place to roll out my sleeping bag and relax for a couple of days of sightseeing before moving on to my next assignment.

I was anxious to go to the American Express office to pick up my money and to see if Phil sent any more news. The news was better than I expected. "Packages at hotel have been found. Official line is that this is an internal matter. Family will handle. Take a few weeks before beginning return trip. Package in Istanbul still awaiting your attention. Same procedure preferred. Good job. Enjoy India."

Based on Phil's message, I wouldn't have any problems going back through Afghanistan. Regardless, I planned to make it as quick a journey as possible. For the time being I planned on following Phil's advice and to enjoy India. Everything about the country was exotic; the sights, architecture, religion, smells—everything. Delhi was a good transition because it was cosmopolitan but maintained plenty of the traditional Indian trappings.

The city was divided into two sections, with New Delhi to the south of what was known as Old Delhi, or simply Delhi. "New" is actually a bit of a misnomer. New Delhi was built on what had been previous cities and civilizations. I spent the next few days exploring all of the sights. My favorite was easily the *Jamia Majid*, which, as far as I know, was the largest mosque in India. According to an Imam in the mosque, six thousand men worked every day for six years to construct and decorate it.

Visiting the Hindu temples gave me an intense desire to leave the big city and get into the essence of India. To begin, I bought a bus ticket to Agra, 125 miles southeast of Delhi. Agra was the capital of India under the Mughals until 1634, and is the site of the Taj Mahal. The Taj Mahal, a mausoleum for the wife of the Mughal emperor Shah Jahan, was built over a twenty-year period from 1630 to 1653 and is more impressive than its pictures suggest. Unfortunately, I was not able to stay there long. I was tossed out while playing Frisbee on the grounds with another tourist.

I had studied Hinduism and Buddhism at Purdue and so had a rudimentary knowledge of what lay ahead as I continued through India. But no amount of study prepared me for my next stop in Benares, also known as Varanasi and Kaasi. The best way to describe Benares was "concentrated India." Benares was widely accepted as the most sacred pilgrimage site in India for a number of reasons, not least of which was that it sat on the Ganges River. The Buddha frequently visited Benares and supposedly gave his first sermon about the principles of Buddhism (Dharma) in Sarnath, about 13 miles away. It was also the home of one of the manifestations of the Hindu deity, Shiva, also known by the name Kasi Viswanatha. Last but certainly not least, Benares was also the home of Ravi Shankar, a sitar player who had become very popular with the hippy culture.

From Benares, I took a train to Calcutta. Traveling

by train in India was an experience in and of itself. Every square inch of usable space was packed with people, even on top of the train. I was disappointed by Calcutta because it was formed in 1698, making it a fairly new city, as far as India was concerned. While people from all over the world lived in Calcutta and created a diverse, melting-pot environment, the city really did not exude the exotic atmosphere I experienced elsewhere in India. Consequently, I lost little time finding a train to Bhopal.

Bhopal is the capital of the state of Madhya Pradesh and is located roughly 360 miles south of New Delhi. I stayed briefly in Bhopal before moving on to the ashram of Prem Nagar. Several travelers I met in Asia spoke to me of "finding enlightenment" in Prem Nagar, and I was interested to visit. The Sri Prem Nagar Ashram is located two miles from the city of Hardwar. Located on the banks of the Ganges, Hardwar is itself one of the holiest pilgrimage destinations in India. Situated at the foothills of the Himalayas, the Ganges is like ice in Hardwar, but that did not stop me from bathing in it.

On my first evening at Prem Nagar a lengthy service was held by the ashram's guru, fifteen-year old Maharaj Ji. Maharaj Ji's organization, although originally founded by his father, had grown in popularity around the world during the last few years due to his magnetic personality. His Divine Light Mission had established more than two hundred centers in the United States. His followers, popularly known as *premies* or "lovers of truth," praised him as the holiest man alive and believed, among other things, that: Maharaj Ji (also known by his given name, PremRawat) was the one and only *Satguru* (master); his legitimacy as the only *Satguru* was unquestionable; knowledge is the ultimate truth, and its techniques were revealed by Maharaj Ji; his three brothers were the incarnations of the Hindu gods Shiva, Brahma, and Vishnu; his mother was the Holy Mother of the Universe; and finally, that God was certainly great, but Maharaj Ji was greater, because he revealed God and without him to reveal

God, there would be no God for humans to experience and know.

There were thousands of *premies* at Prem Nagar from all over the world, enraptured by every word the Maharaj Ji spoke. He was dressed as a Hindu god and his priests wore saffron robes like Buddhist monks, clothing that made the *premies* believe his teachings were based on ancient Eastern beliefs and mysticism. In reality, his message of one God and one way to know God was much more akin to the messianic message of Christianity than it was to the polytheistic belief system of the Hindus. The bottom line is that his religion fell victim to a severely confused and contradictory belief system that, on the one hand, preached that there was only one God, while on the other hand held his entire family up as reincarnated Hindu gods. But I was not going to raise that theological dilemma in front of thousands of his rabid believers. Instead, I did something equally as stupid.

While I was at Prem Nagar, India was gearing up for the *Holi* festival. Originally a celebration of a good harvest, *Holi* had also become a symbolic replaying of a Hindu myth concerning the worship of Vishnu and the death of the demon Hanika. One of the traditions of the festival was that people chase each other around, throwing brightly colored powder dyes, known as *gulal*, and water over each other. In principle, I had nothing against being pelted with the brightly colored dyes; what did bother me was that some person hit me in the head with an entire can of dye, still in the can. I literally saw red, lost my temper, and hit the offender with a spinning back kick to his head. At that moment, as the crowd rushed at me, I thought the whole town of Hardwar was related to the man I had kicked. I was severely beaten with sticks and fists, and the next thing I knew, I woke up covered in blood and bruises.

I was a mess and the only thing I thought to do was pick myself up, wash off in the Ganges, and hope that there was some truth to the claims of the river's restorative powers. After cleaning myself I crawled into my sleeping bag at the ashram, planning to stay there for a few days to heal. Unfortunately, I woke up with a burning fever and felt much worse than I should have after a simple beating. A couple of days later, my skin started to turn a sickly shade of yellow. I checked in with an Indian doctor at the ashram and learned that I had contracted hepatitis. Although I never thought about communicable diseases on my trip, it made sense. I had already stopped eating vegetables because they gave me intestinal parasites. Considering how food was prepared in the small villages I passed through, where people wipe themselves with their hand after defecating and then go on to cook their meals without washing, I figured I was lucky to have stayed healthy for so long.

I spent the next ten days so sick I thought I was going to die. A local Ayurvedic practitioner was sent to help me. Ayurvedic medicine in the foothills of the Himalayas is much different than the sanitized version practiced in the United States. Whereas in Western countries, Ayurvedic medicine emphasized massage, herbs, and proper diet, in rural India it relied heavily on superstitions, cow urine, the dung of goats and birds, spells, and the chanting of mantras. Whether it was owing to the treatment, which was in and of itself enough to make me sick, or the passage of time and a naturally strong constitution, I started to feel better after about ten days. When I was able to walk a little, I took a bus back to Delhi and the Kesri to plan my return trip to Istanbul.

CHAPTER 13

DISASTER IN IRAN, RECKONING IN ISTANBUL

I booked myself back into the Kesri and spent another couple of days in my sleeping bag nursing my wounds. When I began to feel almost normal, I started visiting the American Express office with the hope of lining up a ride heading west. I felt that I had to be much more selective about my ride for the return trip because I wanted to spend the least amount of time as possible along the route, especially in Afghanistan. My sole focus now was to reach Istanbul, complete my mission, and return to Munich.

After a few days I saw an American putting up an index card on a bulletin board looking for somebody to share the cost of gas and driving to Austria. Eric was a documentary filmmaker who had been shooting footage in India and, as it turned out, had been in Prem Nagar the same time I was. A non-practicing Jew from New York City, he was quite taken with his own talent and was looking for somebody to listen to him talk about himself as much as anything else. Twenty-eight years old, 5'10", and weighing about 140 pounds, he had long, black, thinning hair and a superiority complex usually reserved for those more physically imposing than he. He had seen enough of Asia and wanted to drive straight to Vienna. That suited my plans perfectly. His Mercedes van was packed with video equipment and film, which momentarily made me apprehensive because he seemed to be a perfect target for thieves who would not hesitate killing anybody they robbed so that there would be no potential witnesses. However, he had made it this far so I figured we would be safe.

We arranged to meet the next morning at American Express and I returned to my room for my last night in India. At 8:00 the next morning I loaded my backpack and sleeping bag into his van and we left. Our only stop before the Pakistani border was the City of Amritsar, the city of the Sikhs. Eric insisted on seeing Amritsar, which means "pool of ambrosia," and I was happy that we stopped, although it was not part of my plan. Before it was a city, Amritsar was only a small lake where seekers of wisdom such as the Buddha would come to meditate. A couple thousand years after the Buddha spent time there, Guru Nank, the founder of the Sikh religion, moved to Amritsar and, after his death, his followers turned it into their central shrine. The original, and many shrines thereafter, were destroyed by a number of wars. The current structure, known as the Golden Temple of the Sikhs (*Hari Mandir*) is a combination of Muslim and Hindu architecture, gilded in gold and decorated with marble statues and precious gemstones. Starting at sunrise, the Sikhs chant prayers and poems all day and well into the evening. With instruments like flutes, drums, and Indian strings playing along with the voices, the atmosphere around the temple was haunting and hypnotic. An added bonus was that the Sikhs had a tradition of housing and feeding all visitors, regardless of nationality or religion.

It was easy to understand why so many people were seduced by the peace and tranquility of Amritsar and threw off their responsibilities in favor of a life of quiet meditation. But Eric and I were hard pressed to continue, each for our own reasons. Crossing into Pakistan went smoothly and the ride along the Great Trunk Road was easy. The Mercedes van was comfortable enough, except for Eric's incessant prattle about himself. The positive side to his nonstop talking was that I didn't have to say much except for the occasional "uh huh" and "yup," exactly the kind of conversation I had grown accustomed to over my many years of isolation.

We drove straight through Pakistan, stopping briefly to eat or to use the bathroom. As we approached Afghanistan, I began to worry. Although I was confident that there was nothing to tie me to the events at the Hotel Kabul, I wanted to avoid the hippie haunts like Sigis and Chicken Street. As we cleared Pakistan, I tried to also clear my mind of negative thoughts and worries. It was important to be perfectly calm and nonchalant. The procedure at the border between Pakistan and Afghanistan was the same as when I crossed it from the other side: declaration of what I had with me and inane questions, the answers to which the guard entered into a logbook. After he stamped my passport, I returned to Eric's van, fighting the urge to look back over my shoulder.

A few hours later we were back in Kabul and my nerves were screaming. Had anybody at the Hotel Kabul seen me and passed my description to Abdunabi's family? Would they be looking for me now? All I could do was repeat to myself, "You're clear. You're clear. Be cool." I hated stopping there at all, but we had to eat. I mean Eric had to eat. I had absolutely no appetite. We bought kebabs and a coke, stretched our legs at the Babur Shah gardens, and then continued the drive to Kandahar. At Kandahar we went through the usual border-crossing procedures and were waved through to proceed to Iran.

As we neared the border of Iran, I began to breathe a sigh of relief. Once out of Afghanistan, I would be able to focus my attention on Istanbul. Again, Afghani exit procedures posed no problems. And again, I saw people unloading the drugs they were carrying. One had to be crazy to try to smuggle drugs into or through Iran. The warnings on the signs were clear; the consequences could mean death. I was totally clean, so I started the Irani border-crossing process without a care in the world.

I was making my currency declaration when the next thing I knew, two large, plainclothes Iranian cops grabbed me from behind, swung me around, and pushed me face first against the wall. I felt my nose break as they handcuffed me and hit the back of my knees with something resembling a police nightstick. As I dropped to my knees, I looked over to the side and saw the same thing being done to Eric. Stunned as much by the surprise as by the pain, I started to ask what the problem was but was quickly slapped across the face. The Iranians were yelling in Farsi as all the other border crossers backed as far away from us as they could.

I was in shock. What the hell was going on here? I tried to focus my thoughts and figure out what was happening. Had this happened in Afghanistan, I would have understood; I had half expected it. But there was no reason to hassle me in Iran. Had that egomaniac Eric stashed some drugs in his van? Was I being attacked because I was traveling in the same vehicle and therefore guilty by association? I had no clue, and it was obvious that the Iranians who cuffed me were in no mood for questions. Eric had not figured that out yet. He kept screaming that he was an American and that they couldn't do this. All I could think was, "Yeah, you're an American, and a Jew, and this is a Muslim country, and if you don't shut up, you're going to get us both killed." The more Eric screamed, the more they punched him. He was clearly unfamiliar with the protocol involved in being beaten; it boiled down to keeping quiet, especially when on the receiving end.

After a couple more punches he stopped screaming and lay on the ground crying quietly. They then made us stand and half dragged, half pushed us outside, where we were made to get into the back of a truck with the four Iranians who attacked us. It was difficult to stay seated on the bench as, being cuffed, we couldn't hold on to anything. The Iranians laughed as the two of us were bounced around and beat up more by the jostling of the truck on the unpaved road. After about half an hour we pulled up to a gate with a uniformed man in a guard shack. We drove through the gate and up to a white-washed building that looked like a prison. We were blind-folded and pushed out of the truck.

The guards roughly forced us to our feet and pushed us forward. Someone pounded on the door and I heard it unlock and swing open. Although I couldn't see where we were, my other senses were unimpaired. I was struck by a horrible stench that reminded me of the sewer I was dumped into when I was a child. Then I heard voices. I had no idea what they said, but several voices seemed to be saying the same thing over and over again, almost in a pleading way. I was led straight ahead for several feet, turned, and then walked for a few minutes more until I was forced to stop. I heard a key in a lock and a door swing open. My blindfold was removed and I was pushed into a room as the door was shut and locked behind me.

The room (actually, it looked more like a closet) was about 3 feet wide, 5 feet long, and 5 feet high, and had an empty bucket at the far end. The only light came from a 2-inch square opening in the door. With not enough space to stand or lie down, all I could do was sit with my knees folded. Sit and think, think and sit. This was not good. The Hippie Trail was full of stories about trials on the spot and summary executions in Iran. Explaining that I was an American would do no good (it certainly didn't help Eric any). I could claim innocence, but I didn't know why I was there in the first place. I was in no position to demand anything; that would only anger the guards. There was nothing I could do but sit and wait for what-ever might happen next.

The sounds of pleading and moaning droned on endlessly, making sleep impossible. I had no idea how long I sat there before the door opened and I was pulled out and blindfolded again. I was led to another room where the blindfold was removed. This room was much bigger, about 120 square feet, and had a plain wooden table in the middle of it. In front of the table was a wooden bench and behind it was a chair. This was apparently an interrogation room. I was made to stand in front of the table. After a few minutes, the door opened again and in walked three men. One of them, well groomed and dressed in European-style clothing sat at the table; the other two, both scruffier looking with heavy beard stubble and stained clothes, flanked me.

The man at the table started talking to me in what I took to be Farsi. Every so often he would pause as if to allow me to answer or say something, but since I didn't understand a word he said, I only responded by saying I didn't understand. He pulled a sheet of paper and a pen out of his jacket pocket and indicated that he wanted me to sign it at the bottom. Again, I couldn't read what was written and so I refused to sign. He then started yelling at me and nodded to the two others who grabbed me, took my jacket and shirt off, and tied me to the bench, face up. They took off my socks and pushed them into my mouth. They then bent my legs from behind and attached my ankles to my thighs with two belts, causing me to wince in pain. The interrogator showed me the piece of paper again, pointed at the bottom and offered me the pen, indicating that all I had to do was sign and they would untie me. I wouldn't do it, figuring I could be signing my own death warrant.

One of the two goons pulled out a very wide belt, about 4 inches wide, much like the belt a weightlifter would wear to protect his back, and started to beat me on the stomach with it. Again they showed me the paper and pen, and again I shook my head "no." Then he started using the belt on my upper legs. With the socks in my mouth I couldn't even yell. Again the paper was shown and again I refused. This time he used the belt to whip my groin area. Each strike hurt so badly I thought my eyes would pop out of my head, if my head didn't burst first. After the third hit, I was seeing bright flashing lights. And then, nothing. I woke up against the wall of what seemed like the same small closet I was in initially.

It had been some time since I had used a toilet, and I felt that my bladder and bowels were about to burst, but I didn't dare call for help for fear of what might happen. Figuring that that was the purpose of the bucket, I relieved myself as best I could and then dozed on and off for an indeterminate amount of time. It was a light sleep, so when I heard the key in the lock I was immediately awake. I was pulled out of the room. One of the two guards sniffed the air, walked into my cell, and came out with the bucket, which he then poured over my head as they both broke into laughter. I was blindfolded and led to what I expected would be the same room I had been in earlier. I was wrong. This time, they took me to a suffocatingly hot room with a scalding floor and little breathable air. I was alone for about half an hour. After that, I was whipped with the belt and given the opportunity to sign that damned piece of paper. This was repeated about six or seven times; I lost count. Through the whole ordeal, I didn't hear a word of English, though I suspected the guy doing the interrogating knew it well enough.

Then it was back to my small cell, which was beginning to look good to me, because it was the only place where I was not beaten. Again, I relieved myself in the bucket. I assumed the same thing would happen, but there was no alternative in that small space. After sleeping fitfully, jumping at every sound I heard, the door opened again and I was hauled out. Again I was given my shower of feces and urine, blindfolded, and led away. When we passed through a door I could tell that we were outside. They took off my blindfold and led me to a white stone wall that was filled with holes and had steel rings affixed to the stone about waist high. They handcuffed my wrists behind me to one of the rings and walked away. A man I had not seen before walked up and told me, in perfect English, that I had been tried, found guilty, and sentenced to death. The sentence would be carried out immediately. He barked out some orders and five uniformed men with rifles appeared about 10 yards in front of me. He blindfolded me. It was a cold night. Here I was, about to die, and all I could think about was that I was not wearing a jacket or shirt. Then, in the silence, I heard the rifles being loaded. An order was given and I heard the sound of gunfire. My knees collapsed as I felt the impact of the bullets hitting the wall. I slumped forward, held up by the cuffs attached to the ring; I thought I was dead. Then I heard the guards laughing. Then I passed out.

I woke up naked but clean as far as I could tell. Furthermore, I was lying in a clean bed in a bright room. At first I thought the whole thing had been a horrible dream, but the welts on my stomach, legs, and hips brought it all back (that and the fact that I looked like I had lost about 30 pounds). It had all been real, including the mock execution. My clothes were on a chair next to the bed, cleaned and folded. My backpack, sleeping bag, and other possessions were all there too, including my knife. I felt weak from hunger and my whole body was throbbing. Nevertheless, I dressed, packed my stuff, and tried the door. It opened onto a hall with several other numbered doors. I was in a hotel. Moving down the hallway, I came to a staircase that led down to a lobby with an Iranian woman standing behind a counter. I asked her where I was and she told me that this was the Arya Hotel in Tehran. It was April 3, seven days after I had been arrested. I had spent my twenty-first birthday in that hellhole of a prison, wherever it was.

It was clear that the clerk did not know anything about what happened to me and, for the time being, it wasn't important. All I cared about was leaving Iran before somebody's mind changed about my release. I asked about a bill and she told me it had been settled in advance. I asked for directions to the American Express office and limped out of the Arya. It was slow going, but I arrived. Phil had wired money and a letter. "Bad choice of travel companion. Van was loaded. Did what I could when I heard. Will explain later. Too bad about your friend. Pick next ride a little smarter."

My friend, my ass. Judging from the note, he was no friend of anybody's anymore. That was fine with me; nobody would have to listen to that arrogant bastard again. And how was I to pick a "smart ride"? *Everybody* on the road was some kind of dope fiend; that's why they were there in the first place.

My body was broken and my mind was in a state of shock after my mock execution. Walking was difficult (I would learn several months later that the beatings I had suffered would require me to wear special shoes to compensate for spine damage), and I needed time to sit and heal, but I had no desire to stay in Iran one minute more than necessary. On top of everything, I had a job to do. So I bought a bus ticket to Tabriz, figuring I could find a ride from there to the Turkish border.

When I reached Tabriz, I checked into a hotel that cost seventy-five rials (slightly more than one dollar) a night. A sleeping bag on the cold ground wouldn't suffice with the aches and pains I was experiencing. I decided that in lieu of real medical treatment, I would spend some time nursing myself (*not* medicating—especially after my scare in prison) and learning about the city. Though I was broken and in much pain, the history of my surroundings interested me. Legend said that Tabriz was the birthplace of Zarathustra, or Zoroaster as he is known in Greek, religious teacher and founder of Zoroastrianism. That was debatable because every tribe that converted to Zoroastrianism created legends about his life to claim that he was "one of them." During the day I hobbled over to a large park with an artificial lake and a central hexagonal pavilion. From this garden, called El Goli, I could see a large red cliff overlooking the valley of the Tailkel River, which runs through Tabriz. It was a great place to relax and organize my thoughts.

I managed to catch a ride with four British travelers—one guy and three girls—who were heading back to

England. I met them at a kebab stand and we started talking. Quite naturally, they were curious about why I looked like I had just crawled out of the wrong end of a meat grinder. I didn't want to blow my chance of riding with them, so I said I was mugged in Afghanistan. They believed that and, mainly out of pity, agreed to take me as far as Istanbul if I contributed to fuel and shared the driving. The first leg of our drive took us to Bazargan, on the border with Turkey.

As we approached the Irani exit station, I started to feel dread again; my last encounter with Iranian border guards had, after all, been less than ideal. The guard took my passport, looked at the picture, and then at me. He called out to his superior and they started a long discussion with much hand waving. By now I was extremely nervous; I didn't think I could survive another stint in an Irani prison. But after a telephone call and some more discussion, they gave me my passport back with an exit stamp. If I had the strength, I think I would have run to the Turkish side, but I was so scared I could barely walk.

The Turkish immigration officials also gave me the once over, but that was probably owing to both my bruised face and the fact that I was walking like an old man. We moved through the border crossing fairly quickly and decided to share a room in Erzurum that night. Under normal conditions, I would have considered having two single girls in a hotel room to be ideal. Under the current circumstances, however, any form of physical exertion was the furthest thing from my mind. I contributed money for Jack, my male travel companion, to buy some hashish; it would deaden my pain. I was starting to have serious concerns about engaging my target in Istanbul since I did not have the strength to pull off anything like I did in Kabul. But the hashish relieved me of my concerns that night and after some inane chatter, I drifted off to sleep.

The morning was half gone when we started off for Samsun, our next planned stop. Samsun was situated between two river deltas jutting into the Black Sea. According to local legends, the delta east of Samsun was the land of the Amazons, the female warrior tribe described by Homer in his *Iliad* as, "those who go to war like men." The legend of the Amazon tribe has been distorted by various and conflicting reports; however, it was intriguing to visit the site where all those tales may have originated. When we arrived in Samsun we ate, found a hotel room, smoked hashish, and went to bed.

We wanted to reach Istanbul by the next night, so we did not sleep late; instead we left soon after dawn. We bought some bread and cheese in Samsun so we wouldn't have to hunt for anyplace to eat on our way. We took turns driving and made only a few stops for gas, to use a bathroom, and once in Ankara to check for messages at the American Express office. There was a letter at the office from "home," which read:

> Have arranged for a room at the Hilton in Istanbul (Taksim). Room secured with mom's credit card. Explained to hotel management that our son has been traveling and might be a little disheveled. They understand (I told them to include a decent tip for any services rendered—I'm sure that helped). Take a bath. Get your clothes cleaned. Glad you left your car at the Hippodrome. Should ease your trip back to Munich. We are proud of what you have done.
>
> Love you.
>
> Mom and Dad

Taksim was across the strait from the old Sultanahmet part of Istanbul, which contained the hippie enclaves. I was familiar with the Hilton because the American Express office I first used was located there. The puzzling part of the letter was what Phil wrote about my car, but I could think about that later. We arrived in the outskirts of Istanbul late that night and I asked to be dropped off at Taksim Square. We said our good-byes, wished each other luck, and I walked toward my hotel.

I entered the Hilton not knowing how I would be received. I was carrying a backpack, limping, slightly dirty, and I didn't exactly smell like aftershave. Luckily, my clothes were cleaned in Tehran, so I was not nearly as dirty as I could have been. The hotel was accustomed to people who looked like me entering the lobby to visit the American Express office, but not walking up to the front desk. The desk clerk sniffed the air and kind of looked away as I stood in front of him. When I didn't leave he directed me toward the American Express office. I told him that I had a reservation and gave him my name. Giving me a look that said, "Sure you do," he checked his book. His expression changed, but barely, when he saw that I did indeed have a reservation.

I filled out the registration card, which had already been partially completed telephonically by "dad." The clerk handed me a key and a small package that had been waiting for me. I took the elevator up to my room and collapsed on the bed for a few minutes. Since waking up in Tehran, I experienced periods of extreme dizziness, as if I had just disembarked from a roller coaster. I then called the front desk and asked to have my laundry cleaned. Taking all of my clothes off, I put them and my few reserve articles of clothing into a bag and set it outside my door along with my sleeping bag. I then took a hot bath and soaked for more than an hour, adding more hot water when it became tepid. After my bath, I ordered food from room service, which, being without clothes, I had them leave at the door. It had been a while since I had substantial western-style food, so I ate slowly and deliberately. Then I fell asleep, knowing there would be time to plan tomorrow.

Being alone, I slept more soundly than I had in some time and didn't get up until 9:00 the next morning. My clothes were cleaned and folded, waiting for me outside my door. I ordered a breakfast of Eggs Benedict, toast, and tea, which I savored while I thought about what to do next. At that point, I remembered that the desk clerk had given me a small package. It contained a key, apparently a car key, wrapped in cotton. Remembering Phil's reference to "my car," I figured I might as well ride a bus to the Hippodrome and see what I could find.

As usual, there were many vehicles parked at the Hippodrome. Just as I was getting frustrated, I saw an Opel Kadett, the same model I had owned when I attended Purdue. I don't know why I didn't recognize the shape of the key I had as an Opel key. I stuck the key in the door and was only slightly surprised to find that it turned and unlocked the car. I sat down and looked around. The car was empty, except for a package under the front passenger's seat. I tried the key in the ignition and it started. The gas gauge indicated a full tank. I now had much more data to digest. I decided to leave the car where it was and took a bus back to the hotel to check out the package.

I returned to the hotel and ordered a couple of beers to be sent to my room. Although I was not a beer man, it sounded better than a coke. When the beer arrived, I opened the package. Inside was a metal case, about the size of a large cash box. Flipping up the clasp, I found an M1911 .45, a couple of clips of ammo, a pair of black gloves, and a silencer. I had been wondering how to proceed in my diminished physical state. Here was the answer. Phil knew that I had gone through some heavy crap in Iran; apparently, my target in Istanbul was too important to postpone or cancel the mission.

I put on the gloves, picked up the pistol, and screwed on the silencer. Silencer is not the best term for the equipment, though, because a pistol can't actually be silenced. I was instructed on silencers during my M1911 training. Silencers, or to be more accurate, sound suppressors, look and sound impressive in the movies. But before my training I did not understand how a relatively small attachment on the end of a gun could squash such a loud bang.

I learned, in fact, that this fancy-looking steel attachment was not even necessary. Something as simple as a potato over the end of the barrel did the trick.

The principle behind noise suppression is simple. In discharging a gun, there are two sources for the loud bang. When the trigger on a gun is pulled, gunpowder is ignited behind the bullet. The ignited gunpowder creates a high-pressure wave of hot gas, which forces the bullet down the barrel. When the bullet exits the end of the barrel, the effect is like uncorking a bottle of champagne. But the pressure escaping behind the bullet is much more intense than that which is behind the cork, and therefore the sound is more explosive. That is the first source of a bang. A silencer screws on to the end of the barrel and has, in comparison to the barrel of the gun, a much larger volume of space. When the silencer is attached, the highly pressurized gas behind the bullet has more space into which it can expand. With the pressure of the hot gas greatly reduced, the sound the gun makes is also greatly reduced, resulting in more of a pop than a bang.

The second source of the loud noise from a gun cannot be suppressed by a silencer. When a bullet moves faster than sound, at supersonic speeds, it cannot be silenced because it creates its own sonic boom as it travels, creating a cracking sound at each object that it passes. Many high-powered loads travel at supersonic speeds. Therefore, a weapon that fires bullets at subsonic speeds combined with a good silencer results in the most quiet discharge. The M1911 is perfect for this purpose. The .45 was designed to have a quarter-ounce bullet travel at a relatively low speed (slightly more than half the speed of sound), thus giving the bullet enough foot-pounds of energy to cause hydrostatic shock on impact, kill the target, and not cause any supersonic banging along its path.

Silencers do affect aim, so they are much more effective when used up close. Of course, at close range, the best silencer is the target's own body. Then the best tactic is to ram the weapon into the person's torso between the ribs and the belt and squeeze the trigger. All of the highly pressurized gas from the weapon then expands into the target's body and all the only sound is a light thump.

All of the pieces of my puzzle came together. I had an ideal weapon, silent and lethal, to compensate for my weakened physical state. I would drive to al Zarqa's house, eliminating the need for public transportation and the risk of being noticed as a foreigner in a residential area normally devoid of tourists. I would also drive to the train station to catch a train to Bulgaria, Vienna, and ultimately Munich. When I checked in, the hotel desk clerk told me that the room was reserved for four nights with allowance for room service and incidentals like laundry. I had three more days to pull this off.

The next day I rode the bus to the train station and bought a ticket to Vienna. A train was leaving Thursday at 11:15 P.M. That was two days away. Then I drove to al Zarqa's house. He lived in a fairly large house, a *Yali*, along the banks of the Bosporus, which represented his prosperity. A solid-looking, pinkish, wooden house, it was surrounded by a concrete wall with a gate leading into the courtyard. The front of the two-story house had two doors and windows on the ground floor and two doors leading to a balcony and two windows on the second floor. All of the doors and windows had shutters. I parked down the street, slouched in my seat, and waited. I spent the next several hours waiting and watching.

There was not much traffic on the street, and no sign of al Zarqa until 9:00 that evening. He pulled up to the gate in a large white Citroen; there were four men in the car. A large man exited the front passenger door and unlocked the gate. Then the car pulled in while the man locked the gate behind it. After they all entered the house, somebody closed the shutters. I drove back to the Hippodrome, parked the car, and took the bus back to the Hilton. By 8:00 the next morning I was watching his house again. At 10:00 A.M. the Citroen arrived with three men in it and picked up al Zarqa. I had some bread and goat cheese with me so I sat there all day waiting to see when he would return. At about the same time as the night before, they returned and went through the same routine; the man seemed to be a creature of habit.

After returning the car to the Hippodrome and locking it up, I returned to Taksim Square for my last night (one way or the other) in Turkey. I needed a good meal, so before going to the hotel, I stopped at a decent restaurant to eat. The dinner started with *mete*, appetizers similar to Spanish *tapas*. I had *Arnavut Cigeri* (chopped and fried liver with onions), *Dolma* (wine leaves wrapped around rice, ground lamb, and herbs), and *Patlican Salatasi* (pureed eggplant salad). Although there is a prohibition against alcohol in the Muslim faith, the Turks have a long tradition of drinking liquor with special meals. I had wine and raki, a licorice liqueur, also called "lion's milk," and often referred to as the national drink of Turkey, which tasted similar to Greek ouzo. A few skewers of lamb and chicken, accompanied by *pilav* (rice) followed.

By the time I finished my meal, I was fairly tipsy (I was never able to handle sweet liqueurs), so I walked back to the Hilton and went to bed. The next morning, I packed my things and checked out at the desk. I waited while they ran the credit information, and about twenty minutes later they thanked me for choosing the Hilton and wished me well. I took my last bus trip to the Hippodrome, picked up the Opel, and drove to al Zarqa's house. I was not yet sure how to complete the job. My first goal was to park within half a mile or so of the house and walk the rest of the way. I was surprised and somewhat relieved that I did not encounter anybody along the walk. Perhaps that was because many of these houses were summer homes for the wealthy, and it wasn't summer.

Trees lined both sides of the wall around the house, which made it easy to climb over to the other side. I had seen no other activity when I watched the house and assumed that it would be empty during the day. I broke the glass of one of the windows farthest from the front door and crawled inside. The silence that followed confirmed that the house was empty.

My natural inclination was to look around the house to see what I could find. But I was not there as a thief or out of idle curiosity; I was there to kill somebody. I also didn't want to risk being stuck in another part of the house if al Zarqa came home earlier than I expected. I needed all the men who might be with him to be close together. The elements of surprise and speed were necessary. So I sat on an overstuffed ottoman, pulled on the gloves, and examined my weapon. Then I waited. As it grew dark, I realized that the night would also work in my favor.

When I finally heard a vehicle pull up and the gate creak open, it was 8:45 P.M. I positioned myself behind the front door and waited as I heard the key turn in the lock. The door swung open and the first man entered the room, turning to his left to turn on the lights. Close behind came another guy, then al Zarqa, and finally the fourth person. As the last man swung the door shut, I aimed at the back of his head and pulled the trigger. *Pop!* As the impact of the slug thrust him forward, I killed the second man with a shot directly above his left ear as he was turning to see what was happening. The third man was reaching for what I assumed was a gun in the left side of his jacket when I shot him through his right eye. That left al Zarqa. I intentionally left him to be last because he was least likely to be armed. He stood there with his mouth open, pointing at me, seemingly in shock. As he started to say something, I shot him once in the center of his forehead.

I checked each one of them; they were all dead. I looked at my watch. It was 8:47 P.M. Barely two minutes had elapsed since they had entered the house. I had a train to catch.

I unscrewed the silencer and slipped it into my

pocket. I left the gun on the floor next to al Zarqa's body. There was no point in taking the weapon with me; it was untraceable and would get me into serious trouble if I were stopped for any reason. The silencer was another matter altogether. It indicated a sophisticated hit. I knew that the killings would be investigated as part of an ongoing struggle between rival drug operations and I suppose that in some ways it was.

After locking the front door, I left the house the same way I came in, through the window. I looked over the wall and saw that the street was clear, so I quickly walked back to the Opel and drove to the train station. At that point, I realized how huge of a role luck played in everything I had just done. I could plan for days and weeks, but had no control over things like somebody driving by as I climbed over a wall or walking by as I broke a windowpane. As I drove over the Galata Bridge to the European side of Istanbul, I threw the silencer into the waters of the Golden Horn. Immediately after exiting the bridge, I parked the car close to the Sirkeci train station and went to meet my train bound for Vienna, via Sofia, Belgrade, and Trieste. It was 10:05 P.M.—I had plenty of time to spare. Al Zarqa would not be missed until the morning, so there was no need for concern or panic.

The train was already at the station, but I decided to have a couple glasses of Doluca wine (one of the few Turkish wines worth drinking) and some lamb kebab with bread. After eating, I boarded the train and found a seat in one of the second-class compartments. Almost on time, the train took off and quickly reached the Bulgarian frontier. Exiting Turkey was easy; entering Bulgaria was much more of a hassle. The Bulgarians were convinced that every American coming from Turkey had hashish on him. Given the countries that had stamped my passport, they were all the more intent on finding drugs in my possession, so they thoroughly searched my backpack and my body. I was thankful that everything I owned had been washed at the Hilton in Istanbul. I was as clean as a whistle. The guards, like the ones at every other border I crossed, wanted to know why I had such a big, sharp knife, and if I was willing to trade for it.

When they were finally convinced that I had no contraband they moved on to other passengers. After about forty-five minutes of sitting idle, the train began to move through the country. Unlike today, Bulgaria had a horrendously grim reputation during the Communist rule of Todor Zhivkov, one that did not promote any interest in sightseeing. I had no intentions of getting off anywhere along the route within that country, so I settled in for the more than twenty hours it was going to take to get to my next stop, Trieste, Italy.

CHAPTER 14

RECOVERY AND REFLECTION

As the train rolled toward the Yugoslavia border I tried to rest. I sorely needed to restore my body and mind as much as possible under the circumstances. In addition to resting, I had time to reflect seriously about what I had become. I had taken the lives of seven men. Was I a killer? An assassin? Was there a difference? I did not care for any of the definitions or terms with which I labeled myself. After hours of equivocation, I decided that if I really needed a label, "assassination" was the best word to describe my actions.

Assassinations, or as they are often called, "targeted killings," are nothing new to the worldwide covert intelligence community and have been used as a political tool since before recorded history. The Roman Senate acted as a body to kill Caesar. Was that done for personal gain or to protect the Roman Republic from being taken over by a tyrant? Did I consider Caesar a tyrant to provide justification to Caesar's killers and make myself feel better about what I had done?

Any country that denies using targeted killings is simply denying the truth. Although it might be as a result of heightened media attention, there seemed to be a dramatic rise in the number of political assassinations with the onset of the cold war. For example, there has been a long-running debate among historians on whether President John F. Kennedy knew about the CIA plots to kill

Fidel Castro based on what was called the "Executive Action Program" or whether the repeated attempts on Castro's life were simply rogue operations.

The Soviet KGB eliminated threats to their regime using creative assassination means such as darts poisoned with ricin fired from the end of an umbrella. In 1956, Col. Mustafa Hafez, the Egyptian commander of military intelligence in the Gaza Strip who sent Fedayeen infiltrators into Israel, was killed when a book he received in the mail exploded. From its inception, the State of Israel and its Mossad have resorted to assassination to eliminate Palestinian guerrillas and terrorists. Here again, I wondered whether I chose to see my targets as guerrillas and terrorists to excuse my actions. In their own communities, guerrillas and terrorists are described as freedom fighters and martyrs, implying that their deaths were murders, not assassinations. If the person pulling the trigger belonged to the group writing the history books, he or she was said to have been driven to extreme means to achieve a higher good. If not, he or she was an evil, cold-blooded killer. The characterizations stem from subjective points of view. I chose to include myself in the former category.

I fell asleep with these ideas in my head. I awoke as the train approached Yugoslavia. Entering Yugoslavia I felt safe for the first time in months. Yugoslavia, or the Socialist Federal Republic of Yugoslavia, was, by definition, a Soviet Bloc country. Although Josip Broz Tito was the absolute ruler and people who did not agree with the way he ran the country tended to disappear, he was somewhat of a maverick and maintained a certain autonomy from his Soviet superiors. Yugoslavians were allowed to travel outside of the country and many of them ended up taking jobs in West Germany, something unheard of in all other Soviet Bloc states. Conversely, many Europeans chose to take their vacations on the coastline commonly known as the Yugoslavian Mediterranean.

I slept most of the way to Trieste, Italy. My healing

had already begun, and I decided to travel through Trieste instead of heading straight north to Vienna from Zagreb. With white limestone cliffs to its back and the blue Adriatic to its front, Trieste was an ideal place to recover more before returning to the chilly north.

Trieste has a long, colorful history. It was founded as a Roman colony and in the thirteenth century it joined the Austrian Empire. In the nineteenth century, it became the center of an Italian nationalist movement that called for Trieste and two other former Italian cities, Istria and the Trentino, to rejoin Italy. After WWII, Yugoslavia and the Allies fought over Trieste until 1954, when the city and a connecting corridor finally became a part of Italy. Along with its idyllic setting, Trieste also appealed to me because one of my favorite authors, James Joyce, called it home for sixteen years. There, he wrote *A Portrait of the Artist as a Young Man*, most of *Dubliners*, and *Ulysses* while he taught English classes for Berlitz. Freud also spent time in Trieste as a medical student, and it became one of the first centers of Italian psychoanalytical thought.

I had money left from my last American Express pickup in Istanbul, so I looked for a good, clean, medium-priced hotel. I settled on the Hotel Roma, a little place located in a nineteenth-century building in the Theresian Quarter, not far from the railway station. After checking in I bought a liter of Terrano, a locally produced red wine so popular it had a street named after it. The wine dulled my mind and body, and I slept deeply until mid-morning.

That morning, I decided to eat breakfast at Pirona, a small bakery and pastry shop on Largo Barriera Vecchia. According to the locals, James Joyce ate breakfast there every day between 1910 and 1914. After breakfast, I walked around the town to build up my lower body strength. Being situated on the coast, there were plenty of seafood restaurants. Almost all the seafood I ate relied heavily on fresh herbs like dill and tarragon, and was different from what most Americans expected from Italian food. Aside from seafood, Trieste was also known for its prosciutto, gnocchi, Montasio cheese, and a soup called *Jota*, which consisted of smoked pork and sauerkraut, obviously a holdover from Trieste's ties with Austria and Hungary. And with every meal, of course, there was the Terrano.

After three days of exploring the city and gaining strength from the food, the warm sun, walking in the fresh sea air, and rest, it was time to get back on the train to Vienna. I used the cultural, historical, artistic, and gastronomic diversions offered by Trieste to avoid thinking about what I had experienced, but I could not stay there forever. I was not sure what waited for me in Munich, but I knew that I would not be able to avoid it forever.

I did not want to travel through Vienna because I could have taken a direct train to Munich, but I had been given instructions to stop there first. When I arrived, I went straight to the American Express office. I was happy to be back in a German-speaking country, a language I was at ease with, but Vienna was an expensive city, and I had no reason to stay there any longer than to check for money and messages and catch the next train to Munich. I didn't think I would have to wait long because Vienna was Central Europe's main rail hub, making connections plentiful.

Of course, there was a wire for money (five hundred dollars) and a letter. I exchanged seventy-five dollars for Austrian currency to pay for the train ticket to Munich and some food, pocketed the rest of the money, and took the sealed message with me. Outside, I sat on a bench and opened the message: "Good job. Message delivered in Istanbul is having desired effect. Glad to see you took some time in Trieste. See you soon."

So he knew I stopped off at Trieste. Why was I surprised? Phil had explained there was an ample supply of eyes and ears to report status or progress. What was in short supply were people like me, the "shooters." Somebody was probably waiting at the train station when I boarded in Istanbul to make sure I was keeping to the plan, even though they most assuredly did not know who I was and what I had done, or even why I had to be on that train. He or she probably knew my itinerary minutes after I bought my train ticket. Somebody was waiting in Trieste, too. Although not part of the plan, my side trip was probably viewed as harmless, if not necessary. I was beginning to believe someone, somewhere, knew every time I made a move.

I headed back to the train station and learned there was a train leaving in two hours, giving me time to eat and drink a beer. Although I did not like regular beer, Vienna had a brewery that produced a beer called Ottakringer Bock, which was a much darker, heavier, and more potent beer than lagers. After three beers and a sandwich of lox and a boiled egg on heavy rye I started to feel good.

While sitting on the train for Munich, it occurred to me that, although I had written a number of cards and letters to my parents all along my route, I had not once communicated with any of my family in Munich. Unless they had heard something from my parents, they would not know I was on my way back. I had gained a few of the pounds I had lost since starting this mission, but there was no way to pretend that I had not changed physically. My muscle tone had diminished, owing to the lack of the high-protein diet I generally followed and my normal training regimen. And there were the beatings, hepatitis, and my little "vacation" in the Iranian prison, all of which had caused extensive damage, some of which I wasn't aware of at the time.

The train pulled into the Munich Hauptbahnhof and I took the S Bahn to Unterpfaffenhofen. After the fifteen-minute walk to my uncle's house I decided to ring the doorbell rather than use my key. After all, they weren't expecting me and I didn't want to cause any heart attacks. When my aunt Ilse came to the door I realized how much I had changed and how bad I looked. She took one look at me, put her hand over her mouth, and broke into tears—and not tears of joy. Then my cousins Angelika and Robert came to the door and started crying, too. I wasn't sure if they were glad to see me or disturbed by how bad I looked. All of a sudden I started crying, too.

I had been gone five months but it felt like five years. It was too late to register for the current semester at Ludwig-Maximillians so I had plenty of time on my hands. I started lifting weights again and spent time in the Unterpfaffenhofen community sauna. I also swam, enjoying the cool, soundless water in the pool. As I began to feeling normal again, I started to take the train in to the university and meet friends in the cafeteria. Then one day, as I had expected, Phil fell into step right next to me. Speaking German, he shook my hand and invited me to join him for lunch back at the Matthaeser. It looked like I was going back to work.

CHAPTER 15

BACK TO WORK:
EXTRACTION FROM THE DDR

Although I had been expecting to hear from Phil sooner or later, his manner of popping up out of nowhere rattled me. It made me feel that I was a fish in his aquarium; he seemed to know where I was and what I was doing at all times. We rode the U-Bahn (streetcar) to the Hauptbahnhof and walked the rest of the way to the bar in silence. When we arrived at the Matthaeser we sat down at one of the unoccupied tables and ordered two liters of beer. Phil did not start talking until the beer arrived.

"Got pretty rough a couple of times, eh?"

"Rough? I guess you could say that—and you know damn well it did! Why didn't you get me out of Iran sooner? I don't think I could have made it another hour. I'm still not sure I made it out with my head in one piece. I can't sleep more than a few minutes at a time at night, and the slightest noise has me jumping for cover. When I least expect it, I'm hit with dizzy spells and extreme nausea. Now and then I find myself breaking down and starting to whimper for no reason. It's downright embarrassing."

"Sorry. I did what I could as soon as I knew what was going on. Anytime the Iranians make a drug bust involving Americans, they let us know. Who do you think trained SAVAK in the first place? They kind of owe us. Normally, we don't do anything about it. It's their internal affair; that's the deal we have with them. If the person they busted is well connected back home, they might let them pay an enormous fine in exchange for a lighter sentence. But most of the time they just lock them away. If the bust is big, they go with a death sentence. Although they'll do it with or without a confession, they prefer it with one— it gives them credibility and makes it look cleaner to the outside world. Everybody figures the idiot had it coming. There were two problems with your bust. First, your buddy had a ton of drugs packed into that van, making both of you prime candidates for a bullet to the head. Second, it took a few days before the report that they had you made it down to me. I know you went through some kind of hell there, but actually that worked to your advantage."

"Getting my balls busted by some greasy goon swinging a thick belt like he's Zorro with a whip or something is to my advantage? Unless I'm hoping for a career with the Vienna Boys Choir, I don't see it. And that phony firing squad. How do you figure that one was to my advantage?"

"First of all, that was no phony firing squad. They were doing a dry run to see if you would confess. The next one would have been the real McCoy. The fact that you didn't sign a confession right away kept you alive until I found out where you were and could get you out. Your buddy . . ."

"Quit calling hi that! The only buddy that asshole had was himself."

"Okay. The guy you caught a ride with. How's that? In any case, he wasn't that tough. From what I could gather, he rolled over at the first hint of pain."

"What do you mean?"

"He signed a lengthy confession that included things he probably had nothing to do with. I really can't blame him. At that point he would have probably admitted that he was 110 years old and had four breasts rather than go through half of what he saw happening around him."

"And?"

"And nothing. That's it. Executed and buried. At least I assume they buried him. His body, or what's left of it, could be in some trash heap. You were messed up, no doubt about that, but at least you're alive—and lucky to be that. The Shah and his French-loving jet set in Tehran might like America, but the average Iranian out in the sticks considers us all decadent scum. By getting rid of people like you, they figure they're doing their families, their country, and Allah himself a favor. And though they would never admit it out loud, they would just as soon get rid of the Shah, too."

"Let me guess, now you want me to go in and take out the Shah of Iran?"

At that he laughed so loud that people actually stopped what they were doing and looked over at us.

"Don't flatter yourself. You did okay. Alright, better than okay; you did good. But keep it in perspective. The guys you took out were small fish. And, the way I hear it by all accounts out of Afghanistan and Turkey, you were also damned lucky. Now don't get me wrong, luck is a good thing. It's an important part of the equation. But it is a variable that you can't count on. It would take more than good luck to take out a target like the Shah and walk away. And even if that scenario about the Shah was in the cards, you wouldn't be the guy I would pick for the job. You're still too green, too cocky."

"Green? Give me a break! You intentionally kill one time; you're a killer. Am I missing something here? I don't know whether to be relieved or pissed. But whatever, I don't think you dropped in today to tell me what a lucky guy I am."

He stopped laughing, pulled out a thick manila envelope, and told me to open it. I tore open the envelope and pulled out maps, a few pictures, and directions.

"The guy in the picture—call him Klaus—is currently in Leipzig, where he is supposed to stay for the next two weeks. We need to get him over to this side of the curtain. That's all you need to know about him personally.

A week from Friday, he will take a trip to Erfurt for the weekend. He's a devout Lutheran who has had this pilgrimage to one of Martin Luther's main stomping grounds planned for over a year now, so the side trip won't cause any undue suspicion, even from the *Stasi*. You will meet him in Erfurt on Saturday and see that he makes it to West Germany safely. You'll have less than forty-eight hours to get him out before the fact that he is missing will raise an alarm and tighten the borders around there more than they normally are."

"Let me guess. I get a phony ID and drive over posing as a German on vacation. The rest is up to me."

"Not even close. You can't drive over the border this time. I don't care how convincing you can be as a German. They would make a copy of your phony passport and follow up on checking you out. They have hundreds of people who live for this stuff. It wouldn't take but a few hours and they would be connecting your passport picture with the one they made a copy of when you legally went into East Berlin when you first got here in the fall. That alone would get you arrested and locked away for a long time. No, I'm afraid we're going to have to drop you in for this one."

He explained that I would be flown to a point close to the border and would do a HALO jump to minimize hang time. My target drop zone was the town of Gotha, about twenty miles inside of East Germany. From there, I would walk fifteen miles to Erfurt. I would make contact with Klaus in a church in Erfurt at 10:00 o'clock on Saturday morning and from there we would drive his Trabant in a southeasterly direction to the Czech border where we would cross through a prearranged breach late that night. Once in Czechoslovakia, we would drive to the border with West Germany and cross over, again at a designated "weak point." If all went well, the whole operation would take less than thirty hours. If anything held up our progress, we would have one more night to pull it off before Klaus was missed in Leipzig.

I had a couple of questions. "Why go to all the risk of adding another border breach by going into Czechoslovakia when the border between East and West Germany is so close to Erfurt? And why send somebody in? Isn't there somebody already over there who could get this guy over to the West?"

"Trying to breach the border between the two Germanies is way too risky; it's probably the most militarized border in the whole world, except for maybe Korea. The border troops are organized into three border commands and two independent regiments. The ones that will concern you are Border Command South, with its seat in Erfurt, which guards the border from Nordhausen to the Czechoslovak border and the independent border regiment which patrols the Czechoslovak border and is headquartered in Pirna. The fortifications along the whole border consist of double fences made of steel mesh with razor sharp edges. All along the fence there are watchtowers, one within sight of the next. Some of the areas between the two fences are mined, but even those that aren't are considered death strips where anybody found within them is immediately gunned down by machine-gun fire from guards patrolling the zone. In other Soviet Bloc countries, the border defenses between the West and the East are much lighter. Take the border between Hungary and Austria; that one consists of a simple chain-link fence. But you don't have the time to get to Hungary. The border between East Germany and Czechoslovakia, although not as loose as the Hungarian and Austrian one is considerably easier than the one between East and West Germany. Besides, we have reliable, well-placed people there with access to the border to help you out. Why not use somebody already over there to bring him over? Our people are there for a reason. We can't risk breaking up our network. Anything else that you will need to know is in the envelope. Study it closely and be at the Hauptbahnhof at 9:00 A.M. the Friday after next. That's June 1. You don't have to bring anything with you; we will get you outfitted with everything you will need."

"Now let me get this straight. The East German Border Command South is headquartered in Erfurt. And you want me to pick this guy up in Erfurt? You couldn't pick a more quiet, less-populated place than that?"

"Actually, you would stick out more in a more secluded setting. Sometimes it's best to do these things in full view, because that is precisely where nobody is watching. Haven't you ever heard the old line that the best place to hide something is right under a person's nose? Besides, he has a good excuse for being there; he will be right there where he is expected to be."

"And one more thing. I seem to recall reading about a U.S. military jet being shot down somewhere close to Erfurt a few years ago. What's the story there?"

"That was 1964. One of the Air Force's training jets strayed over the border, was intercepted by Soviet fighters, and shot down."

"Casualties?"

"All three crew members dead. Chalk it up to mistakes in judgment and some bad luck."

Somehow, his explanation didn't make me feel any more at ease, but once again, I was the doer not the planner. I went back to my uncle's house and told my relatives that my class was going on another field trip and that I would be gone for a few days. They reacted with their usual indifference and did not ask me where I was supposedly going this time. Then I resumed my normal routine of visiting the university during the day, working out, and sitting in the sauna in the evening.

On Friday, June 1, I went to the train station and met Phil. We took a train to Frankfurt where we were picked up by a civilian who drove us to Wiesbaden Air Base. I was briefed further on the mission. I would leave at 1:00 A.M. and fly toward the border. Before the border, near the town of Eisenach, I would jump, from about

Roland Haas in 1959 at six years of age in Buffalo, New York

Haas at eighteen upon graduation from high school in 1970 in Lakewood, Ohio

The author as an NROTC midshipman seated second from right on board the USS *Guadalupe* in 1971.

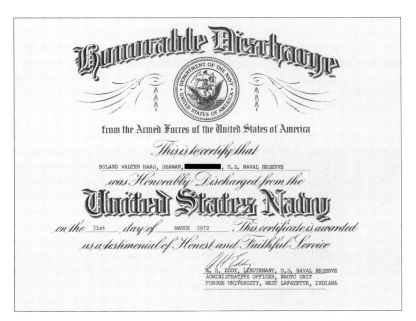

Although Haas was supposedly drummed out of the Navy due to felony counts, as arranged by the CIA, he was still given an honorable discharge on March 31, 1972. Normally, the circumstances involved with him leaving the uniformed services would have resulted in "Discharge under Other Than Honorable Conditions."

Diese Karte wird ungültig am:
1. MAI 1973

I. Netzkarte für den Innenraum mit zusätzlichen Zonen im Außenraum:

Monatsmarke DM **33,--**

4010

Stammkarte Nr 045957 | **Studenten**

II. Gültig für die Zonen:

Monatsmarke DM **26.--**

045957

Nº der Stammkarte

| 4010 | 3900 | 2700 | 1600 |
| 0000 | 1200 | | |

16 N 754 B 002600M

Benutzungsbestimmungen siehe Rückseite

Haas's Munich mass transit pass for 1972 and 1973.

The courtyard of the Najib Hotel in Kabul, where the author stayed on his first CIA assassination mission in 1973.

BRENDA LANE-WORTHINGTON

Tribune photo by Kenneth Green

Roland Haas, right, works out with former Mr. America, Don Ross.

A thinking man's jock

Oakland's **Roland Haas** may be the only English teacher in town who can get professional athletes to drop by his place regularly.

His guest list includes **Joe Harris** of the Los Angeles Rams, **Rod Martin** and **Lindsey Mason** of the Raiders, **Sherman White** of the Buffalo Bills, and Mr. American of 1978, **Don Ross.**

But they don't drop by to discuss Beowulf or to recite Elizabethan poetry.

When Haas is not teaching comparative literature at UC-Berkeley, he can be found at the Olympia Health Club on Grand Avenue. He's one of the owners.

If he looks like a weight-lifter, that's because he is. He became acquainted with barbells when his family moved from Germany to Buffalo, N.Y.

"I didn't speak very much English then," says Haas. We moved to one of the roughest parts of town. I was picked on and beaten up quite a bit by some of the kids."

The slender youth quietly began training in his basement. In 1972 he placed third in the National Collegiate Powerlifting Championship. He had long since convinced neighborhood bullies to find another weakling.

Today, Haas wears an impressive 220 pounds stretched across a six-foot two-inch frame. His chest is 49 inches, his arms, 16.

He and his partners — **Craig Aho** and **Kenly Morrison** — opened the club in January and membership has been steadily growing.

Says Rams' Joe Harris: "There aren't many gyms like this in the country. A professional athlete must have equipment that keeps him in shape off-season. We need the kind of flexibility that can only be kept up by working with heavy machinery. Steady workouts here make the transition to going back to the field less difficult."

Not surprisingly, Haas agrees. He says that he designed a lot of the gym's equipment. "There wasn't much machinery being made that was heavy enough. Most gyms today are health spas. This is definitely not a spa. In many of those places the owners don't want anyone who's likely to talk loud or even sweat. They discourage serious athletes."

But Olympia is not just for men only, or just for professional athletes.

In addition to the impressive line-up of male poundage that pours through its door from 6 a.m. until midnight, there are also housewives, office workers, teens and seniors.

"More than half our members are women," says Haas. "In the beginning, a lot of them were afraid that working out would give them bulging muscles, but there's a difference between body-building and power-lifting. A lot of my Olympic lifters are so light that they look anemic. Getting strong

doesn't mean you have to bulge.

"Besides, the muscle structures on women are so different from men, that they'd have to take hormones to look like Mr. America."

There are also karate, aerobic dance, exercise and yoga classes available — enough to keep Haas and his partners very busy. They each work about 90 hours a week. But Haas says he still looks forward to his time in the classroom.

"Physical exercise helps me concentrate on my books. And it keeps me in shape. I have colleagues at the school who are my age (29) and they look 46."

Maybe his colleagues wouldn't like hearing Haas talk about them that way. But they'll have to take the matter up with him.

Him and his black belt, that is.

Haas (left) outside the Olympia Gym in Oakland in 1982, with Hells Angels vice president "Cisco."

The author at Lake Tahoe in 1982 with country/western artist Waylon Jennings (right) and his Hells Angels bodyguard (left).

Haas in 1990 in West Germany with Soviet special operations (Spetznaz) officers and their families whom he had extracted from East Germany.

Right: The author in 1990, dismantling part of the fence between East and West Germany.

Haas (lower left) in 1991 with a Polish/Romanian CFE inspection team at the U.S. Army base in Wildflecken, West Germany. He was on orders as the site commander.

DEPARTMENT OF THE ARMY
HEADQUARTERS, UNITED STATES ARMY RESERVE COMMAND
1401 DESHLER STREET SW
FORT MCPHERSON, GEORGIA 30330-2000

Orders B-0492   25 NOVEMBER 2002

HAAS, ROLAND W.   ██████████   GM14
                                              USARC DIRP

You are to proceed on temporary duty as shown below and return to your permanent duty station
upon completion of the duty. You will submit a DD Form 1351-2 (travel voucher) for this travel
to the servicing Finance and Accounting Office within 10 days after completion of travel.

Temporary duty at: GUANTANAMO BAY, CUBA
Purpose: Coordinate Military Intelligence Issues
Number of days: 3
Will proceed date: 05 DECEMBER 2002
Security clearance: TOP SECRET
Accounting classification:
      2132080.0000 0 24-2400 121R34.05000 2###   21T2 $ 116.00
      005053 HAA7574TBBH492 5ABH00 028013

Additional Instructions: (1) Government quarters and mess will be used if available. (2) If
all or part of this travel is by commercial air, tourist class will be used when it meets
mission requirements. (3) When traveling to the National Capital Region (NCR), San Antonio, TX;
Atlanta, GA; and TDY to Oahu, Hawaii region, you must contact the Lodging Success Center at
1-800-GO-ARMY-1 (1-800-462-7691) before making lodging arrangements. (4) A copy of paid DD 1351-2
(travel voucher) should be provided to your resource manager / resource POC. (5) The Toll-free
number to reach the HQ, United States Army Reserve Command is 1-800-359-8483.
VARIATION AUTHORIZED. SECURITY MANAGER HAS VERIFIED THE ABOVE SECURITY CLEARANCE TO BE
CORRECT. TRAVEL IS BY MILITARY AIR.

Format: 400

                                         ****
FOR THE COMMANDER: *   OFFICIAL   *
                                         *   HEADQUARTERS   *
                                         * US ARMY RESERVE COMMAND *
                                         *   *
                                         ****
DISTRIBUTION: OVETTA D. ROBINSON
Individual (1)   BUDGET ANALYST, G8
DCS, Comptroller, AFRC-COP-H (1)   FORT MCPHERSON, GA 30330-2000

Haas's 2002 Army orders, showing his "Top Secret" status
for duty to "coordinate intelligence activities" at the detention facility in Guantanamo Bay, Cuba.

32,000 feet, to Gotha. There was a new moon so it would be dark. I was dressed all in black, but my pack included normal civilian clothes, which I would change into before I entered Erfurt. My pack also contained, among other things, food, night-vision scope, a set of black clothes for Klaus, all-purpose wire, a knife, and a silencer-equipped M1911. When I saw the weapons I turned to ask Phil a question, but he beat me to the punch.

"This mission is simply an extraction, nothing more. You will make every attempt to avoid any conflict. The last thing we want to do is risk any harm to Klaus or, for that matter, any civilians. You will use your weapons as a last resort if capture or death is imminent. If you sense anything funny before you leave Erfurt, you will abort the extraction and try to make it back by yourself. This is not Afghanistan. Am I clear?"

As was often the case when I spoke with Phil, I had nothing more to say, at least nothing more that would make any difference. I checked and rechecked my equipment and then had a few hours to sleep before we were scheduled to take off, which was good because it looked like I would not be sleeping for at least a day and a half. When it was time, I suited up and we were off. When we reached the jump point, I was tapped on the back and went out for my first jump since Yuma, almost two years earlier. After forty seconds, I deployed my chute and maneuvered toward Gotha.

As it turned out, I overshot the town by a couple of miles, but that was fine because I had less than nine miles to walk. I took everything I needed, including a worn German knapsack, out of my ALICE pack, I stashed it and my rig in a small depression about 50 yards into the woods, and covered it all with loose brush. I was not going to be in East Germany long enough to be concerned about it being found. And chances were, if it was discovered the finder would keep it rather than report it.

I got my bearings and started walking east along the Eisenacher Strasse toward Erfurt. It was a few minutes after 2:00 A.M., which meant I could take an easy pace of about twenty minutes per mile and arrive with plenty of time to spare. I listened for sounds of traffic. Although I did not expect to encounter any traffic in the East German countryside at that time of night, I made sure that I had the cover which was offered by the nearby woods if I needed to duck out of sight for any reason. I passed by Frienstedt and made it to Schmira, which was about one mile from Erfurt before I ducked into the woods and changed from my black outfit into drab, dark blue pants and a blue-checked shirt. Now, all I had to do was to wait for a decent hour to enter Erfurt.

There was no reason for fear or need for stealth during this part of the mission. I spoke the language without an accent and was dressed like a typical German weekend hiker. In addition, I had been given an East German ID with the name Heinz Dieter Emmert, a student at the university in Leipzig. My grandmother's maiden name was Emmert and I therefore considered my assumed name to be a sign of good luck (no harm in wishful thinking). I also had my phony *Studienbuch*, or curriculum of study, and could have intelligently discussed the classes that I was listed as taking.

I stopped at a small bakery and bought a few German rolls called *Semmeln*, some strawberry marmalade, and a cup of black tea that I doctored with cream and sugar. At 9:30 A.M., I walked to the religious complex comprising the Marien Dom (cathedral) and Saint Severi-Kirche (church) where I was to meet Klaus. The two Gothic structures, built during the thirteenth and fourteenth centuries, stood side-by-side, towered over the city, and were Erfurt's main claim to fame.

I climbed a set of huge open stairs to the cathedral and entered. I was struck by the huge leaded-glass windows. The thirteen windows surrounding the choir area were at least 50 feet tall and breathtaking. Elderly people were spread throughout the cathedral. I saw Klaus immediately. He was sitting alone in a long pew toward the back. He had a slight frame, slate-gray hair, and a bushy white mustache. Stooped over, he seemed older than his picture had led me to believe. I guessed he was sixty-five years old. But even if I had not seen a picture of him beforehand, he would have been easy to pick out as he was the one who, instead of praying intently, was looking around nervously.

I walked to his pew and silently slid in a few feet away from him. He was shaking so badly I thought he would faint. I quietly initiated the prearranged conversation. I said, "Ein Radler wuerde jetzt gut schmecken," which translated to, "A bicyclist's liter [half beer and half lemon-lime soda] would taste good about now." To which he replied, "Ja, aber lieber ohne Limo," or "Yes, but it would be better without the soda." With that out of the way he knew who I was.

It was too early to get on the road because I didn't want to reach the border with Czechoslovakia before dark. I had originally planned to spend the rest of the morning and early afternoon with Klaus playing tourist in Erfurt, but he was clearly too nervous. So I told him to go back to his room at the inn for a few hours and to meet me in front of the cathedral at 4:00 P.M. Although I had not driven in one, I had been told that Trabants were not fast cars, so I planned on three hours to drive the 120 miles to the Czech border. I told him not to check out of his hotel but, if asked, say that he was going out for dinner followed by a long evening stroll.

Klaus left for his room while I went to a local *Gaststätte* for lunch. After eating I wandered around Erfurt to take in the sights. Promptly at 4:00 P.M., Klaus pulled up to the cathedral in an off-white Trabant. Trabbis, as they were called, were not intended to be cars. In the 1950s, cheap transportation was popular throughout Europe. With bicycles, small motorcycles, and mopeds vying with the Volkswagen as the primary means of transportation, the idea for an intermediate type of vehicle arose.

The Trabbi was originally meant to be a three-wheeled, bubble-covered vehicle similar to a golf cart but intended for street use. It soon evolved into the P50, the P60, and finally the P601, a little four-seater with a small, easy-to-repair, 594-cc engine and lightweight construction. The P601 was produced for decades with few changes in design, and became a symbol of East German socialism and the butt of countless West German jokes. It was even claimed that the Trabbi was so short on metal and so recyclable that it could be completely digested by pigs. I stowed my backpack in the small trunk and, given the state of Klaus's nerves, decided to drive. He didn't argue. He seemed to want to talk about himself and why he was doing this, but each time he started, I told him that I didn't care and it was better if we did not discuss the matter. He was Klaus, on vacation, and I was Heinz Dieter, a student hitchhiking, or tramping, as the Germans called it, across the country. I didn't want to hear about his family, his work, or his life.

We drove east in silence, passing by Hochstadt, Mönchenholzhausen, and Weimar before taking a short stop in Jena. We had traveled about 30 miles, but Klaus was so rattled he already needed to use the bathroom. Leaving Jena, we headed south toward Schleiz, where we turned east again toward Plauen. We drove the 80 miles or so to Plauen in less than two hours and then took another bathroom break.

At that point it was after 7:00 P.M. and not dark enough to proceed, so we decided to grab a quick bite to eat. In the middle of town I saw the Stadt Hotel, which looked like it would have a decent restaurant. Klaus couldn't stand the thought of food, so he nursed a glass of wine; I was hoping it would steady his nerves. I ordered a small sausage platter and a lemon-lime soda.

By 8:30 P.M. we were back on the road toward Zwota. When we arrived we parked the Trabbi and walked two miles toward the Czechoslovakian border. Along the way, I made Klaus change into the black slacks and shirt I brought for him. It was dark and there was hardly any moonlight overhead. From the cover of a wood line, I scanned the fence with my night-vision scope. Klaus asked me what I was looking for. "A rabbit," I replied. "I'm looking for a rabbit to show me how we will proceed." This pushed him almost over the edge toward a total nervous breakdown, so I explained. If the plan had been carried out, a trusted agent in the area would have cut out a small section of the meshed-steel fence for us to cross through and loosely put it back so the hole would not be noticed. A stuffed rabbit, set to look as if it were munching on the grass, would mark the spot.

I almost laughed when Phil had explained how I would recognize my exit point. My last name is Haas, which is German for rabbit (*haase*). My nickname at Purdue had been "rabbit." When Phil introduced me to the various instructors I had during my training phases he also referred to me as "rabbit." It seemed, for better or worse, that "rabbit" was now my signature and my code name.

Klaus asked who set up our escape, how I knew they could be trusted, and how I knew it was not a trap. Too may questions. I had no idea who was supposed to prep the fence. It could have been a local working with the West for political reasons or maybe an East German border guard. Presumably some guards were in a position to help in situations like ours. I didn't know, nor did I care. If I saw a rabbit, I would go. At that point it was blind faith. And then I saw it. A fairly large brown rabbit was standing close to the fence.

After waiting a few minutes to make sure it was not a live rabbit and there was not a patrol near, I pulled Klaus out of the woods and we quickly crept the few hundred yards past the warning signs and up to the phony hare. I picked it up and took it along (no point in leaving it to possibly compromise the method). I dislodged the cut piece of mesh, which looked like a barbecue grill, and we slithered through the hole. Replacing the piece of fence, I pulled Klaus straight ahead to the next fence where a similar piece had been cut. We squeezed through that one, replaced the mesh, and were in Czechoslovakia.

It was after midnight when we arrived in the town of Kraslice, about three miles from the Czech border. The first car I saw was a white, four-door Škoda. There was not much crime in Czechoslovakia so it was natural for the doors of the sedan to be unlocked. If a car has a standard ignition system, is not fuel-injected, and does not have an electric fuel pump, hot wiring will usually start it and keep it running. I pulled the wire out of my backpack and ran it from the battery to the coil, positive to positive, jumping the starter and turning the engine over. The only thing I could not know with the car running in this state was how much fuel it had, because the gauges were powered through the ignition switch which I bypassed when I jumped the car. We didn't have much farther to travel, so I hoped for the best.

Klaus sat in the passenger seat and we headed southeast toward Karlovy Vary. I did not want to travel too close to the border before we were near our designated crossing point. At Karlovy Vary, 25 miles down the road, we switched direction and headed southwest toward Cheb, a trip of 32 miles. Along the road, I threw the stuffed rabbit out of the window; it would pose no threat of exposing anything there. When we arrived in Cheb we drove through and abandoned the car in the woods about 4 miles past the town. It was about 2:15 A.M. and we had another three miles to walk to our exit point.

We stayed away from the road as we walked toward the border. The walking was taking its toll on Klaus and he started to slow down considerably. I had to remind him of how close we were and what would happen if he gave up here. Going back was impossible and getting caught would result in a lengthy prison sentence—if he were lucky. His only hope was to keep moving.

I saw the Eger River, my next landmark, shortly before

4:00 A.M. I pulled out my scope and scanned the fence line. Klaus said, "More rabbits?" in a half joking tone. I answered him, "Yes, more rabbits." He didn't believe it. But actually, it made perfect sense. The less complicated the plan, the less that could go wrong. This was so uncomplicated it was almost insulting. I had no idea who was responsible for each exit point being ready and marked. Although not very likely, for all I knew it really could have been done with the collusion of border guards who were sympathetic to the west. I didn't know it at the time, but after the Iron Curtain came down, it was determined that the number of border guards who actually defected to the west between 1961 and 1985 totaled more than 2,500.

We walked another couple of hundred yards before I saw a twin to the first rabbit. After a quick check for any patrols we crept up to the fence on our stomachs. I removed the two-foot-square piece of fence and we crawled through, again taking the rabbit with us. Twenty more yards and we breached last barrier; we were in the Federal Republic of Germany. We walked a mile and a half, passed the town of Schirnding, and reached Arzberg three miles later. I located the pay phone I had been instructed to use and called Phil at the number he had given me. Fifteen minutes later, two cars came for us. Klaus entered one and was taken away. I sat down in the back seat of the other one. It was 6:20 A.M. The whole mission, from the jump into East Germany to the pickup at Arzberg, had taken slightly more than 28 hours. It was time for a nap.

CHAPTER 16

THE SEARCH FOR NORMALCY

Over the next few days, I did much thinking about the future. My conclusion was that I did not have one. It's not that I stopped believing in what I was doing. Although I didn't know who was calling the shots or why, I was convinced that I was working for or toward a higher good. I was bothered because my affiliation with the Agency was nonofficial; I technically did not have a job. I could not imagine living on piecemeal payments and being considered a bum by my family.

These thoughts continued for a couple of weeks when, once again, Phil "dropped in" and we went to the Matthaeser for another meeting. He complimented me on the extraction of Klaus, which I had not even thought about after we parted ways. Compared to what I had already gone through, that mission was a piece of cake. I laid out my concerns to him and told him that I wanted to go back to Purdue and finish up my degree. With all the classes I had tested out of or received credit for on the basis of my advanced placement (AP) high school courses, I wouldn't have lost any time and would be able to graduate with my original incoming class in the spring of 1974. But considering the conditions under which I left, I didn't think the school would reaccept me.

Phil didn't say anything while I talked; he sat and listened. When I finished he looked at me and asked,

"So, you want to quit?"

I thought about that for a minute before I assured him (and myself) that I did not want to quit. However, I wanted to earn my degree for a couple of reasons. It would give me credibility on paper in case I ever wanted to get a "real" job. Also, it would ease the burden on my parents. Although they were not the kind of parents to tell me they were proud of me, I thought they had a desire to boast about their children to their friends and family. Without trying to sound bitter or facetious, I was depriving them of the satisfaction of a real desire. Instead of giving them a reason to brag, I was forcing them to make excuses for why I was not living up to their expectations.

A few more minutes passed before Phil spoke again.

"I understand where you're coming from on this. I really do. But there are a few things I want you to consider. First of all, you're not the same person you were when you left Purdue. You've looked into the eyes of men whose lives were draining out of them, and you did that knowing that you were the reason they were dying. There are not many people on this earth who can say that. You weren't even the same person when you left Purdue that you were when you first got there. You've changed so much from the eighteen-year-old freshman from Ohio that I'm not sure you could ever make it back in that life. And then there is all the money and time we put into your training. That's not something we would just want to throw away. But I believe you when you say that you don't want to quit. And I also think that you've earned a break. Let me think it over and get back with you. Give me a week. I'll meet you here next week, Monday, same time."

I agreed and he went to wherever he stayed in Munich. The week went quickly. I went to the mountains for a few days with my cousin Angelika and some of her friends. At twenty-one, I was the oldest person in the group and the second oldest was sixteen. But that was fine; I played the role of chaperone.

On Monday, I found Phil waiting for me at the

Matthaeser when I arrived. He wasted no time on small talk, not that he ever did (which is something I admire to this day).

"You made a couple of good points. And I'm glad that you're more than willing to stay on, so this is what we'll do. Go ahead and apply for readmission to Purdue. I just happen to have the forms with me. While you're at it, go ahead and apply for a room in the graduate house. That way you will be able to be around people who are a little older."

Although I hated to interrupt, I had to break in.

"What makes you think they'll readmit me when they threw me out a just a year and a half ago? And even if they did let me back in, how could I live in the grad house when I'm still technically a senior? Sounds like a real stretch to me."

Phil let me rant for a few minutes. When I was finished listing all the reasons why this could not or would not work, he continued.

"Haven't you learned anything about trusting me? If I tell you it will work, it will work. Do I have to remind you that I got you out of a death sentence in Iran? And who arranged for a couple of dead rabbits to show you the way to an escape route from the DDR? Do you think it was all just dumb luck? You do the paperwork and I'll handle the rest. I'm taking you at your word that you're still a member of my team, and if I come calling, I will expect you to do whatever it is that needs to be done. Do we have an understanding?"

He was right, of course. If my experience as a guest of the Irani prison system had been the subject of a movie, I would have been freed amid massive explosions and a blaze of gunfire. But no, the reality was that I faced a firing squad one day, and woke up in a hotel the next, bruised and broken, but alive. The extraction from the DDR was also a lesson in reality. I didn't crash through the border in a bulletproof sports car. Nor did I lob grenades into a manned guard post. As incredible and simplistic as it sounds, a couple of goofy yet realistic-looking stuffed rabbits pointed the way, which had been prepped equally as quietly by somebody with access to the fence. No flash, no drama; instead there was quiet, low-key efficiency.

I agreed with Phil. He gave me an envelope with a thousand dollars inside, slapped me on the back, which was definitely out of character for him, and left. After sending the paperwork to Purdue, I wrote to my parents that I was coming home and told them what I wanted to do. They were skeptical but went along with it. My mother was convinced that once marked by the police, a person wore a big, neon scarlet letter that implicated his or her family. If I were back home, my family would have to bear the shame publicly. My German relatives protested my plans to leave, though I was sure that they were perfectly happy to have me go; they had done their duty to my father and, more importantly to them, paid off their guilt. So I bought my return-trip ticket and left Munich the same way I arrived, wondering what would happen next.

Contrary to what Phil said, I relished the quiet life back in Lakewood, Ohio. My younger brother Bob had set up a summer business of painting houses. I joined him in July, and we did quite well. The days were spent painting while the nights were dedicated to smoking marijuana and drinking beer (I still didn't like beer, but I was beginning to feel like I had to have it) under a bridge at the Rocky River Reservation, locally known as "the valley," with my high school friends, Fritz and Jim. I gave a slide show and address at the Lakewood Kiwanis Club on my "travels" to India and back, couching the whole story as a journey for knowledge and a rite of passage, and, of course, leaving out most of what actually occurred.

All of my remaining physical ailments (and there were quite a few) I credited to the beating I received in Prem Nagar. My story was well received, and I soon found myself something of a local celebrity. This acceptance by people of influence within the community went a long way in soothing my mother's concerns for the family's reputation.

I quickly received a letter of acceptance from Purdue along with an offer to be a resident at Graduate House East. Everything Phil had promised came to pass. There was no mention of having left the university in disgrace. The one explanation I imagined was that my records had been changed, and almost certainly not by a university employee. I met with my academic counselor and found out that if I wanted to graduate in the spring, I would need to take twenty-eight hours during each of the remaining two semesters, which would be a challenge, but was possible. So I registered for eight classes for the fall semester and tested out of two more.

When I was back into the swing of college life, I decided that I wanted more money as well as more excitement, so I took a job as a bouncer at the first, and at that time only, bar close to the university. I arrived every night and set myself up at the door with an eight-ounce glass of tequila, checked IDs, stopped fights, and threw out rowdy drunks.

There was not much challenge in dealing with college guys who had too much to drink other than the occasional idiot who got drunk and felt he could fight the whole world. That kind of drunk could be hit over and over again without knowing that he was hurt. Those encounters never ended until the offender was knocked unconscious and the cops hauled him off.

Phil dropped into my life again before the Thanksgiving break. I was studying in the student union when he plopped into the chair next to me. He explained that this was a friendly visit to maintain contact and to give me material to work on to "broaden my horizons." He handed me what appeared to be a slightly larger-than-normal pen and told me to open it. I pulled off the cap and ten pieces of metal with strangely shaped tips fell out on the table.

"Okay, I give up. What is this?"

"A lock-pick set built to look like a pen. And here's a manual to go with it. Read it. And more importantly, practice."

"On what? Do I just go up to somebody's door and try to break in?"

"Eventually, yes. But to start with, just go out to a hardware store and buy a few different locks. Be patient and stick with it. I think you'll find it both easier and harder than it looks. You'll understand once you get started."

After about an hour of small talk, he left. I was fascinated. I associated picking locks with the cloak-and-dagger missions I had anticipated when I was first recruited. My lock-pick set brought back the excitement I had felt when I was learning how to parachute jump and use different types of weapons. I immediately put away the schoolbooks and read about locks well into the night.

Apparently, although locks came in all shapes, sizes, and designs, most are based on fairly similar concepts. Take for instance the pin and tumbler design, which consists of pairs of small pins of different lengths which sit in a tube that runs through a central cylinder plug and into a housing around the plug. When the unit is locked, the bottom pin of each pair is entirely inside of the plug while its partner on the top is halfway in the plug and halfway in the housing. This is what keeps the plug from turning. What a proper key does is to push each pair of pins up just enough so that where they meet will line up with the space where the cylinder and the housing come together, forming what is called the shear line. This in turn will remove any obstructions and will allow the plug to turn and the lock to open. The trick is to accomplish the same thing without a properly notched key.

This is where the pick set comes into play. One of the pieces of metal in the set was what is known as a tension wrench. The first step in opening the lock is to insert the tension wrench and turn it (apply tension) in

the direction a key would normally turn. Next, you se-
lect a pick, insert it into the lock and attempt to lift each
pair of pins to the point where each top pin is completely
in the housing, forming the shear line. The experienced
lock picker should be able to hear and/or feel as each
pin falls into its correct position, allowing him to move
onto the next set. Keeping the tension on the lock would
form a kind of ledge which would keep the pin from falling back into its original position once you got it where
you wanted it. When all of the pins are in the correct
position, the pressure you exert in the tension tool is able
to turn the plug completely and the lock is open.

Although this was easy in theory, it was very frustrating to put into practice. You have to gain a familiarity
with what pick to use and how much pressure to apply.
What was most difficult was developing the sensitive
touch needed to actually feel the tiny pins moving into
the proper position. It helped to take apart dozens of
different locks to be able to see and visualize the pro-
cesses used in the various lock designs so that you could
then apply that knowledge to an intact lock. As was the
case with any assignment I was given, I threw myself into
learning everything I could about the task at hand. There
were other lock types and other techniques, like raking,
which made it seem like a task you might get reasonably
good at, but never really master.

I spent hundreds of hours practicing this difficult
craft until I could open almost any door in the dorm.
After that, I would wander around the campus at night
and break into various locked buildings. I did not take
anything but I felt a tremendous adrenaline rush roam-
ing around the open rooms by myself. Had I been a thief,
I could have made a handsome living with my new hobby.

In the movies, burglars break locks with hairpins and
paper clips, often using a screwdriver or nail file as the
tension wrench. I had enough trouble learning how to
use the highly specialized picks designed for the job. I
doubted that a thief could actually have success with the

method used in movies. And in real life, a thief, or in my case, an assassin, would not waste time picking a lock when breaking a window or forcing a door, drawer, or cash box would be so much quicker. Thinking back on the killing of al Zarqa and his crew in Istanbul, I really don't think I would have wasted the time or risked being seen picking the front door's lock when breaking a window out of sight accomplished the same purpose. But if a lock had to be bypassed without a trace, which is so often a necessity in espionage work, picking the lock would be the best way to go. The bottom line was that if Phil told me I needed to learn this stuff, I was in no position to question him, so learn it I did, adding one more skill to my toolbox. And as it turned out, I have had to rely on this unique ability on more than one occasion.

I dated many women during my senior year at Purdue. Being one of the few sober guys in a bar full of college coeds made meeting women easy. As the bouncer I could let a girl in even if she was not twenty-one. However, I was a private person, and I kept what I did, and whom I did it with, to myself. But my brother Bob, who was attending Indiana University in Bloomington, had recently met and become engaged to his future wife, Joyce, and I felt that it was the right thing to do—find somebody I was compatible with and eventually settle down. Unfortunately I was not comfortable or compatible with anybody I met.

When spring semester arrived, I signed up for the last nine classes necessary for graduation. The next few months went by quickly with all of the work I had, and I graduated in May 1974, with a Bachelor of Arts in German with a Russian minor, and maintained a B-plus/A-minus average for the last two semesters, despite the massive course load. I had contact with Phil, who continued to give me things to read and study, in the spring. He told me I remained a part of his team, but there was no need for my particular talents at that time.

That summer my brother Bob and I again painted by day and smoked by night. I was twenty-two and my experiences in Europe and Asia, although they occurred a year ago, seemed like a distant past. With no other prospects knocking at my door, I applied for graduate school, again at Purdue. I also applied to be a dorm counselor. Although my felony arrest record should have made me ineligible for the job, Phil assured me I would have no problems. Sure enough, I was accepted to graduate school and offered a job as a counselor at Cary Quadrangle, the same dorm I lived in as a freshman.

I went back to Purdue in August 1975 to work on a Masters of Arts in German, again with Russian as my secondary language. I also went back to my bouncer job at the bar. When I had my first meeting with the guys on my floor (there were no coed dorms at Purdue in 1975), I made it clear that I expected to have a symbiotic relationship with them. It was not part of my game plan to lurk around, trying to catch them breaking dorm rules. They would promise to stay out of trouble, thereby making me look good to the administration. For my part, I would let them into the bar without proper identification. But they would be responsible for their actions. If they caused trouble while drinking, all deals were off. As it turned out, my floor was a model of good behavior and we were all happy.

I was dating one girl, Dale, more steadily. Dale was a French major who lived in a small apartment, part of a duplex, directly across from the bar. When the bar closed, well after midnight, I would go to her apartment, take a shower, and spend the rest of the night there. Since her father was a professor of agriculture at Purdue, her family lived in town. They were devout Methodists with roots in rural Iowa. They were also good, simple people who readily accepted me as her boyfriend, especially since we never flaunted the part about my spending nights at her apartment.

As my first semester of grad school progressed, so

did my thoughts about getting married, and I proposed to Dale. However, she was seeing another guy steadily, a teacher at a school where she had done her student teaching. Dale asked me for some time to visit him and straighten out her feelings. When she returned, she accepted my proposal and we planned a wedding for the end of the school year.

I did not do right by Dale, and that has been one of many mistakes that continues to bother me. Our marriage was doomed to failure because I considered marriage to be a social obligation rather than a lifelong, total commitment to another person. I saw the joy my brother's marriage to Joyce brought my parents and felt the pressure to do the same. I was still looking for their acceptance and praise.

I also rushed into marriage because I thought my life would become what it had been before I was an Agency contractor. (I have trouble with the label "killer.") I believed that if my life resembled the families portrayed on television—a wife, two kids, and a house in the suburbs—I would have everything that went along with that life (e.g., peace, tranquility, and security). But Dale and I were too different to make the relationship work in the long run.

Initially, at least, the marriage and life in general seemed idyllic. For our second year of graduate school, we were both teaching assistants, she in French and I in German. We lived in a nice, two-bedroom apartment in a new complex that had a club house and a pool. I had committed myself to some rigorous religious training so that we could be married in the Methodist church, something her parents had requested. And although I was not a believer, we attended church every Sunday with her family. Dale was against drugs of any kind and her family was opposed to drinking alcohol, so I spent the next couple of years almost totally sober. Her mother, Barbara, an organist at the church, and her sister, Phyllis, a librarian, thought the world of me and let me know it.

My dream of a television-style family was coming true and Dale and I were thriving.

As we approached graduation in May 1976, I applied to schools to pursue a doctorate in comparative literature. While working on the masters, I, along with a professor friend named Jan Wojcik, had published some articles and scholarly translations in the field of cultural and literary hermeneutics, based on the lectures of an obscure German philosopher, Friedrich Schleiermacher. Together, we reconstructed Schleiermacher's work, which had survived only as aphorisms in German, Latin, Greek, and Hebrew. Jan, an ex-Jesuit priest who earned his PhD at Yale, inspired me to go the Ivy League route, so I applied to Harvard, Yale, Princeton, and Columbia, as well as the non-Ivy league Berkeley and Purdue. I was accepted to all of them, but Berkeley offered the best financial incentives, so in July 1976, with our masters degrees in hand and visions of me becoming a university professor, Dale and I packed our belongings in a trailer and, with her parents in tow to help us settle, we headed to California.

Going to California from Indiana was like entering a different world. Property values were already sky-high and the rentals were almost cost prohibitive. We found a small apartment in Oakland and while I explored the Berkeley campus, Dale searched for a job. My tuition and fees had been waived, and I was offered a teaching position by Berkeley, but that would not be enough to keep us afloat; Dale would have to work full time. In a few days she found an administrative job at the Oakland airport and we were set.

If California was a different world than Indiana, Berkeley was a different solar system. "Head shops" specializing in drug paraphernalia were all around the school. On any given day you might see Jane Fonda or Country Joe McDonald speaking on campus. A few times a week, there were free, impromptu concerts with dozens of people in various stages of nudity engulfed in clouds of smoke. Rallies against the government and the military were regular events. Initially, these antigovernment rallies angered me considerably. But when I considered what fueled them, I could accept them. The demonstrators were, in essence, idealists.

I attended graduate courses in Russian, Latin, German, and comparative literature and taught undergraduate comparative literature classes. In my free time, I continued my studies on the Soviet military and honed my lock-picking skills. I became an expert on the Soviet order of battle and Soviet military training and tactics. I immersed myself in all things Russian: Russian history, literature, art, and thinking. I took a hermeneutic approach to the Russian psyche. My mentor, Czelaw Milosz, was a full professor of Russian literature who specialized in the work of Dostoevsky. He had been an underground Polish partisan behind Nazi lines in WWII and had become a celebrated poet, winning the Nobel Prize for Literature in 1980, and while he traveled the world giving talks I had the opportunity to teach several of his classes.

In my personal life, Dale and I were growing apart. On the surface things appeared happy and normal, but I was beginning to see how different we were. Although she worked outside of the house, her universe revolved around her family. I, on the other hand, was rapidly becoming bored and wanted to return to action. I decided to take a part-time job both to earn more money and for a reason to leave the house when I was not at the university. I took a job as a commissioned carpet salesman for a department store in Oakland. They were reluctant to hire me because of my extensive education, figuring I would not be happy and quit. I convinced them that I was sincere in applying for the job, and they relented.

I enjoyed being a carpet salesman. Customers would come into the store and look over samples of floor covering. When they found something that interested them, I would go to their homes, measure the areas to be covered, and give them an estimate of the total cost. In many ways, I was my own boss and did not have to spend much time in the store. Going out to measure homes turned out to be much more interesting, and at times dangerous, than anybody would have expected. I ended up in homes where the people were drunk, stoned, tripping, and even butt naked. I was propositioned by men and women, young and old. One guy even asked me to have sex with his wife while he would watch from a closet. I declined.

One incident almost cost me my life. I was measuring a small house off of 14th Street in Oakland, a very dangerous area and a hotbed of black gang activity. After doing my measurements I was told by the customer that they had changed their minds and did not really need any carpet at that time. I packed up my materials and headed outside only to find three young black males sitting on the hood of my Volkswagen Jetta. As I approached the car, one of the guys said, "Blood, you in the wrong neighborhood." That had become very evident to me, but I was already there. Not wanting any trouble, I apologized for my obvious error and explained that I was on my way out. The next thing I knew, I saw a knife come down toward me and felt the pain as it cut into my face. As I backed away, they hopped off of my car and started to slowly approach me. I had heard it said that you can tell who the winner of a knife fight is by seeing who dies last and I did not want any part of that. But my hands were tied; I had tried to talk my way out and it didn't work.

I'm sure that they figured me to be an easy mark, considering I was a pasty white guy wearing a Seiko watch and a tie, so they were not as wary as if they had been facing other street punks. The guy with the knife lunged forward with it using the same movement you use when extending your arm to shake hands. I took one step back, grabbed the wrist with the knife coming toward me and, using his own momentum, swung his arm in an arc 270 degrees, causing him to bury the knife deep into his upper thigh. The combination of his screams and the massive amount of blood (most probably from the femoral artery) that started soaking through his pants caused the other two to stop, turn, and run. What to do next? After my brief encounter with the incompetence of the authorities back at Purdue, I knew that I didn't want any involvement with the police; you never knew what interpretation they would have of an event and jail was not something I wanted to risk. So I made a snap decision to just go home. The cut on my face would heal without medical attention, and I didn't really see these guys going to the cops and having to explain what they were doing in the first place. And as far as the guy with the knife in his thigh—he would either bleed to death or he wouldn't. Not my problem.

The lesson in all of this is that I had been longing for some normalcy in my life, but in many ways, "normal" ended up being almost as bizarre and dangerous as what I had been doing overseas. I didn't have to go all the way to India to be attacked by somebody for no reason; the same kind of things happened in Oakland, California. And as it turned out, things were about to get even worse.

CHAPTER 17

THE HELLS ANGELS

I had not heard from the Agency in a long time and my life was quiet. I attributed the lull in communication to something that happened a few years earlier in Washington. In 1976, President Gerald Ford issued Executive Order 11905 to clarify U.S. foreign intelligence activities. In the section of the order titled "Restrictions on Intelligence," Ford decreed political assassination to be illegal: "Prohibition on Assassination. No employee of the United States Government shall engage in, or conspire to engage in, political assassination." The order was reaffirmed by President Jimmy Carter in 1978, and by President Ronald Reagan in Executive Order 12333, which further restricted the activity: "No person employed by or acting on behalf of the United States Government shall engage in, or conspire to engage in, assassination."

When I met with Phil after my missions in Afghanistan and Turkey, I had asked him when I would contribute in some other way than targeted assassinations. At that time, I had visions of classic espionage activities (by that I mean what I saw in spy movies), dealing with secret documents, plans, etc. His answer was deflating.

"People in this line of work are specialists at what they do. Some field agents deal with information; others with people. You are a people person. But you don't have the credentials or the cover to deal effectively in the open. That and the fact that you look to be about sixteen years old rule you out for many things. However, all of that does act in your favor because it allows you to get close to people. Looking at you, the last thing anybody would expect is a bullet, or even less a knife, coming their way.

"Although I can see you doing some other things down the line, for now you are, for lack of a better word, a triggerman; call it a hired gun. Please don't misunderstand where I'm coming from with this because I don't mean it as a judgment. You simply have absolutely no qualms about taking a person's life. Your whole childhood has molded you into this. With you there is no hesitation, no moral or ethical equivocation. You simply do what you are sent to do. That's why you are successful, and that's why we have you in the lineup. You never send a pitcher up to hit when you really need a home run and you never ask the right fielder to play shortstop. A good manager always goes with the right player."

So that was it. I worked on an extraction, but apparently that was because nobody would suspect me of something like that and there was a high probability that somebody would have to die if anything went wrong. I have to admit he was right. If faced with being captured and imprisoned in East Germany or killing anybody who stood in the way of my escape, I wouldn't have hesitated for a second. It was beginning to make sense to me that if the United States took assassination out of its toolkit (although I still didn't believe that would ever happen), I would probably be obsolete and should start focusing on a new career.

Shortly after I began working at the department store it closed, so I was out of the carpet-sales business, at least for the time being. But I did not know if I wanted to become a professor. It had become painfully clear to me that a life within the ivory towers of academia was in many ways boring, surreal, and sometimes disappointing. For example, one of the best known Russian Literature professors at Berkeley, generally recognized worldwide as the primary expert on the writer Gogol, was blatantly gay, a fact that should have been nobody's business but his own. Unfortunately, to receive a decent grade on anything a student wrote for this guy, the focus of the paper needed to be on how the concept of homosexuality worked in every piece of literature ever written. I did not know what I wanted for the future but knew that it was time for a change. This very prestigious program at one of the top universities in the country no longer represented my idea of higher learning.

Weight training remained one of the most important parts in my life, so in 1981 I decided to open a health club. I had recently made the acquaintance of a very large milk-truck loader named Kenly, who was also interested in the health-club business. Although a man of limited intelligence, he did have an unbridled imagination and enthusiasm and had recently received an inheritance after the death of his father.

We began to train together every day, and I was deeply impressed by the intensity with which he attacked his training regimen. I had not been pushed like that in years and usually collapsed, completely exhausted, after our workouts. Together, with an extremely dull-witted friend of his named Craig, who had also come into a modest inheritance, my twenty-five thousand dollars from a second mortgage I took out on a small home Dale and I had since managed to purchase in Oakland, and a silent partner with ten thousand dollars, we entered into a partnership to build the Olympia Health Club.

The Olympia had potential greatness written all over it from the start. We found an empty furniture store at 600 Grand Avenue in Oakland. The location was ideal for a health club. The building itself was located on Lake Merritt, which offered joggers a beautiful setting in which to run and gave the gym a ready-made pool of potential members looking for a convenient place to shower and change clothes. The interior of the building was huge and radiated *big*, with a spiral staircase leading to a balconied second floor where we planned to have locker rooms; a giant, coed, twenty-person hot tub; a steam room; two saunas; and offices. We persuaded the building owners to give us a balloon lease, which would afford us lower rent at the beginning of the venture to help with the high costs of renovation and equipment acquisition.

We leveraged the space of the building by investing in huge, high-quality mirrors to cover the walls on the first floor. Looking in any direction, the gym patron would have the illusion that the weights and machines continued forever, like the hall of mirrors in the palace at Versailles.

We personally designed almost all of the free-weight machines, contracting a local bodybuilder who owned a foundry to construct the machines with tubular iron and steel. We lined the walls with dumbbells in 5-pound increments, ranging from 5 to 150 pounds, and ordered a large number of 100-pound plates—not that anybody would ever need to use 150-pound dumbbells, but their mere presence radiated power. Nautilus machines and aerobic classes (which were not yet the rage back then that they have become today but were still starting to catch the attention of a middle class America that was becoming more health conscious) ensured that we would appeal to literally every need when it came to fitness.

I hired Don Ross, a charismatic, Mr. America title-holder and professional wrestler from Detroit, to be the primary trainer for the club. Don was also an author and a regular contributor to all of the mainstream bodybuilding magazines like *Muscle and Fitness, FLEX,* and *Iron Man.* At that time he was training for an upcoming International Federation of Bodybuilders (IFBB) Mr. Universe contest which was going to be held in conjunction with that year's Mr. Olympia in Australia. I gave free memberships to professional athletes from the Oakland Raiders, San Francisco 49ers, Oakland Athletics, and members of athletic teams across the country who called the Bay area home.

With professional athletes as members, the Olympia enjoyed instant credibility especially with those armchair athletes who gained their own sense of importance through association with people who had actually accomplished something. I also contracted the biggest names in the bodybuilding world, such as Tom Platz, Boyer Coe, and Dennis Tinnerino, to present fitness seminars and posing demonstrations at the Olympia. As part of their contracts, they were required to say that the Olympia was the only place in the Bay Area for serious fitness buffs. The reputation spread quickly; the Olympia was not a lightweight spa.

The business was going far better than Kenly, Craig and I believed was possible. The *San Francisco Chronicle* even ran a feature by Brenda Lane Worthington on my personal rise from skinny immigrant kid to successful body builder/powerlifter, business owner and university instructor. Unfortunately, it was a classic too-good-to-be-true case. The trouble began with the arrival of Hell's Angels leader and president Ralph "Sonny" Barger. I said that I was looking for a little more excitement, and I was about to get a lot more than I bargained for.

A silent investor had recently approached us with a favor. He said Sonny was having legal problems with federal authorities and needed to prove a legitimate source of income. He asked that Sonny be put on the payroll in exchange for unspecified future "favors" should Kenly, Craig, or I ever need them. All we had to do was list Sonny as an employee of the club. He would choose his own hours and would not interfere with daily operations. It seemed like an easy enough favor to grant. Also, I saw a mystique to having an authentic American rebel, an American legend, actually, in the club. We had professional athletes, politicians, and people in show business as members, why not an "outlaw"? I don't know if we were incredibly naïve, stupid, or both.

It's hard for people today to really understand how

totally ruthless the Hells Angels were back in the 1960s and 1970s. With something like 2,000 members spanning 20 countries, the Angels tried to project an image of respectability by incorporating under the title Hells Angels Motorcycle Corporation. A more appropriate name would have been Murder Incorporated (but that name was already taken). The group has been linked to extortion, prostitution, trafficking in narcotics (especially methamphetamines, or meth as it is called on the street), witness intimidation, and murder. Anytime one of the Angels was implicated in these crimes, the club took the official position that these activities were committed by individual members and should not be seen as an indictment on the "club" as a whole.

When I first met Sonny Barger, I was struck by how unimpressive he was physically. He was not tall or particularly muscular; I wondered how he maintained his hold over the notorious Hells Angels organization for as long as he had. After speaking to him a number of times and observing him around his fellow Hells Angels members I began to understand. In Sonny's eyes I saw both power and pure evil; I saw a man who would do anything to acquire what he wanted and what he felt life owed him. I also sensed that he was a man who did not care about pain and death—his or anybody else's. But along with instilling fear, Sonny also radiated charisma. People flocked around him as if he were a rock star literally everywhere he went.

The higher echelon of the Hells Angels called him "chief," and they worshipped him and would do whatever he asked of them. Although small in stature, he commanded absolute respect. The Hells Angels organization may be decentralized on paper, consisting of numerous local, autonomous chapters, but Sonny Barger sat at the top of it all as the supreme commander. Despite claiming to be retired now (he had surgery for throat cancer and is a motorcycle dealer in Arizona) he will always be the leader of the Hells Angels.

My partners and I started to lose control of the Olympia soon after Sonny became a fixture there. At one point, Kenly and I decided to buy motorcycles. I had previously owned a small motorcycle, a Honda 250 cc and would have been happy with a medium-size "rice burner," but Sonny's vice president, Cisco, a man I had already known for quite some time, so tough and ruthless that he was the only person in the history of the Hells Angels to be made a member by Sonny himself without starting as a prospect, convinced me that a Harley-Davidson was the only bike worth owning. When Cisco talked, people listened, and I was no exception.

Being a homeowner with a job at the university, I qualified for a loan. Kenly was another story. He had quit his job at the dairy and did not have a record of regular income from the club yet. He did not qualify for a loan. Sonny offered to loan the money to him and Kenly jumped at the opportunity. Sonny called his wife Sharon on the phone and said,

"Hey babe. Go out to where we keep the meat and bring me 10 pounds of steak as soon as you can."

Within an hour, Sharon Barger walked into the Olympia with ten thousand dollars in cash, and Kenly bought his Harley. Of course, Sonny Barger doesn't loan ten thousand dollars to a man because he likes him—his loans come with a price. From then on, Sonny figuratively owned Kenly and played a large role in the Olympia's affairs.

More favors began to come our way with increased frequency. The Hells Angels provided crowd security and bodyguard service to a number of musicians, particularly country western acts like Willie Nelson, Waylon Jennings, and Merle Haggard. When they came to the San Francisco Bay Area, or to nearby Lake Tahoe and Las Vegas, Kenly and I were given backstage passes to party with the band. I can still remember going drink for drink right out of the bottle with Waylon Jennings before a concert in Tahoe. Pictures taken at the concert show me clearly glazed and ready to drop while Waylon was still going strong. Meanwhile, anytime Kenly needed money, another call would go out to Sharon Barger, and she would bring the required amount of "meat," so that Kenly could be "fed."

Before long, members of the FBI joined the Olympia to keep an eye on Sonny. The ones we knew about didn't hide their identities, but I'm sure there were undercover agents present, too. It was almost a game and was similar to normal intelligence-gathering activities between countries. On the surface, we knew who their agents were and vice versa, but the same did not hold true with deep-cover activities.

The Olympia was soon home to many illegal dealings. Don Ross had his own profitable sideline going with the sale of anabolic steroids, the use of which had not yet become illegal. Don was well connected in the body-building and medical communities and had lined up a reliable number of sources for anything from orals like Anabol, Anavar, and Dianabol, to injectibles such as Testosterone Cypionate, Testosterone Propianate, and Deca Durobolin. He was even able to find exotic drugs such as Equipoise, a steroid used on horses, as well as some East European products that had not yet been named.

A large number of local professional football players were publicly claiming that they never had and never would resort to these drugs, and that they had attained their 6'4", 340-pound frames of solid muscle relying solely on tuna, steak, and sound training principles. All the while, they would buy their "special supplements" from Don at the Olympia. Some of them stored their drugs in their gym lockers and injected them while in our offices so as to avoid having them at home or at their team training facilities. There were also a few women who were heavily using the androgenics, turning them into freaks.

The silent investor I mentioned who introduced Sonny into the club happened to own a jazz record label but made his main income from marijuana sales. He would regularly invite a number of people, me included, to go to lunch at the Tadish Grill, a well known San Francisco eatery in the financial district at 240 California Street, with him and his girlfriend, Cindy, a Nevada hooker whom he kept on retainer as his personal "girlfriend." He always paid for everything, and all of his transactions were strictly cash. He avoided banks, preferring to keep a shoe box of Krugeraands in his closet.

At his request, we also hired a karate instructor, Gary, who went by the moniker "G." and who had recently been convicted of cocaine dealing. He was still dealing coke after his conviction and had since added China White and Persian Brown heroin to his inventory, but needed this karate income as a visible means of support to mask his drug income. Olympia quickly became one of his main distribution centers. The same elite athletes who were buying their steroids from Don were also buying massive amounts of coke from G.

But all of that was about to change—at least my part in the dealings. My partner Kenly had come to the conclusion that he wanted the club for himself. There was no need to get rid of Craig, as he did everything Kenly wanted him to do anyway, and the silent partner played no part in club operations. Kenly had become close to Sonny Barger and was firmly in Sonny's pocket. He wanted to be the sole active owner of the club, and Sonny and the Angels wanted that also so that they could use him to control the Olympia. One night, around midnight, I received a call from Sonny. He asked me to meet him at the club.

I thought nothing of it, hopped on my Harley, and headed to the Olympia to find Sonny waiting in my office. He told me graphic stories of what the Angels had done to people who had offended them over the years. He also made it clear that he had a vested interest in the Olympia and that it was in my best interest to relinquish ownership. He told me how unreliable drug addicts were, that they couldn't be trusted, and had to be disposed of. All of a sudden it became clear to me—Kenly had convinced him I was addicted to cocaine, opium, and God knows what else, His intention was to kill me that night; nothing personal, mind you, just a good business decision. I had survived communist East Germany, Afghanistan, Iraq, Turkey, India, Pakistan, and torture in an Irani prison, but I was not prepared for this situation. I could not resort to my overseas tactics, and I could not rely on the Agency's help as they tended to avoid "domestic operations," at least of this nature And even if I could have relied on Phil, it was a little late to be calling for help. There would be no Lone Ranger rescue this time. I was left to my own devices.

I knew better than to trust Sonny but I had been caught with my guard down. However, after some two hours of slow and careful conversation, I was able to convince him that I was not a drug addict and posed no threat to him or the club. I did not deny that I used cocaine. As a matter of fact, G. was a big ticket dealer who moved massive quantities of coke. He would freely give me rocks of the stuff that were taken out of his shipments before he cut it with milk sugar. The supply was steady, as pure as you could find anywhere outside of South America, and it was free. I can honestly say that I generally had at least a thousand dollars worth of fairly clean cocaine in my possession at all times. But as much as I enjoyed doing it, I was no junkie; I easily gave away much more than I personally consumed. Despite knowing that I was not a drug addict, Sonny expected me to run and hide as soon as I left the office.

But I did not run and hide, and the fact that I didn't had consequences. A few weeks after my meeting with Sonny I was riding my motorcycle to the Olympia when I heard a loud noise and suddenly felt a sharp pain in my left forearm. Barely managing to control my bike, I saw the blood oozing out of my arm. I had been shot. I made it into the club and extracted the slug myself. I had been through far worse pain on more than one occasion and I was not bothered by the wound. I was bothered by what the wound foreshadowed. A couple of days later, I was visiting Marilyn, an aerobics instructor at the Olympia and my future wife. I was standing on the balcony of her apartment, and looked down to see a man in Hells Angels colors (the vest with the club badges and accomplishments displayed) aiming a gun at me. I instinctively covered my face and head as the shot rang out. I felt a hot, searing pain and saw that most of the middle finger and the tip of the ring finger of my left hand were hanging by a meager piece of skin, a mangled, bloody mess. I called G., wrapped a towel around my hand, and waited for him to take me to the hospital. The hospital was required to notify the police of all gunshot wounds, and the Oakland Police Department was quick to respond.

I told the police officer who came to the hospital what had happened.

"Look," he said when I had finished speaking, "You don't want to tell that story. Believe me. On the Oakland PD there are two types of officers when it comes to dealings with the Angels—those who are on the take or those who are deathly afraid of them. Either way, your story will bring you more trouble than you can handle. Why don't you say that the whole thing was an accident and let it go at that? You were cleaning a gun on your balcony and it went off. It happens all the time."

I couldn't believe what I was hearing. I insisted on giving the officer an accurate account of my injury and he reluctantly took my statement and left. I went into surgery and a skilled doctor managed to save a fair amount of my fingers.

A few days later, the Oakland Police Department responded to my statement by interviewing me and repeating to me what the officer at the hospital had suggested, that I shot myself. (I owned a .357 magnum with hollow tip bullets, a weapon that would probably have shot off everything from my elbow on down, not just my fingertips.) They also suggested that I might have been shot by my sister, Sharon, or my wife, Dale. To clarify their position, the Hells Angels stole my motorcycle. It was stolen in front of the Olympia, on Grand Avenue, a busy street in Oakland, but there were no witnesses and no leads. The police dropped the investigation almost as quickly as I filed the report. I understood the message that was being sent by all of this. Drop the issue and think about survival.

But law enforcement was not finished with me. A few weeks later I was visited by FBI agents who offered me a deal. I would testify to a grand jury about Sonny Barger, both first-hand information and details I learned by watching him interact with other Hells Angels in the Olympia, and the FBI would enroll me in the witness protection program. I asked for clarification. They explained that I would be given a new identity, a new life somewhere far away, and Sonny would be imprisoned. They also openly said that, should I agree to testify, I would probably be killed regardless of the witness protection program. According to the agents, most people in the witness protection program as the result of organized crime were often murdered eventually.

I thanked them for their honesty and respectfully declined their offer. First of all, I was in the employ of the CIA, not the FBI. When Sonny first became a part of the Olympia Health Club scene, I contacted Phil and asked him if there was anything he or the Agency wanted me to do with respect to the Hells Angels. He was very adamant that this was a domestic matter (i.e., an FBI and local law enforcement concern). He also was concerned with the fact that were I to get involved, I would come under too much scrutiny by the FBI, which could in turn have compromised my cover and any future effectiveness in my CIA capacity. The whole conversation gave me the very strong suspicion that there was a lot of competition between the two agencies. The CIA was not in any hurry to help the FBI or the local cops look effective or even competent. Phil did ask me to keep my eyes and ears open in case I came across anything the CIA could and would act upon.

The bottom line was that if the Feds wanted Sonny Barger, they would have to get any evidence against him themselves. I might have been a killer (and in that respect, except for motivation, I was the same as Sonny), but I was not ready to be an informant, nor would I become one if it meant that I would have to compromise my years of training and service, or that I and probably my family, would be killed. I was not afraid for my own life, but my parents, brothers, and sister had done nothing to deserve what Sonny was capable of. I knew that I had to leave Oakland, California, and possibly the United States to survive. I had defied Sonny Barger, a man who does not allow people to defy him. The government was not going to help me unless I first helped them, but I had no help that I was willing to offer at the time. I decided to move to Germany.

Meanwhile, Dale and I were divorcing. The divorce was my fault. I chose to marry for all the wrong reasons. Since the opening of the Olympia I spent more and more time working and meeting with my new, high-profile friends. I had recently moved out of my house, and in with Marilyn. She had become my soul mate. I knew I could spend my life with her had circumstances been different.

Dale and I had no children despite our attempts, a fact that aided my decision to move. I thought I would be moving to Germany alone; alone was something that I understood, and I felt confident I could handle it. However, to my great surprise, Marilyn offered to go with me. I was extremely moved by her willingness to leave her life for an uncertain future with me. She too was going through a divorce, but she was doing well in California. She was an aerobics instructor, a talented artist, was popular with quite a few guys, and had come into an inheritance from her mother. The last thing she needed was to be tied down with me, but that was exactly what she offered to do.

I let Dale have all our possessions: the car, house, and everything in it; I owed her that much and more for dragging her across country and walking out on her. I did have my teaching position at Berkeley, but I felt that the great American dream of owning my own business and raising a family in suburbia had come crashing down around me. I knew a large part of it was my own fault. Naiveté, stupidity, greed, and drugs all were major factors in the closing of that chapter of my life.

I recently read Sonny Barger's bestselling autobiography, *Hell's Angels: The Life and Times of Sonny Barger and the Hell's Angels Motorcycle Club*. His recollection of our time in Oakland doesn't resemble mine. Sonny would have readers believe that he was nothing more than a free spirit who was hounded by the law for things he had not done and knew nothing about. According to him, he was constantly persecuted for pursuing true freedom. He wanted to be left alone to ride his bike and enjoy life. As I would have expected, nowhere in his book does he mention anything about "working" at the Olympia.

CHAPTER 18

GERMAN DEMOCRATIC REPUBLIC CALLING

It was now the fall of 1982 and I had recently turned thirty years old. Before making any permanent decisions about our future, Marilyn and I decided to take a trip to Europe. She had her modest inheritance, and I had an American Express card with no spending limit. We didn't consider this a permanent move, but we knew we had to let the situation in Oakland settle. We traveled to Germany, Amsterdam, France, and Switzerland, and stayed in first-class hotels. Between hotels, meals, and incidentals, I managed to put about eleven thousand dollars on my American Express card before they left a message at the desk of our hotel in Zurich. They thought I had spent more than enough money for three weeks and they would approve no more charges until they received a payment from me. That was my signal to return to Oakland and see how things were going there.

The climate in Oakland was not good. My partner Kenly had contacted the Oakland police and accused me of taking illegal drugs and stealing money and equipment from the Olympia. But when the police told him that they could not pursue the accusations unless he signed a sworn statement, he balked. Apparently, he was not willing to face the consequences if I submitted to a polygraph test. I knew it was not safe to go to the Olympia, and friends told me it wasn't safe to be in Oakland at all. Marilyn and I decided to store our possessions and stay with various friends and family until we planned our next move. Knowing the Angels had chapters throughout the country, we decided to return to Europe.

A cousin of mine in Germany assured me he could find a job for me, so we decided to head for Germany. The Angels did not have a vendetta against my sister, Sharon, and Sonny assured her she was safe in Oakland. I believed in "honor among thieves," absurd as it may sound, so when Sonny said my sister was safe I did not hesitate to leave her.

We landed in Frankfurt, rented a car, and drove to Würzburg, my mother's hometown. I had quite a few relatives living in the area. My cousin Peter, who lived in the farming community of Stahldorf, outside Würzburg, had promised me that he could secure a job for me as a translator, so we moved into his basement temporarily. Unfortunately, Peter's promise was false. He did not know anyone who could offer me a job, so I had to search for work on my own.

I found temporary employment at a video-rental store in Dettelbach, a nearby farming community, and then as a bouncer at a Veterans of Foreign Wars (VFW) club called the House of Lights, in Kitzingen. The town was home to two military posts, Harvey Barracks and Larson Barracks, and had a heavy U.S. military presence. Bouncing there was different than bouncing in the bar at Purdue. Drunken soldiers were much tougher than drunken students and racial tensions added to the trouble. Usually there would be a white, country-western group which took over one end of the club while a black group took the other end. Sometimes a man would cross the line between the two groups, usually over a girl, and a fight would ensue. I had to hope that I was more sober, and a dirtier fighter, than the men involved.

One night I was sitting behind the bar sipping ouzo, when I looked up and saw Phil staring at me from a table. I joined him and started to talk:

"Long time no see."

"Yeah, a few reasons for that. I was giving you some space; and it looked as if you were going to become a model citizen in the 'burbs for a while. Hard to compete with that. But you ruined that, didn't you? Couldn't you have picked a more sane man than Sonny Barger to mess with? But I guess the real reason I didn't bug you is that I didn't need you. No offense."

"And you couldn't give me a hand in Oakland? I was almost killed.

"What was I supposed to do? Make Barger disappear? The Angels would have had a problem with you either way. You created that problem alone and had to solve it the same way. Or not."

"And now you're the one who needs me, or else you wouldn't be here."

"Still not much for small talk, I see."

"Would you rather I pretended that I care? You know me better than that."

"Right to the point as always. You're right; I could use you again. And by the looks of things, you could use me, or at least some of my money."

He was right about the money. Marilyn and I didn't stay in Peter's basement for long. We used what little money we had to rent an apartment in Veitshöchheim, a small suburb outside Würzburg. And although we had a place to stay, we didn't have any money to buy furniture. I was ready to hear what Phil had to say. But first I needed clarification.

"I thought I was a guy with a specialty—a specialty that is now illegal."

"You're talking about that 'no killing' law that supposedly went into effect? There are so many loopholes in that thing. Officially, the United States is not allowed to conduct or allow assassinations. But that's a policy, not a law. On top of that, the United States has always distinguished assassinations as separate from military operations directed against an enemy in the course of self-defense. Whether the intentional killing of somebody is defined as an assassination or an acceptable military operation depends on whether the countries involved are at peace or war, how you define peace and war, the status of the person doing the killing, and how the killing is carried out. And even countries at peace are allowed to use military force in self-defense; it all comes down to your perception of the threat. A combatant is a legitimate target at all times, and again, it boils down to your definition of a combatant. So a military operation—you supply the definition—to kill an individual combatant—again, you supply the definition—is considered okay."

"What are you, some kind of lawyer? I thought the law was clear. If it's not a declared war, you don't go around killing people on the other side, or any side for that matter."

"No it's not a law, and no laws addressing the issue were ever enacted. That's the beauty of the executive order. With that in place, people believe a law isn't necessary. But like you've probably figured out by now, the order is subject to interpretation. It purposely does not define assassination, or the terms 'engaging' or 'conspiring.' And as long as a plan does not specifically include assassination, any 'incidental' death that results from the action is just a tragic by-product. Now, with an executive order, a president can repeal it, amend it, or approve a 'one time' exception to it; all things he could not do if the prohibition were spelled out in a law."

"So, what you're saying is that the executive order is nothing more a smoke screen for a president to make himself look moral while allowing the training and use of assassins to continue, as well as anything else he might want to do?"

"Bingo! So are you ready to come back to work?"

I was trying to understand everything Phil had said when a loud commotion broke out on the dance floor. I had been lucky up to that time; all of the fights in the House of Lights had been fistfights. That night I was not so lucky. A white soldier had taken offense when a black soldier approached his German girlfriend. Knives appeared on both sides of the club. The owner yelled out for me to break up the fight. I surveyed the scene and walked out with Phil.

I had been hitchhiking to and from work, so Phil offered to drive me home.

"What's the gig this time?"

"For now, strictly DDR. But that could change. Your AOR [area of responsibility] will be the Meiningen area. There is a large concentration of Soviet troops stationed there, including some Spetznaz [from the Russian специального назначения, or Spetsialnogo Nazncheniya, literally meaning "special purpose units"] But that's not the only reason for your mission. We've identified and further developed a breach in the fence close to Meiningen. You should be able to come and go without much trouble. Of course, while you are over there you will be at considerable risk."

"And what's my cover? How do I bring in cash? I'm not here alone, as I'm sure you know. I can't just show up back at home with a lot of money."

"Simple. You have a master's degree and have finished all of your coursework for your PhD. You can teach for one of the colleges giving courses to soldiers and their dependents. That will only take a few hours a week of your time, leaving you plenty of time to do what we need you to do. You won't teach anything at the local *kaserne* [barracks]. You will go down the Autobahn to Fulda and Wildflecken. That will give you an excuse to leave your place early and come back late. A couple of the classes will be 'dummy' classes. They'll only exist on paper. You won't have to do anything, but you will collect the pay. This should get you by for now. You'll find some instructions on applying for teaching positions with Central Texas College and the University of Maryland, both of which have contracts to provide higher education to soldiers stationed in Germany. You won't have any trouble getting on with both of them. There's also some stuff in there for you to read. Get familiar with all of it and then burn it."

With that, he tossed me the by now familiar manila envelope. Inside I found one thousand U.S. dollars, and three thousand German marks, and about two hundred pages of information pertaining to my mission, including pictures. When we arrived at my apartment complex Phil told me he would be in touch soon. Before I left the car, I wanted an answer to one nagging question.

"What about Sonny and the Angels? Sooner or later he's going to find out where I am. I'm not exactly hiding here."

"He's got nothing to gain by killing you now. You split, remember? You left him with Kenly and the club. He won and saved face in the process. Besides, he knows that you didn't say anything about him or he would be locked up right now based on your testimony. That means something to a guy like him. Stay out of California and away from the Feds, and especially out of Sonny's backyard, and you've got nothing to worry about. You've got a lot to do, so I'll leave you to it. I'll get back to you in a few weeks."

The following Monday, I submitted my applications with the University of Maryland and Central Texas College representatives at the Leighton Barracks education center. The senior education services officer informed me that, as part of the application, I was required to be fingerprinted and undergo a background check. If I was hired I would be given a U.S. government identification card and be subject to the Status of Forces Agreement. I was initially concerned that my connection with the Hells Angels would surface in the background check, but I remembered that my record was cleaned before returning to Purdue. I assumed Phil had repeated the favor this time.

After my applications were submitted I began studying the materials Phil gave me. I first read about the Soviet Army presence in the German Democratic Republic

(DDR). The highest concentration of Soviet forces outside the Soviet Union was the Group of Soviet Forces Germany (GSFG). In the early 1980s, the GSFG consisted of more than three hundred and fifty thousand soldiers and it was strengthened continually. It was more than two times the size of the East German National People's Army (NVA) and almost two times the size of the combined Soviet forces in all other occupied East Bloc countries. The GSFG was organized into five armies, equipped with over five thousand battle tanks, and a number of tactical nuclear weapons. There was also a Spetznaz brigade working in East Germany and one Spetznaz company assigned to each GSFG army. The best-trained and equipped part of the Soviet Air Force was also stationed in the DDR with about two thousand aircraft capable of carrying nuclear weapons.

The Soviet armed forces in the DDR enjoyed a better standard of living than those in the Soviet Union. Once soldiers were exposed to living conditions farther west, they were often unwilling to return home. This made for a large number of defection attempts, many of them successful. My AOR was Meiningen, a city in the southwestern portion of the state of Thuringia, 12 kilometers from the border. In 1972, an official border crossing between the Federal Republic of Germany and the German Democratic Republic had been established near Meiningen.

My reading material included an extensive study of the border itself. I had crossed the border between East Germany and West Germany in 1973, but since then both sides had made considerable improvements to border defense and surveillance. The East Germans had replaced most of the original barbed-wire fencing with wire mesh, a practice begun in the early 1970s. The 22-foot-high wooden observation towers were being replaced or supplemented by prefabricated concrete towers. The East Germans had also reduced the number of border-guard personnel. In 1983, the two Germanys entered into new trade and business agreements, and in the spirit of those moves both sides tried to reduce tensions along the Inner-German Border.

Beginning in 1972, SM-70 mines were deployed along 412 kilometers (30 percent) of the border, but the high cost of mines brought an end to the practice by the early 1980s. Also, a proposed one-billion-Deutsche-Mark loan to East Germany from West Germany stipulated the removal of the mines along the border. Their removal would mean less risk to people crossing surreptitiously.

I also read that East Germany was suspected of building tunnels under the border defenses. They allegedly used these to insert reconnaissance patrols and covert agents into West Germany. There were also reports of East German border patrols being caught and detained on the West German side of the border. These patrols were trusted officers highly loyal to the East German government, and therefore not believed to be defectors. It was assumed that they were in West Germany on covert missions.

Later that year I read in a German newspaper that in 1983 alone, four tunnels originating in the East had been discovered and eight East German patrols had been apprehended. Later it was reported that one particular East German was alleged to have worked as an assassin from 1976 to 1987 while part of an East German commando squad. *Stasi* experts now believe that hundreds of operatives were involved in eliminating traitors and defectors on the West German side of the border.

On the Western side, two restricted zones were established next to the border. There was a 50-meter warning zone marked with a sign that stated: "Attention. 50 meters to the border." There was also a 1-kilometer restricted zone for all U.S. military personnel not authorized to operate in the border area. In addition, signs were placed along roads leading to the border stating:

"U.S. Forces Personnel. HALT. 1 kilometer to the German Democratic Republic. Do not proceed without authority."

The 11th Armored Cavalry Regiment, stationed in Fulda, was responsible for patrolling the V U.S. Army Corps' border sector. Their arsenal included a Combat Aviation Squadron that provided aerial surveillance along the entire V Corps' sector.

Phil had also given me a considerable amount of material on the group known as the Red Army Faction (RAF), which took its name from the Red Army, a Japanese leftist terrorist organization. The RAF called itself a faction to give the impression that the group was part of a larger, international Marxist movement. The RAF was more commonly known as the Baader-Meinhof Gang, the names of two of its founders. The group had its roots in the West German student protests of the late 1960s. Andreas Baader was captured in April 1970, but freed by Ulrike Meinhof shortly thereafter in a violent shootout. Along with two other group members, Baader and Meinhof went underground to a Palestinian guerrilla camp for training. When they returned to West Germany, they began their "war against imperialism" by staging bank robberies to raise money for explosives and arson attacks against U.S. military facilities, German police stations, and symbols of the West German press and economy.

In June 1972, after an intense manhunt, Baader, Meinhof, and other key leaders of the group were captured and imprisoned. These RAF members were jailed individually in solitary confinement. A second generation of the RAF emerged in the early 1970s, consisting mainly of sympathizers with the cause who were independent from the inmates. Numerous bombings and kidnappings by this second generation ensued during the 1970s while the original leaders sat in prison.

The troubles peaked on October 13, 1977, when a flight from Palma de Mallorca to Frankfurt was hijacked. Four Arabic men took control of the plane and demanded, among other things, the release of the Baader-Meinhof group. The plane flew to a number of other stops, both to refuel and in an attempt to find a destination which would accept them. The last of these stops was Mogadishu, Somalia. There, in a high-risk rescue operation, the plane was stormed by the GSG-9, an elite German federal police unit. Half an hour after the assault, German radio broadcast the success of the rescue operation, and the Baader-Meinhof inmates were allowed to listen to the broadcast.

That night, Andreas Baader was found dead with a gunshot wound to the head. Another member, Gudrun Ensslin, hanged herself in her cell, and a third, Jan-Carl Raspe, died in a prison hospital the next day, also from a gunshot wound to the head. Although the German government claimed the deaths were the result of a suicide pact, exhaustive evidence suggested otherwise. How was Baader able to obtain a gun? How was Irmgard Möller (who survived) able to stab herself in the heart four times? Conspiracy theories abound that implicate German authorities in the deaths.

In 1980, with most of the gang's leadership dead, new members of the "third generation" RAF established an alliance with the French group Action Directe. It was determined, though not officially, that the RAF was receiving training as well as financial and logistic support from the *Stasi*. I knew Phil had not given me reading material to pass the time and assumed my mission would address these threats.

A few days later I was cleared to teach English composition, German, Russian, and literature by the University of Maryland. I would teach my first class when the new semester began in January 1983. I welcomed the steady stream of income, especially because, shortly thereafter, Marilyn became pregnant.

I started teaching my first class, English literature, for a serviceman's wife who was one class away from graduation. Teaching one class for one student did not require much preparation or grading time. I told Marilyn that I had three classes that term, the other two being in

Fulda. I told her one class met in the afternoon and the other one met in the evening. I left early in the morning to "prepare" for class. My two-hour drive to Fulda, the three hours between my phony classes, the hours I claimed to need to counsel students, and the two-hour return trip to Veitshöchheim gave me almost twelve hours, three days a week, of free time to work on my mission. My cover also accounted for the extra money I was given by Phil.

I had a message at the Leighton education center to meet with Phil at a restaurant in Fulda. When I got to the Gasthof Drei Linden, which was on the Neuenberger-strasse fairly close to the center of town, Phil was already sitting there and eating. It seems that the owner of the Drei Linden was also a master butcher who owned an adjoining butcher shop, so the meats were always plentiful and fresh. I sat down at the table and ordered what he recommended, which was roast goose and a beer, and he started to talk.

"Settling in to your teacher's life?"

"It's okay."

"Do you ever say more than four or five words at a time?"

"Not if I can help it."

"You must be a real joy to live with. I hope Marilyn at least has a television or radio to keep her company. I assume you read everything I gave you. Any questions so far?"

"What you gave me is clear. I understand what I read; I just don't know why I read it."

He slid three photographs across the table to me. The pictures were of three different women—the first sitting down in a car, the second crossing a street, and the third sitting at an outdoor café—all clearly surveillance photographs taken without the knowledge of the subjects. They were all young, in their mid- to late twenties, and fairly attractive. They were casually dressed—jeans, sweaters, and boots. After I looked at photographs for a few minutes, Phil continued:

"These shots were taken in Frankfurt. The young ladies are members of the Red Army Faction. Up until recently, they would pick up soldiers in bars, get them
drunk, and take them to an apartment. There, the soldiers would be drugged and dumped a few blocks away,
but not before they probably divulged information about
their units, equipment, missions, and the like. They woke
up without their IDs, credit cards, and other personal
effects. Most of the soldiers were too embarrassed to report what happened to them but a few did. The number
of reports of lost IDs indicated that this happened much
more than initially thought. The women weren't arrested
because, frankly, they were worth more to us walking
around. The hope was that they would eventually lead
us to bigger game. Problem is they disappeared a few
weeks ago. It is thought that they slipped over the border
to the DDR and are now part of a group training for something bigger."

He stopped speaking and ordered another beer. I
supposed he was pausing for effect, to let me dwell on
the potential impact. I did not see it.

"So you wait until they come back, let the Germans
arrest them, and they go to prison for a long time."

"I wish it were that easy. While it's true that the Germans are tough—a lot tougher than we are—they won't
arrest them until they actually break the law. We're concerned that by then it might be too late and we could
have another fiasco like the German embassy bombing
in Stockholm in 1975 or the hijacking in Somalia, this
time involving American personnel and property. That
has obviously been the subject of their preoperational
surveillances. They have enough valid IDs to get a couple
dozen of their folks into a vulnerable area at the same
time. We can't afford to let that happen."

"Stupid question, and I'll probably be sorry I asked,
but do we know where they are? And since I'm sure that's
an affirmative, what is it you want me to do about it? You're
obviously telling me this whole story for a reason."

Phil explained that the three women had been spotted in a bar in Suhl, an East German city known for its custom-built firearms, about 20 kilometers northeast of Meiningen. The assumption was that they were undergoing training in the area. I was to go to the East, assess the situation, and take appropriate action.

"What do you mean by 'appropriate action'?"

"You go in a few days and try to get close enough to them to start a dialog. Personally, I don't see that happening. They are pretty committed to the RAF ideology and I don't believe that they would waste any words on anybody outside of the group. They have been trained not to trust anybody, and they don't break training. You're going to have to take them out of the picture. When that happens will depend on how things unfold once you've been there a little while."

"And what's my story to cover being gone?"

"You shouldn't need to be gone overnight at all. You cross the border in the morning and come out at night. You should be home by midnight at the latest. Since you're supposedly teaching until 10:00 P.M. and talking to students for a few minutes after class ends, you should be covered."

"You make it sound like getting in and out of the DDR will be like crossing the street. I don't remember it being like that at all."

"Times have changed. The stuff I gave you to read mentioned that at least four tunnels constructed by the East Germans have been discovered. That's not a secret. As a matter of fact, it was in the newspapers. It shouldn't be too much of a stretch that we have a tunnel or two ourselves. The tunnel is just north of Eussenhausen. It starts a few hundred yards from the border and goes about half a mile under East German territory. We'll take you to the tunnel and be waiting for you when you come back out at the end of the day. I don't want to underplay the risk. Something could go wrong, in which case you would be on your own. Whatever happens, you don't want to compromise the tunnel. Don't get anywhere near the opening on the other side if you think that you have been followed."

"Do these women have names?"

"Lots of them, but none that would do you any good. I'm sure they're going under assumed names where they are."

"How do I get to Suhl once I get over the border? It must be at least 40 or 50 kilometers. That's way too much to walk and I can't steal cars every time I go over."

"We have a contact in Henneberg, just a couple of kilometers over the border. He will provide you with a car to travel to Suhl and back."

I had about as much information as I could hope for. I was supposed to go over the following Monday, so I had the weekend to think out possible scenarios I might be faced with.

Marilyn noticed that I was quieter than usual, something she didn't think was possible. She would talk, and I would nod or grunt in agreement every couple of minutes. I was thinking about more than my mission. For the first time since I began working for Phil I was worried, although not about myself. Marilyn had given up everything to come to Europe with me. If anything happened to me, she would be lost. But it was too late to dwell on thoughts like that. Instead, I wanted to escape from my thoughts, and alcohol served that purpose. I was drinking a minimum of one liter of wine every night, and had been since living in Germany.

I left before dawn on Monday and drove to Ostheim, where I would be picked up and taken to the tunnel entrance. The timing had been arranged to avoid contact with the West German Border Police and U.S. military patrols. The entrance to the tunnel was in a utility building on a farm, far from any curious eyes. A stairway led down about 40 feet below the surface to the tunnel. The shaft was about 4 feet in width and 7 feet in height and was equipped with lights every 50 feet. I walked along the shaft for several minutes and reached a ladder leading up the shaft into total darkness. There was a switch on the wall at the foot of the stairs that I had been instructed to flip. It would signal my contact to open the exit hatch. I flipped the switch and after a few seconds, light spread into the tunnel as the hatch opened.

I climbed up the ladder and entered a room in a farmhouse. I was met by a man in his late thirties or early forties. He invited me to sit at a table and we discussed the expectations for the day. I was to stay at the farmhouse until late afternoon or early evening and then drive his Trabbi to Suhl. In Suhl, I would go to the Gasthaus Goldener Hirsch, where my targets had been seen on several occasions. Then I would have to play it by ear.

Knowing I had time to kill, I took a nap and then read some information about Suhl and the surrounding area. The population of Suhl was about forty thousand people. Founded in the fourteenth century, it was now the capital of the East German Bezirk Suhl district. Suhl was famous for its weapons and had a respected weapons and armor museum. Hunting was a favorite pastime of the locals. Suhl was also the home of the East German national shooting facility, which regularly played host to a number of international-level marksmanship competitions. The sound of gunfire was not unusual in the Suhl area.

I began the thirty-minute drive to Suhl. When I arrived I parked in front of the Goldener Hirsch and went inside to wait. I sat at a table and ordered a beer. East Germans were said to be paranoid and suspicious in the 1980s, so I was ready when the waitress asked me what brought me to Suhl. I explained that I was a student at the university in Leipzig (a cover that had worked for me before,) and was in the area to see the museums and do historical research. I sensed her apprehension fade as I finished my story.

The three women I was waiting for arrived at about

7:15 P.M. They sat away from the other patrons and ordered beers. After about twenty minutes, I went to the restroom, which took me close to their table. As I passed, I smiled and greeted them with a cheery "Guten Abend meine Damen." They looked at me, scowled, and didn't say a single word. I knew immediately that I could not build a rapport with them. Each woman seemed to have a sensitive radar on at all times. I knew further attempts at conversation would arouse their suspicions and they would report me to whomever they were working for.

When I finished in the restroom, I paid my tab and sat in the car to wait for the women to leave. At about 8:30, they left the Gasthaus and went to their Trabbi. I had no intention of following them, but I wanted to know which direction they took to leave town. They headed west toward the town of Dietzhausen. I waited a few minutes and drove back to Henneberg; my work was done for the day.

On Wednesday, I visited the weapons museum in the afternoon and then parked outside the Goldener Hirsch to wait. Knowing another face-to-face meeting would be fruitless, I did not go inside the bar. The women arrived at about the same time they had on Monday. I waited in the car while they were inside, but when they left there were so few cars on the road I could not risk following them. I would have been spotted immediately. I repeated the visit to the Goldener Hirsch on Friday. They arrived at 7:15 and left at 8:30, as they had on Monday and Wednesday. I assumed they had a strict curfew.

When I returned to West Germany that night I briefed Phil on the situation and told him that any attempt to move closer to the women would alert them to the fact that they were being watched. He nodded and said:

"The buzz on the street is that something big will happen soon. If we can't get any info from these girls, we'll just have to take them out. It's better if we do it over there. They technically don't exist in the DDR so there should be no official response to their deaths."

"So what do we do?"

"You tell me—this is your operation now. You know the lay of the land. But it should look like an accident. Not that that will fool their handlers, but in a way that's a good thing. I want them to know that we can get into their backyard and take care of business. Tell me what you need."

I had anticipated this happening, so I had already thought about what I would do. I asked that a gun, a roll of reflective tape, and a five-liter can of gas be waiting for me when I returned next week. I would wait until the following Wednesday, if that was acceptable. He agreed.

I went home to Veitshöchheim to finish my preparations and wait for Wednesday. Marilyn had developed a craving for Chinese food (I should have seen the signs, but I can be pretty slow when it comes to the obvious) and we had been eating at a Chinese restaurant across from the Hauptbahnhof in Würzburg quite frequently. The owner had taken a liking to us and had been giving us complimentary plum wines with our meals. Marilyn had also been leading aerobics classes on base which was good in that it kept her busy while I was otherwise occupied.

When the day arrived I drove to Ostheim, parked my car, and was driven to the tunnel. I put the tape in my pocket, the gun in my belt, carried the can of gas, and headed down the ladder. In East Germany I waited until 7:30 P.M. before driving to the Goldener Hirsch where, as expected, their car was parked. I made sure I was not being watched and then tore off two small pieces of reflective tape. I attached the first piece to the front of their car on the left bumper and the second piece above the driver's side window.

At 8:20 P.M. I drove toward Dietzhausen. Before the town, there was a bend in the road with trees on either side. I pulled off the road to the left and turned the car around so that it faced Suhl. As 8:30 approached, I turned on my headlights, stepped out of the car, and lay down on the ground. I heard a car coming and waited to see the two pieces of tape reflected by my headlights. As the car approached, I aimed six inches below the top piece of tape and pulled the trigger. The Trabbi swerved off the road and hit a tree.

I didn't think the shot would attract any attention because hunting and shooting were so popular in the area. The crash itself didn't make much noise, not surprising given the small amount of actual metal used to build the Trabbi. Regardless, I didn't want to waste time. I drove my car to the wrecked Trabbi and looked inside. The bullet had hit the driver directly above her lower gum line, exited her left cheek, and then gone through the window. I was relieved that the bullet had not lodged in her head. If it had, I would have had to extract it. All three were alive but unconscious. I knew what I had to do, but hesitated.

Slumped in their seats they looked like fragile young women who needed help. I had never hurt a woman. But I had to think about the broader context. Those women were willing and capable of bombing schools and killing innocent family members of soldiers stationed in Germany. They were enemy combatants without uniforms. I had my orders and I had to carry out my mission quickly. But before I doused the inside of the car with gas, I snapped their necks. I might have been a killer, but that did not mean I had to make them suffer. Then I poured the gas over them, threw a match in the car, and ran to my vehicle. As I drove toward Suhl I heard the explosion. Local officials accustomed to seeing the women in the Gasthaus every night would assume they had too much to drink and missed the curve; a tragic accident. What their handlers believed was up to them.

CHAPTER 19

MEININGEN AND THE SPETZNAZ

After unsuccessfully trying to start a family for a few years with Dale, I had been told by my doctor that a low sperm count all but ensured fatherhood would never happen. I had always wanted to have children but had given up on the idea. But Marilyn's cravings for strange foods increased, which bore checking out. My mother's cousin, Anneliese, had married an obstetrician named Gottfried Schwabe, who volunteered to be Marilyn's physician at no cost. I wasn't sure how interested she would be in having a relative as her Ob-Gyn, but she didn't mind. He gave us the definitive news that she was indeed pregnant and should be due in August.

We went to a furniture store and applied for a credit account to purchase furniture. Being a foreigner with no credit history and a limited income, I was not hopeful for our chances, but the store gave us a phenomenal amount and we were able to do a decent job furnishing the apartment. Then we went to a German bank in Würzburg and applied for a line of credit. With the Schwabes as cosigners, we received more credit and bought furniture to outfit the coming baby's room.

Having a child in Germany seemed more economically feasible than in the states. Companies involved in baby products—diapers, formula, baby food bottles, clothes, you name it—sent us free samples. My Uncle Gottfried was a phenomenal doctor and saw to it that

Marilyn received the best in prenatal care. Marilyn continued to lead aerobics classes, thinking that the better shape she was in, the easier the birth process would go. Relatives from throughout Franconia started visiting and offering to help in any way they could. Things were definitely looking up.

I continued to teach and began purchasing weight-lifting equipment, which I used to set up a small gym in a room outside of our apartment. My boss was pleased with the way the Suhl situation was handled. The deaths of those three RAF terrorists (I call them that because that was their intent) halted whatever had been in the planning stages. I didn't for a minute believe that what I had done would have a major or lasting effect on the political situation in Germany or the terrorist threat American soldiers and their families faced there, but it did at least temporarily dent the RAF operations.

I also continued with my occasional forays into the East which, for the time being, were tame and innocuous. Since Meiningen was supposed to be my AOR, I thought it would be in my best interests to become as familiar with the people and area as I could. I settled on three spots to be used as meeting points should the need arise, as I was sure it would. The first was the Meiningen Theater, a turn-of-the-century building that was bustling with people, making blending in easy. The second was the Saechsischer Hof, the oldest hotel (Gasthaus) in the city, which was built in 1798. It attracted tourists and, being a Gasthaus, it was a place to expect seeing unfamiliar faces. The third was the memorial to Johannes Brahms in the English Gardens. This was a more secluded spot and offered a higher degree of privacy.

Going undercover to Meiningen was actually enjoyable. It reminded me of being back in Berlin back in the early 1970s. By now, past the age of thirty (but feeling more like fifty) I was looking too old to pass for a student; my new cover was as a German high school teacher from Goettingen, a city further north in lower Saxony. I would have preferred posing as a university professor, but college educators seemed to be high on the *Stasi* suspect list. I duly memorized facts and figures about Goettingen so that if the need arose, I could reasonably pass myself off as a denizen.

Whenever Phil wanted to meet, he sent a note to me through my box at the Downs Barracks Education Center. On Friday, July 8, I received a message from him telling me to meet him at the Drei Linden the following Tuesday. When I arrived at 11:30 A.M. on Tuesday, July 12, he was already eating his lunch. He told me that contact had been made through a German agent with a Spetznaz officer stationed in Meiningen who had expressed a willingness to pass some documents to us that might be of interest.

Meiningen was at the core of what had popularly become known as the Fulda Gap, a corridor that began in the Erfurt–Eisenach region, crossing the border into the Phillipstal–Rasdorf region where there was a break in the Vogelsberg mountains through which the Iron Curtain ran. It was the shortest route from the DDR to the Rhine and was widely believed to be the point of entry for any Soviet invasion of the west. In case of a Soviet invasion, its 8th Guards army would need to cross only one secondary river, the Fulda, and if the invasion occurred during the summer, troops would not even have to do that.

The American answer to the threat of Soviet invasion came in the form of Operations Plan (OPLAN) 4102, a top-secret document that detailed how every soldier, tank, and piece of equipment would be used to repel the Soviets the moment they crossed the border. The Soviets held presumed military superiority; should they attack, the Americans planned simply to hold them off as long as possible until reinforcements could be sent from all the NATO nations. Obviously, any information that might have a bearing on those plans and possibly reveal anything in regard to the Soviet's military strategy was invaluable to our own war planners.

My job was to act as a courier for anything the Russian might want to pass over to us. I was to be at a prearranged spot in the English Gardens, reading Dostoevsky's *The Brothers Karamazov*. My contact was supposed to approach, sit down beside me, and say, "Такое тяжелое чтение на таком свету, дне лета." (Such heavy reading on such a light, summer's day.)

To this I was supposed to respond, "К сожалению, мое настроение намного более темно чем день вокруг нас." (Unfortunately, my spirits are much darker than the day around us.)

After that, he would rise from his seat and depart, leaving behind whatever he had for me to take. Aside from being an American with a phony East German ID receiving highly classified military documents (which meant that if caught I would be tried and probably executed as a spy), compared with other missions, this seemed like easy stuff.

I went to my spot in the English Gardens for two days with no success. My instructions were that we could not be sure exactly what day he would show up, if at all, as changes in his duty schedule were possible (and if the Soviets suspected his activities, he was as good as dead). On the third day, I became concerned when I noticed a man walking toward me from my left. He had a dark complexion like a native of one of the more eastern Soviet states, was slim and muscular, and wore ill-fitting civilian clothes. He sat down beside me, looked at my book, and spoke the agreed upon greeting. I answered with my part of the line. Then he pulled an envelope out of his light jacket, placed it between us, and without another word he got up and left. I casually picked up the envelope and put it into my book and continued to sit there and read. After another thirty minutes or so, I got up and headed back.

I was still being chauffeured to and from the tunnel

and Phil himself had been present in the car for the last two days, so I knew that he was anxious to get his hands on whatever was in the envelope. As I gave it to him, he looked at me and asked:

"Did you look it over?"

"Nope. Does it look like I opened it up?"

"Since I don't know what it looked like when you got it, I would have no way of knowing. So did you open it up?"

"Like I told you already, no."

"Aren't you the least bit curious?"

"Not at all. I'm just the delivery guy."

He shook his head as he opened the envelope and started to read the contents. Surprised, I said, "I didn't know you knew Russian."

"Don't you remember the first day we met back in Indiana? We spoke Russian back then."

Of course he was right. But why hadn't I remembered? It was not like me to forget something as important as that. I didn't make the connection, but I'm sure the increasingly heavy drinking was starting to take its toll on my cognitive abilities. I had added peppermint schnapps and ouzo to my nightly bottle of wine, and I was starting to forget small details more often. But like any emerging alcoholic, I rationalized that I must have had a temporary blip of memory loss or I was a bit tired, or I was preoccupied with the impending birth of my daughter. I blamed everything except the real problem.

I went back the following Wednesday, July 20, and took up the same position as before. Like the first time, my contact approached cautiously and went through the same ritual of commenting on the book. I gave him the same answer. This time he left me a much thicker packet, which he had slipped into a newspaper. I commented on that fact as I handed it to Phil, who chuckled as he asked me,

"Do you know what he gave us last week?"

"We've been through this already. I have no idea."

"The envelope had nothing more than a recipe for Borsch."

"Excuse me?"

"He was obviously not too sure about the arrangement. If it were a setup and he was being followed, he could say that you had asked him for the recipe. The worst they would have on him would be fraternization with an East German. This was his way of testing us. What you received from him this time should be more along the lines of what we were expecting. I doubt that I'll need you to go back over for a while. Sit tight until you hear from me."

Some time off sounded good. My Uncle Gottfried had determined that Marilyn was due at the beginning of August, and that time was almost here. For the next couple of weeks, I relaxed around the apartment and played Atari games on my television. The first week of August came and went and so did the second. We had one episode when Marilyn thought that she was starting labor, but it was a false alarm. Our nervousness at the delay reached a point when we tried things like walking up the big hill leading to the Marienberg Fortress (Festung) to move things along. Standing on the site of the first church built in Germany in 700 A.D., the Festung stood atop a fairly high hill. I figured if Marilyn marched up the hill a few times, it might induce labor. It didn't work.

Then on the night of August 24, she said that she was sure she was going into labor. We packed up what she needed and hurried off to the Theresien Klinik, where my uncle was on the staff. The Theresien Klinik was operated by Catholic nuns called the Sisters of Redemption (Erloeserschwestern). Although the nuns were notorious for their sometimes callous demeanors, the fact that I was a close relative of their main Ob-Gyn doctor resulted in graciousness toward us from the moment we arrived. They determined that Marilyn was indeed in labor and she was taken into a delivery room to await the birth.

After about eighteen hours of labor pains and with no signs that she was dilating any further, my uncle decided to perform a Caesarian Section. And with that, our daughter Annemarie was born.

I remember a German friend of ours, Lindy, who when she felt her labor pains start, drove herself to the hospital, delivered her baby within an hour, and drove herself home later that day. We, however, took the more prudent path. With Marilyn having had a Caesarian, she remained in the clinic for a few days. Since I had yet to be summoned by Phil, I was able to spend a lot of time with her and the new baby. Annemarie was a perfectly healthy baby with top scores in all aspects at her first physical, so as soon as Marilyn got clearance from my uncle to leave, we returned to Veitshoechheim.

There were still some minor details to handle associated with the birth. Marilyn and I were not married when Annemarie was born, so as prescribed by German law, we went to the city birth registry in Würzburg to register her birth, as well as for me to sign an affidavit attesting to the fact that I was indeed her father. By virtue of the fact that Annemarie was born to American parents overseas who were not in the country under any U.S. government sponsorship, she was in the enviable position of being a dual citizen.

I checked my box at the education center daily, and on September 12 Phil sent me a message that read simply, "Need you to go out of town on the 14th to pick up another recipe." My vacation was over for now.

When Wednesday arrived, I followed the usual routine and drove to Meiningen. When my contact arrived, he did not look at all well. Although this was a straightforward delivery-courier relationship that normally did not call for any talk, I could tell he had something on his mind, so I initiated a conversation,

"Что случилось, Вы выглядите больными." (What's wrong? You look sick.)

"Они подозрительны. Они знают, что кое-что

не правильно." (They are suspicious. They know some-thing is not right.)

"Если бы это было верно, то Вы не сидели бы здесь теперь." (If that were true, you would not be sit-ting here now.)

"They don't know it's me, they just know something, somebody is not right. The only reason I am allowed to leave the base is that I am a higher ranking officer and I have family that is connected at home. I am even sup-posed to help root out the traitor. The others, the en-listed men, are confined to the base. There is talk that we are all being sent back to Russia."

"What do mean by 'we'?"

"My whole unit.

"And?"

He explained it was not his unit's normal time for rotation. But if they were indeed sent back now, it would be precisely because somebody suspected foul play. Once back in the Soviet Union, the interrogation would be re-lentless and would continue until somebody confessed to something. Once somebody confessed, he would be shot. The rest would be sentenced to hard labor in the gulags for having harbored a traitor. The entire unit would be disgraced, and that disgrace and punishment would extend to their families.

"What are you proposing?"

"There is no more future for me if it all plays out like I think it will. I will either be dead or wish that I were. I must leave, and soon."

"And what of your family?"

"I am not married. As far as the rest, to hell with them."

"You know I can't take you out with me right now. I need clearance for this kind of thing. This could cause an international incident and could jeopardize other ongoing operations. I will be here again on Friday, if God allows. I will also bring more documents—contingency plans for war as far as this sector is concerned. If you are not here, I will have to do something else, possibly even kill myself. But I know that I can't go back to Russia."

That evening, I laid it all out for Phil. This was something that was too explosive for even him to decide on how to proceed. He said that he needed clearance at the highest levels, but based on what I had already brought back with me, he felt that the possibility of getting our hands on confirmed Soviet war planning would sell the idea. But concerns remained:

"Of course, there is the possibility that he is a double agent, giving us totally bogus materials to throw us off."

"Not my problem."

"No, and not mine either. You know, if they do suspect him and he is followed, it will mean death for you. There won't be any possibility of getting you out once they apprehend you."

"Can I go in armed this time?"

"*If* you go in. And if you do, I recommend it, even if it's to use on yourself because there is no other way out."

That was a sobering thought. I had never been programmed for self-destruction, despite what my drinking was doing to me (which I still considered as recreation, not a death sentence). I also thought about my wife and daughter as I spent Thursday at home with them. These thoughts had not occurred to me during the previous mission in Suhl. What had happened to me since then? All I knew was that this was not a job for a family man. But it was my job, and turning my back on it now would assuredly mean the death of my contact in Meiningen and possibly others as well.

Leaving on Friday morning was one of the hardest things I had ever had to do. I wouldn't know until I reached my vehicle drop-off point whether or not I was going over to deliver bad news or if I were going to pull an extraction. After kissing the baby good-bye, I had to go out the door smiling, as if this were simply another day of teaching in Fulda. I needed to control my emotions about this or Marilyn would worry. As I slid into the back seat where Phil was sitting, I could tell by his demeanor what the decision had been. He handed me a shoulder holster with a .45 in it. Then he spoke:

"It's a go. But there are strict instructions. If you sense anything out of the ordinary, you walk away. I know you want to pull this guy out, but he knew the risks when he got into this. The .45 is a last resort only. Nobody wants to see an instant replay of you involved in a gunfight on East German television. But if you have to shoot, you shoot. And you don't compromise the tunnel. If you're being pursued and you can't shake them, steer clear of the tunnel. If there's no way around capture . . . use your own judgment."

Before entering the tunnel, I checked out the .45; it had a full clip of seven rounds, and the shoulder holster contained one additional clip. After crossing under the border, I drove my Trabbi to Meiningen where I parked it at the Bahnhof right across from the English Gardens. I sat there for couple of minutes, trying to assess the situation. Although not particularly scientific, I had come to rely on my intuition in situations. Everything looked and felt normal—everything but my stomach. When I had taken a few more minutes to steady my nerves, I left my car walked to the Brahms Memorial, sat down with my book, and waited. Again, I tried to assess what was going on around me. It was hard not to keep looking around, but I had to look as natural and unconcerned as I possibly could.

I didn't wait long before my contact approached. I figured he had been there long before me and had been anxiously counting the minutes. He walked to me quickly, almost in a power walk gait; he was clearly on the edge. He looked at me. I answered with a quiet,

"Пойдем. Давайте выходить здесь." (Let's go. Let's get out of here.)

He nodded and let me lead the way back to the car, following about 25 yards behind me. I got into the Trabbi and waited for him to slide into the front seat next to me. We drove south down the Lindenallee, turned right onto the Marienstrasse, and after a couple of blocks turned south headed out of Meiningen. I reasoned that if we were being followed, we would have been intercepted by now, that is, unless they wanted to see where we were going. As we left Meiningen, I turned to my contact and asked him to place a hood I had brought over his head. I apologized, but explained that I had to have him do this as a precaution so that he could not identify where we were going. There was still the slim chance that he was manipulating us to find out how we were transiting the border. He understood and I continued to drive.

We were about 5 kilometers out of Meiningen when I saw police lights moving up behind us. This was bad, but it could have been worse. There was a single police vehicle behind us and we were merely 10 kilometers away from the tunnel. My mind was spinning. Running was out of the question; we were in a Trabbi, and besides, there was only one police vehicle, indicating that this was probably simply a routine stop and check. However, a Russian was in the car next to me who could not fake being German like I could. As I pulled over, I yanked the hood off of my passenger and told him to keep calm, that everything was under control. I rolled down my window and at the same time pulled the .45 out of my shoulder holster, keeping it down out of sight in my right hand.

The East German officer exited his vehicle and approached. When he reached my door he said,

"Ausweis bitte (papers, please)."

He was asking for our IDs—no problem for me, but a big problem for the Russian. No other cars were in sight, so I smiled, nodded, and then shot him once square in the chest. I tossed the hood back to the Russian and told him to put it on. Far from becoming agitated and unhappy about what had occurred, he seemed at ease for the first time since I had seen him that day. The Spetznaz is unique among the elite forces. They are in reality trained killers who often are not able to melt back into society after their service time is completed. Shooting this German officer who stood between us and our goal was something he understood. With that single act, I had gained his complete confidence.

There were only about 10 kilometers left before we reached the building containing the entrance to the tunnel. I led my companion inside at which point I allowed him to remove the hood. Several cars waiting for us on the other side in anticipation of our arrival; apparently, getting this guy was a big deal. The Russian (after all we'd been through I still didn't know his name) looked over at me as he was led to the lead vehicle and simply nodded. We both knew that we would never see one another again and there was really no need to say anything. I liked it that way, and I got the feeling that he did too.

Instead of returning to my car, which was what I thought I was going to do, I was taken for a long ride so that Phil and two other people I had never met before could do an out-brief with me. They winced when I started talking about the East German police car pulling me over because they knew that there weren't too many ways that could end positively, not considering I had returned with the Russian. They were far from thrilled when I explained how I had to resolve the problem—but they did understand.

"You're going to have to stay out of Meiningen for a while. As a matter of fact, it would probably be a good idea to avoid the DDR altogether."

"But why?" I asked. "Nobody there can identify me, except the guy who lives over the tunnel."

"Actually, it's not about you at this point. It's going to be too hot for anybody to be in that area for a while. Even if they don't know it yet, soon the Soviets will discover that a field grade Spetznaz officer is missing. He had to go somewhere, and the West is the obvious conclusion. There just isn't anyplace in the East Bloc where he could hide for long. And it will also be obvious that he couldn't have pulled this off alone. Once they figure that out, they'll be saturating the entire border with troops and dogs. They'll go over every square inch of fence line looking for a breech. When they don't find one, they'll go over other possibilities. It's only a matter of time before they find this tunnel."

"What do you mean by 'this tunnel'? There's more than one? And what about our guy operating the other end?"

"He's not stupid. If the pressure starts to rise, he'll grab his family and come over here. Or not. It's his choice and he knows it. He wouldn't be the first guy to go down with the ship by choice."

The fact that he glossed over my question about other tunnels made it clear that there were probably more. I was surprised at the thought, although I didn't know why I should be.

"In any case, it's best that all operations cease for the time being. That means that you get to take a break. Go home and be with your wife and kid for a while. Enjoy it while you can; it won't last."

There was another surprise for me. I hadn't thought about Marilyn and Annemarie even once from the moment I left my car earlier that day. Something else I hadn't thought about was having a drink. When I was on a mission, I was so focused that I didn't think about anything else. I didn't crave alcohol; I didn't think about getting high. Now that I would have some free time on my hands, I was afraid of falling into that pit. I quickly promised myself that I would do everything I could to quit, and just as quickly I realized that I was fooling myself. Instead I compromised and told myself that I would cut back on my consumption, but deep down I think I knew that that wasn't going to happen either. It was better not to think about it at all.

CHAPTER 20

WELCOME TO THE BUREAUCRACY

One quality I possess is patience; I do not rush, and I try not to anticipate. This trait was again tested over the next eighteen months. Phil wasn't kidding about lying low for a while. Although we continued to meet regularly and discuss ongoing situations involving the DDR, as well as the Soviet army and terrorist activities throughout Europe, my active participation in current operations was not required, if for no other reason than my AOR was too precarious an area to be in for somebody who was not local and not absolutely necessary.

Instead I taught classes. I was contracted through the University of Maryland to teach a Russian language refresher course for military intelligence linguists and analysts at Downs Barracks in Fulda. And despite the fact that I had taken few of these classes myself, the University of Maryland and Central Texas College added history, political science, and government to the subjects I was cleared to teach. With the added disciplines, at $1,300 per class and a limit of three classes per term, I was not making enough money to support a wife and child. What helped quite a bit was the fact that I continued to receive money from Phil from time to time. As a "contractor" and not officially on the Agency's payroll, I viewed those payments as a retainer to keep myself mentally and physically trained.

But my income level had to change. We had a nice

207

apartment with expensive Swedish furniture, a Saab 900 Turbo, an exercise room to which I was constantly adding weights and equipment, and we supposedly did it all on an official salary of about $15,000 a year. I was sure that somebody was bound to start asking questions sooner or later. The solution was to find a job in addition to teaching. I talked it over with Phil and we decided that I would apply for a civil service job working for the Army as a training coordinator at the Wildflecken Training Area.

Located 35 kilometers northwest of Bad Kissingen, Wildflecken Training Area (WTA) was close to the border with the DDR, in the middle of the Fulda Gap, which would make it an ideal location for me once I started back working in the east. The high, rolling hills gave it an Alpine atmosphere. The installation itself at Wildflecken opened its gates in 1936 as a Wehrmacht training post and was taken over by the allies after WWII. Now it was one of three Major Training Areas (MTAs)—Grafenwoehr, Hohenfels, and Wildflecken—maintained by the U.S. Army Europe (UAREUR).

I had no experience either working for the Army or as a training coordinator so there should not have been much chance of me being hired for that job, but somehow I knew that I would be. I was hired with a grade of GS-09 (a civilian grade roughly equivalent to an army captain) in June 1985 and began the daily commute from Würzburg. The long drive became tiresome quickly so with the help of the First Sergeant from the 144th Ordnance Company, one of the many units stationed at Wildflecken, we rented a huge house in the neighboring community of Bischofsheim and moved there.

I spent eighteen months working as the installation training support coordinator before a new opportunity presented itself. An internal inspection had uncovered the fact that the installation Security, Plans and Operations (SPO) officer was incompetent and that her operation was in complete disarray. She was relieved of duty and I was asked to step in and temporarily run the office until a suitable replacement could be brought over from the United States. I took over as the SPO in January 1987 and found the assignment fascinating.

The SPO developed and maintained all contingency plans for the area, such as the Command Transition to War (CTW) and the noncombatant evacuation order (NEO) plans. The SPO developed current intelligence reports and safeguarded all of the local classified holdings. The job required regular contact with German military and law enforcement agencies as well as with American military intelligence entities. In short, it provided the perfect cover for continued operations with Phil and the Agency, which I had been told would be resuming again soon. Additionally, it meant a promotion to GS-12, which was comparable to an army major.

I would have liked to have the job permanently but obstacles stood in my way. First, written policy dictated that civil servants working in the security and intelligence fields had to be hired in the United States unless they were retired military personnel who had been engaged in that field while in the service. Except for that, nobody had been hired in Europe into one of those fields. I was told in no uncertain terms that there could be no waiver of that requirement. Second, I had no official experience that I could cite. The GS-12 level was supervisory in nature and as such required three years specialized experience in the field of security or intelligence. There was no option of substituting education. Third, the position required a Top Secret (TS) security clearance owing to the classification of the war plans involved as well as the current intelligence message traffic. I had skated through the investigation for the Secret clearance, but a TS involved a Special Background Investigation (SBI) and was much more extensive. During an SBI, investigators would actually interview my ex-wife, old neighbors, and business associates such as Kenly. A multitude of questions were sure to be raised in those interviews.

I ran the prospect past Phil and he thought I should go ahead and pursue it. So with nothing more to recommend me for the position other than me saying I knew that I could do it, I petitioned the Civilian Personnel Office (CPO) in Heidelberg to be allowed to take it permanently. While I waited for an answer, I undertook every military intelligence correspondence course offered by the U.S. Army Intelligence Schools at Fort Devens and Fort Huachuca, as well as all of the Military Police courses from Fort McClellan. The potential position may have been as cover, but I wanted to do as professional a job as possible. A few of the courses I completed were Intelligence Analysts (Advanced), Electronic Warfare/Cryptologic, Criminal Investigations Warrant Officer (Advanced), Naval Topics for Defense Investigative Special Agents, Signal Security, and Information Security.

The most interesting course I took was the Psychological Operations Officer course through the John F. Kennedy Special Warfare School. The twenty-two subcourses covered such topics as guerrilla motivation, media manipulation, propaganda development, targeting religious and political factors, and insurgency exploitation. Before long—and with the intervention of a ranking Army general—the job was mine, much to the surprise of every CPO official up and down the chain of command. I was even awarded the TS without having to provide written explanations to the U.S. Army Central Clearance Facility (CCF), which is normally the case when any derogatory information on an applicant is developed. How was it possible for a man with a record reflecting allegations of drug abuse and a business association with the Hells Angels to negotiate through all of that with such ease? Hidden connections, that's how.

Now I was in an ironic position. Officially, I was a security and intelligence office worker while unofficially I was a contract covert operative who conceivably could attain the kind of information the official go-to-war contingency plans I had to implement were actually based on. Phil thought that this was the funniest thing he had ever heard. My new office was in the basement of the WTA headquarters building behind a heavy steel door with both a combination and a cipher lock for security. I was responsible for a staff of five people who included a Sergeant First Class (E7) as my Operations NCO, a civilian deputy, two Sergeants (E5), and an administrative assistant.

In addition, I also allowed the 205th Military Intelligence (MI) Brigade to station in the office two plainclothes soldiers who had their own missions. I found having these two men work out of my office hilarious. They were friendly enough but made a point of not being able to discuss their intelligence roles with me as I, "didn't have a high enough clearance or a need to know." They spent most of their time playing golf on the office computers, waiting for missions that did not materialize.

It was now 1988. While the two MI soldiers played Pebble Beach, St. Andrews, or some other world famous golf course on the office computers, I was now going back to the DDR. A local bar owner had come under suspicion of being a spy for the East Germans, and his contacts had been traced back to Meiningen. He was quite popular with the American soldiers on post and his daughter had married an American soldier. Units stationed at Wildflecken included the 1st Battalion (BN) 68th Armor, the 54th Engineer Bn, the 108th MI Bn, the 3rd Bn 52nd Air Defense Artillery (ADA), the 13th Chemical Company, and a host of smaller entities.

All of these soldiers visited this local bar owned by the alleged spy for East Germany, which was the closest one to the installation. The bar was a classic espionage set-up, a perfect way to collect information about troop movements, equipment, and capabilities. What was more ironic was that the two MI soldiers who were so secretive in our secure office environment were long-time patrons at the bar where they would regularly become seriously drunk and drop hints about their work to impress the German women.

There was an official, sanctioned border crossing between the DDR and the Federal Republic of Germany in the Meiningen area, which had been established in 1973. Germans from the west could cross without difficulty, making it easy for those with either political affinities for the socialist east or those motivated by financial gain to establish contacts in the east for the purposes of selling out their country. I had not used this crossing before because although I could easily pass as a native German (I was one), the East German spy network was so vast and meticulous that no cover story would have held up to their scrutiny for long. As an agent for the east, the bar owner (I'll call him "Franz") had no such problems and crossed the border frequently.

Franz was a suspect, but no concrete evidence had been tied to him. First of all, he never met with any DDR agents on this side of the border. Second, he never tried to actively recruit soldiers to divulge secret information, because recruitment was not necessary. Give a soldier enough alcohol and a good-looking woman to impress, and it's hard to stop them from talking. And finally, Franz was being investigated through official channels, meaning German civil and American military intelligence authorities. But being as they were official channels, they were also hamstrung by laws and regulations governing what they could and could not do. I, on the other hand, did not have those restrictions.

Franz's trips to the east were done with surprising regularity for the stated purpose of visiting family. It was not too hard to be parked on the side of the road between the border crossing and Meiningen and wait until his car came driving through. I followed him into town only once, because he always went to the same place, and followed the same routine. He met with a man at the Turmcafe im Hessensall, an upscale Baroque style café located on the Schlossplatz in town. They sat at a table and talked for about an hour, and Franz would hand over an envelope that I assumed contained information or pictures.

We were constantly catching locals taking pictures, from the hills in front of the main gate, of troop movement in and out of Wildflecken. We caught people taking shots at night using infrared film. The installation guards were old, overweight locals who would let people they knew onto the installation proper where they too snapped pictures all over the place. The locals did not take security seriously and I'm quite sure that many of these breeches resulted in *Stasi* files growing larger and larger.

My instructions for this assignment were simple. Follow the man, take pictures when possible, overhear what I could, and report back. I was not supposed to engage him or any of his contacts in any way. This went on for a number of months. It was a long time before the man was picked up by West German authorities and charged. Since he was allowed to continue his activities, I imagine that much of what he passed to his DDR contacts ended up being misinformation. From what I understand, he was eventually given amnesty under what came to be known as the Goldene Bruecke (Golden Bridge) program designed to reintegrate thousands of Germans who had worked for the east back into the united Germany.

The year 1989 was a momentous year for the two Germanys. Other East Bloc countries were experiencing changes in their political systems which prompted the East Germans to begin voicing their own dissatisfaction with the way things were going in their country. The results of East German elections held in May were declared rigged by election observers, which caused small demonstrations to break out. The reaction of the East German government was as expected, with brutal suppression by police and the *Stasi*. The fact that for once the East

German people did not slink back in fear of the brutality was not at all expected.

Then East Germans vacationing in Czechoslovakia and Hungary began storming West German embassies there, seeking political asylum in West Germany. This change in attitude as well as action became prime time news on West German television, which was in turn seen by East German viewers (although it was illegal for people in the DDR to view West German broadcasts, it was routinely done). Germans on both sides of the border were starting to use the word "reunification" more frequently. In September Hungary opened its national borders, resulting in thousands of East Germans rushing in to that country to escape the DDR.

October 7 was the 40th anniversary of the founding of the DDR, but instead of the usual state-staged celebrations, numerous massive demonstrations against the government broke out with one of the largest ones hitting East Berlin. Police and the *Stasi* reacted by beating and arresting more than a thousand people who were then further beaten and degraded in jails and prisons over the course of the next day. Instead of silencing them, the protestors started demanding that responsible authorities be prosecuted for what had happened. On October 9, in Leipzig, an estimated crowd of 70,000 demonstrated against the government. Here, for the first time, the government did not respond with force. Although no official reference to a reunification had yet been announced, there seemed to be no stopping the surge for free and open borders now, and on November 9, 1989, the Berlin Wall came down.

Shortly after the Berlin Wall came down, the CIA managed to acquire an incredibly massive intelligence file which a KGB agent had removed from *Stasi* headquarters (I don't think it has ever been explained why he would give the file to the CIA rather than sending it back to Moscow). They took this file, codenamed "Rosenholz," which contained the names of more than 50,000 *Stasi* operatives back to the Agency headquarters in Langley. Along with the names of the official agents, the Rosenholz files were rumored to contain the identities of more than 200,000 Germans on both sides of the border who had either been targeted by the *Stasi* or who had functioned as spies, informants, or couriers for the *Stasi*. Although the German government repeatedly made requests for the return of Rosenholz, Washington consistently refused for fear that the information would compromise double agents working for both the CIA and the *Stasi*.

However, beginning in late 1999, Washington began to transfer 381 CD-ROMs, containing the 381,000 file cards that made up the Rozenholz file, back to Germany. Remarkably, the records show that some 3,500 West Germans remained active as *Stasi* informants in 1989, the year the DDR broke up. These West Germans ran the gamut of occupations from captains of industry, government civil servants, trades people, and the media. Since the statute of limitations for *Stasi* collaboration has since elapsed, most of the traitors will not be brought to trial to answer for their crimes. Only those cases of high treason can still be prosecuted.

In response to the borders crumbling, Soviet leaders under Mikhail Gorbachev accelerated the massive withdrawal of their military forces from those countries of Europe, which they had occupied. Over a five-year period covering 1989–94, 363,000 Soviet soldiers, all seventeen divisions, were pulled out of what had been the DDR. They also pulled more than 337,000 of their troops out of the other East Bloc countries in central Europe.

While these momentous events were happening in Europe, my own life was undergoing massive change. With the borders being eased, there was no longer a need to have somebody like me who could function on both sides surreptitiously. Also, around my thirty-eighth birthday in April 1990, we found out that Marilyn was pregnant again. Seven years had elapsed since the birth of Annemarie, who was supposed to be our miracle baby, so we were shocked to find out that it could happen again. It would have been hard for me to imagine a more tranquil setting to have a baby than Würzburg, but Bischofsheim would certainly be in the running. We lived at Lilienweg 4, on a cul de sac in a small rural community. There was no industry, no traffic, and no noise.

The one doctor in town, Dr. Hagitte, with his wire-rimmed glasses perched at the end of his nose, looked like he stepped out of a Norman Rockwell print. He took on the prenatal care with grandfatherly concern. With a lull in the covert side of my activities, I spent most of my time running the Security, Plans and Operations office and coaching an army powerlifting team, which did quite well competing across Germany. Marilyn had been hired at the Wildflecken post gym and we had both been certified as United States Powerlifting Federation (USPF) judges.

At about the same time, I had an idea about how to bring in a little extra money. The Iron Curtain had, for all intents and purpose fallen, but the actual wire mesh fence used to separate West Germany from the DDR remained standing, except for where roads crossed from one side to the other. Along with my deputy, Rick Thomas, and my NCOIC, SFC Earl Corp, I went to the exact border areas I used to transit underground and cut down huge expanses of the fence and brought it back to the office. There, we cut these into smaller pieces, mounted them on plaques, and sold them to soldiers who transitioned through the training area. Thousands of these souvenirs of the Iron Curtain were sold at a hefty profit.

As Marilyn's due date, determined to be about Thanksgiving Day, approached, my health started deteriorating. At first, I attributed it to too much ouzo and korn, and figured that if I simply cut back on the drinking, I would feel better. That didn't help, so in typical fashion I ignored my symptoms and continued. Damien was born by planned C section on November 23, 1990, by which time I finally took myself to Dr. Hagitte and explained how I was feeling. He took a blood sample and after a few minutes came back to give me the news. I had diabetes. According to him, my blood sugar count was so high that had I not been in such great shape from the constant weight training, I would probably already have been dead, or at least in a coma.

I would have never suspected diabetes. I exercised daily, ate a high protein, low carbohydrate diet. Desserts and sweets were not part of my needs. As it turned out, I did have an aunt on my mother's side and an uncle on my father's who were diabetic. Bingo—I had the gene and, for whatever reason, it chose to go active on me. More extensive tests followed, which determined that my body was not producing any insulin at all—meaning I would not be able to control the disease with pills. From that point on, I would be insulin dependent.

The news hit me hard. Sure, I had taken all kinds of drugs during my life, but that was recreational. I couldn't stand the thought of having to inject myself three times a day for the rest of my life simply to stay alive. This was totally unfair! There should at least have been some kind of 'high' associated with so much pin sticking. I talked it over with Marilyn and we decided that although it was a crappy situation, we could deal with it. When I called my parents, the reaction was different. My mother wanted to know what I had done to become diabetic. It couldn't possibly be an inherited thing; her family was strong and healthy. It had to be my fault. I guess I should have expected that from her: Forget the evidence, convict the suspect.

Of course I had to run the situation past Phil. The services I was undertaking for him now were all situated within Germany. There was no need to sneak over/under/through borders and no plans for anything in third world countries where health issues could be mitigating factors. Most of what he needed me to do required day trips at worst.

But there were other major changes in my Agency work. Previously anything I did that could be considered "illegal" was accomplished in foreign countries—enemy territory if you will. My current activities were carried out within an allied country and if discovered could cause great embarrassment to the United States. And for that reason, I cannot say any more about them at this time. Suffice to say, he kept me employed.

My official job was also growing in responsibilities. The Treaty on Conventional Armed Forces in Europe (CFE) was signed in Paris on November 19, 1990, by the twenty-two members of NATO and the former Warsaw Pact. CFE was an arms control agreement that sought to establish parity in major conventional forces and weapons between the cold war foes stretching from the Atlantic to the Urals. The treaty set limits for both sides on the conventional (not nuclear) armaments, such as battle tanks, armored combat vehicles, artillery pieces, combat aircraft, and attack helicopters, which could be used in launching surprise attacks as well as larger scale offensive operations. In addition to setting limits on the total numbers of these armaments in Europe, CFE also set limits to how many of each armament could be in each of a number of zones it delineated in an effort to ward off heavy concentrations in certain areas.

Once CFE entered into force, each country which was a party to it would be allowed to conduct a certain number of inspections of sights within other countries to ensure compliance with the treaty. I was selected as the Site Commander for the Wildflecken area and given the task of ensuring that all units stationed there had exactly what they had reported as required by the treaty. I also had to have a handle on every unit that came to conduct training at Wildflecken, which could have been any NATO country at any given time.

My instructions were clear. This had to be a "zero defects" program. There was no room for error—no excuse for mistakes. Owning a single piece of equipment more than what had been reported would be seen as a violation of the treaty and would result in an international incident. The rules of engagement for CFE inspections were specified down to the smallest detail, from the makeup of an inspection team, how long they could stay at an inspection site, to what they could or could not look at, places they could or could not go, things they could or could not touch, what we were required to provide and what we could not provide them. Reading the treaty was like reading *War and Peace*, but I was expected to know it inside and out.

With guidance from our higher headquarters, the 7th Army Training Command located at Graffenwoehr Germany, my deputy, team, and I put together the data and plans necessary should we ever be selected. Once we had our plans in place, we were expected to go through a mock inspection conducted by an agency called The On Site Inspection Agency (OSIA), which had overall oversight for the process. The OSIA hit us on August 28, 1991, and put us through the paces. When they finished with us, my CFE team was cited as having, "one of the best operations in Europe," by the Commander in Chief of the U.S. Army Europe (CINUSAREUR), General Crosby Saint.

The treaty officially went into force in 1992. We were constantly under stress, as a Warsaw Pact team could descend on us with only a few hours notice. As the limit for inspection was being reached for that year, we were selected by Poland. Things immediately switched into high gear. An OSIA team arrived on site to prepare us for the inspectors. It was understood that the OSIA group would also have a number of CIA agents as well as people from the State Department posing as team members. At the same time, we were told that the Polish team would undoubtedly contain KGB agents posing as inspectors.

Although I was the site commander for the inspection, it was a member of OSIA, not me, who was actually in charge. He started barking out orders and informed me that I would be doing the in-briefs and seemingly direct the escort teams. However, virtually everything I said or did was dictated to me through wireless radio. It was made clear to me that I was not to answer any questions on my own volition but to take my cues from the OSIA. Apparently, my entire team and I were to be little more than ventriloquist's dummies for the next eighteen to twenty-four hours.

The inspection team arrived and consisted of uniformed personnel from Poland, Romania, and Yugoslavia. But again, we had been warned that the uniforms were irrelevant as to who or what associations these people had in reality.

The proceedings started off calmly enough but soon degenerated into a comical farce. The inspectors made demands beyond what was sanctioned by the treaty. The OSIA staff members quickly denied those unsanctioned requests, as well as some that were well within the rights of the inspectors. Both sides at times threatened to call off the inspection, which would in turn have voided the treaty. Loud phone calls were sent to the respective higher headquarters as the arguments went back and forth. But in the end, the inspection was completed with no official findings or defects and everybody huddled together in front of the headquarters building for a group picture! The whole experience seemed like a game of dare to see how far either side would or could push.

Meanwhile, another problem came about as a result of the introduction of the West German Deutsche Mark (DM) to the rapidly dissolving DDR during the early 1990s. Although Soviet troops had begun their pullout from the DDR, quite a few of them were left in the country. Their pay was not high to begin with and was of less value for those stationed in Germany because they were paid in Soviet Rubles, a currency people in Germany mistrusted. Anything Soviet soldiers wanted to buy on the German economy had to be paid for in Western currency.

Suddenly, the soldiers started selling everything they could, from mostly insignificant Soviet insignia and uniforms to AK-47s and other Soviet weapons. Anyone who possessed German Marks, British pounds, or—better yet— American dollars, could buy practically anything from the Soviet soldiers. If they did not have it, they would steal on order.

Ever since the border crossing 12 kilometers from Meiningen reopened, my deputy, Rick Thomas, had started a lucrative business with the Soviets who remained stationed there. His most popular items were Soviet submariner watches and uniforms from every branch, which he sold to American soldiers training at Wildflecken who could not leave their bivouac areas. Not unlike a traveling salesman, Rick drove around in his Nissan SUV and hawked his goods. If he didn't have what someone wanted, he took orders and headed back to Meiningen.

One day, Rick approached me with a problem. He had struck up a kind of friendship with two of the soldiers with whom he had been dealing. They had told him that they did not want to return to the Soviet Union and asked him if he could help them find a way to defect with their families. Although there was an open border now, they spoke rudimentary German and could not trust the formerly communist East Germans to be of any help. Rick was now asking me if there was anything I could do to help them.

At first I couldn't believe my ears. Rick had no idea about the extractions I had done or of anything outside of my normal office routine. Yet here he was, asking the one person who probably could help him most. After the shock at hearing the request wore off, I told him that I would look into it. I arranged a meeting with Phil and told him the situation. His answer was a resounding no!

"What the hell has gotten into you?"

"I just thought that this would be easy. We can do these guys a favor."

"Why? This is a no win situation for you. First of all,

there are thousands who would give their right arm to be able to defect. Why do we stick our necks out for these two? If we had a reason, OK, but we're not here to do favors. And what if it's a setup? We know nothing about these guys. There's no plan. Absolutely not."

So much for the Agency sanctioning this, but I had maintained contacts through official channels who might have had an interest in something like this, so I ran it through the military intelligence chain. If I was going to play any role at all, I wanted to make sure somebody was willing to take the Soviets once I had extracted them. I made a few phone calls and was constantly referred to the next person up the chain until I spoke with a major at HQ USAREUR in Heidelberg. It was his opinion that something like this would cause too much trouble politically at a time when the U.S. government was trying to solidify relations with Premiere Gorbachev.

That made it two strikes. My last shot was to call my German government contacts and ask them for guidance. The Germans had offered pardons for their people who had worked with the DDR; maybe they would also take pity on a couple of Soviet soldiers. Their response was a little bit better. They would gladly accept custody of these people but would play no active role in transporting them into Germany. I took that as approval, and totally ignoring Phil's strict guidance not to get involved, I decided to go ahead.

I told Rick that I had an arrangement with the German authorities and sent him on another buying trip to obtain more details on exactly how many people we needed to plan to extract. When he returned he told me that there would be five people involved: the two soldiers, their wives, and one small child. The men were excited but nervous. There was no time for any elaborate plans as they could leave the country any day to return to the Soviet Union. If we were going to help, we needed to act immediately. They were going to take their families into Meiningen the next day to shop; their hope was that we could extradite them at that time. Improvising and pressure are two things I prefer to do without, but here I was faced with both at the same time.

I had no idea what these people would have with them or how they would be dressed, but to be safe, I instructed Rick to find a couple of men's outfits that he though would fit the soldiers. The next morning, we climbed into his Nissan and drove to Meiningen. I couldn't believe how nervous I was, especially considering how much I had been through before. But this was different. First, as I already said, there was no plan of any kind. Second, I had Rick, the two wives, and the child to think about. I didn't want to be responsible for anything happening to noncombatants. I was beginning to think about what Phil said, "What the hell has gotten into you?"

We pulled up to where Rick normally conducted his souvenir hunting, and there they were. The good news was that the four adults were all fairly small; we could squeeze three adults in the back seat while the mother and child crawled into the cargo area of the SUV. As I feared, the men wore their uniforms. When I saw their uniforms, I froze for a second. These were field grade officers and members of a Spetznaz unit. This was something I definitely had not considered, but I was too far along to stop now. We packed them into the car and drove out of town where we pulled over so the men could change clothes. They left their uniforms in the trees and we headed west. I was constantly looking in my rearview mirror to see if we were being followed but all seemed to be going well so far. Although I had been nervous, I did not bring a weapon along because I did not want to risk harm to the child.

After about forty-five minutes, we reached my house in Bischofsheim. I let them into the house and asked my wife to bring out some wine to celebrate. Afterward I called the German authorities and described exactly who I had waiting for them. Soon they arrived with a healthy force of armed soldiers, surrounding the house in the process. After loading the Russians into a bright green government VW van, they took off with sirens blaring. I congratulated myself on what seemed to be an effortless and successful good deed; no muss, no fuss.

The next day at work I received a call from Phil.

"Word is the Germans got their hands on a couple of heavy hitters from the east—a Spetznaz battalion commander and his executive officer. Please tell me you know nothing about this."

What could I say? I wasn't about to lie to the man, so I admitted that I might have played a small role in what happened. He went completely ballistic. I hadn't thought him capable of the tirade he came out with.

"Do you have any idea what you have done here? If your name gets tied to what went down there, there will be hell to pay. You are supposed to be an official of the United States government—a civil servant working in a sensitive field with access to Top Secret classified information. How are you going to explain getting caught up in this?"

He said much more, much of it unprintable. There was nothing I could do—it was done. All I could do was hope the whole incident would fade away and be forgotten. No such luck. A few days later, a high-ranking German military official called an equally high-ranking American general and thanked him for the "two guys Haas and Thomas handed over to us." Apparently they had provided a wealth of information during their out-brief, and the Germans were delighted. Now phone calls started going out from the top on down. The same officers I had asked for guidance from now denied knowing anything had ever been discussed. The obvious conclusion was that this guy Haas was a rogue element who had undertaken this on his own volition.

An investigation was launched, and I was told that I was facing potential espionage charges. Phil had been right, there was no room for good deeds in this business. I could not expect any help from him. In fact, the Agency had nothing to do with this, but if my name was ever linked to the Agency, this would cause an international incident of epic proportions. Luckily, a civilian who headed the Security operation at our higher headquarters was willing to say that I did indeed call him ahead of time for guidance on what to do. I had given the U.S. side the first opportunity to accept the Soviets and they had turned it down. The Germans also readily admitted that they had gladly agreed to take custody of the Soviets. I was cleared, but I had also learned a valuable lesson: No good deed goes unpunished.

The investigation lasted a few months, during which time people avoided contact with me. By the time it concluded, rumors began circulating that Wildflecken might be included on the next Base Realignment and Closure (BRAC) list. Under the provisions of Title II of the Defense Authorization Amendments and Base Closure and Realignment Act or, the Defense Base Closure and Realignment Act of 1990, the Department of Defense periodically reviews its base structure "to more efficiently and effectively support our forces, increase operational readiness and facilitate new ways of doing business." The procedure begins with a threat assessment of our national security, which is followed by a restructuring of our forces and the bases required to adequately address that threat. Some bases might be restructured while others face closure. With three major training areas in Germany and Wildflecken the least important, it made sense that we would be on the list for closure.

Although expected, when the list was released and Wildflecken was on it, I experienced upset and depression. For soldiers and their families, having to move is status quo—they do it about every two years anyway. But for career civil servants and the local economy, a base closure is a life-changing event. I was in a particularly tough situation. First, my official job, my cover, was ending. Of course, I had worked for Phil infrequently over the last couple of years since the Iron Curtain came down (and I was not exactly on his best friend list since I had helped the two Soviet families). One of my options was to find another civilian intelligence job in Europe. But with the great number of closures across Europe, there were more people looking for jobs than there were jobs. I could return to teaching, but that had not paid enough to start with, and now I had two children to support. I could try to move the family back to the United States and look for work there, but for what was I trained? My particular skills were not generally sought after by corporate America. Or I could try to convince the government to offer me a job back in the states, which would require them to pay all relocation costs.

The last option was clearly the best, but it came with a whole other set of roadblocks to overcome. The biggest problem was that since I had been hired in Europe, I had absolutely no relocation rights. The government was under no obligation to find me a position or to pay for my way back if I were to find one on my own. But it remained my best bet. I finally found a prospective job that looked good to me. The Defense Intelligence College was advertising for an instructor in the field of sensitive compartmented information. I met the criteria for education and specialized experience, so I applied. At the same time, I applied for a position as a security specialist at Fort Bragg, North Carolina. One of my past secretaries worked there and let me know that the man who currently held the position was moving to Atlanta to take a job with the U.S. Army Reserve Command. Then, as I was about to be offered that Bragg job, the incumbent changed his mind about moving to Atlanta. I was becoming demoralized. Time was running out as Wildflecken was within a few months of closing.

However, the idea occurred to me that if the man from Bragg had reneged on the Atlanta job, it must be open now. I called my servicing civilian personnel office and asked them about it. Yes, it was open, but I could not apply for it because it was being offered for priority placement candidates first—that is to say, people with return rights to the states. I knew there were certain procedures that needed to be followed, but I was also familiar enough with the bureaucracy by now to know that if I followed procedure I would not be hired for that or any other government job. I called the hiring official and explained my dilemma to her while faxing my resume to her. She agreed that I was more than qualified, but her hands were tied by the bureaucracy too.

Then I called Phil. I told him how grateful I was for him getting me out of Iran, but that I had not asked him for anything significant before. I knew that he remained upset with me, but getting around the red tape in this situation should be easy compared with the manipulations he had pulled before to place me in positions where he needed me. Now I needed him to do this for me. He told me that he would see what he could do. Two days later, I was on the priority placement list, despite the fact that there was no legal justification for it. One more day and I was offered the job. Next, the government agreed to ship my car and my household goods back to the states and paid for airline tickets for me and my family. The final surprise was when they offered to pay all of our expenses like food and lodging for the next two months while I looked for suitable permanent housing.

None of this should have happened, but it did, and I was tremendously grateful. I called Phil and thanked him. The only thing of note he had to say was that as far as he was concerned, I remained a part of his team, and that he would be in touch. I knew what that meant, but for now there was nothing left to say.

We landed in Atlanta in June 1994, and I started as the U.S. Army Reserve Command Information Security Specialist the next Monday. Within five months I was the chief of the Security Division and exactly one year later I was promoted to assistant deputy chief of Staff for intelligence (ADCSINT). For the first time in a long time, I was in complete control of my own destiny, or so I thought. But there was something else far more sinister that was now in control.

CHAPTER 21

INTO THE ABYSS

From assistant deputy chief of staff for intelligence, I had been promoted again and was now the acting director of intelligence for the USARC, a position I had held for the past eight months since the retirement of Col. Mark Fauk. I knew that the position was a temporary one and that I would return to deputy director once a new colonel was identified. When the commanding general announced that the incoming director would be newly promoted colonel known in the command as "Wild Bill," I prepared to turn over the reigns. However, as soon as the announcement was made, people on my staff started to warn me that something had to be done to keep this man from becoming director.

Wild Bill was the boss from Hell. He was severe with everybody, and from my first meeting with him I could do nothing right in his eyes. He berated me during daily "counseling sessions" about my supposed substandard performance. He also let the rest of the staff know that I was persona non grata and that those who associated with me would suffer by extension. For my annual performance appraisal, he gave me an "unsatisfactory" rating, the first negative write-up I had received in my entire civil service career. Luckily, I had a stellar reputation with the command group and was able to show a couple of the generals the review before Wild Bill submitted it. Within minutes, he was summoned to the command group suite.

I don't know exactly what was said to him, but when he returned he rewrote the appraisal in glowing terms—and I was given a substantial cash award for "sustained superior performance." But his behavior toward me did not improve. Each day was so demoralizing, all I could do was go home and pour myself a tall glass of vodka to try and forget about it. I would usually fall into bed in a drunken stupor and get up the next day and have to deal with him again.

I honestly cannot identify exactly when I crossed from moderate to heavy drinker to full-blown alcoholic. I had been drinking every day—usually to the point of total intoxication—since 1987, but I did not consider it a problem. I exercised every day and felt fine physically. But I am sure that one of the primary catalysts in seriously increasing my drinking was Wild Bill's arrival in July 1998.

What saved my sanity during that time was the occasional assignment I received from the Agency. It now seems strange that doing what most people would view as crazy was the activity that kept me grounded. Whenever I received an assignment, I put in for a Temporary Duty Assignment (TDY) at the USARC and took off for a few days. With the great number of Reserve Component elements spread far and wide across the United States, Europe, and Puerto Rico, concocting a reason to go where I needed was not difficult. On returning I continued to file my paperwork along with the hotel, taxi, and other receipts (sometimes phony, sometimes real).

But now there was also a difference in how I completed my assignments. Whereas before I made sure I kept my wits about me when undertaking something dangerous or illegal, now more often than not I was either hung over or drunk. I packed a large bottle of Smirnov Blue (100 proof) vodka in my suitcase or made sure that my destination location could provide a steady supply of alcohol as needed. Since this was early in my alcoholism, neither my mind nor body was yet showing signs of breaking down. I find that remarkable considering that I had suffered through hepatitis while in India; by all rights, my liver should already have been badly damaged.

I survived Wild Bill's two years by carrying out four Agency assignments. The nature of these assignments preclude me from saying anything more about them here. However, I can say that each of them involved the permanent removal of a very real threat to U.S. national security. These were my last jobs for the Agency. I am sure that my handlers realized how I was becoming a liability to them because of my drinking. It was only a matter of time before I would compromise a mission beyond repair. I don't blame them for dropping me. Had I been in charge, I too would have dropped the person I had become, and much earlier than this.

The next director of intelligence and security was not necessarily a bad one for the command but was for me personally. "Big Al" was an honest man at heart. He was devoted to his family and wore the uniform proudly. However, we had a conflict back in 1994 when he arrived at the USARC thinking that he was the new deputy director of intelligence only to find me sitting in that office. He adjusted badly to the reality and carried heavy resentment toward me about which he made public declarations. He also had a horrendous temper that he made no effort to contain. What made the situation bearable in 1994 was that I was his boss and he was limited as to what he could do to directly affect me. However, he did broadcast his feelings to others in authority and made it clear that he would consider it personally disloyal if staff followed my directives rather than his.

Now in 2000, he was returning as my boss. I was naturally apprehensive about the change in our roles, but to his credit (and my surprise) he called me before the decision was made and said that he wanted to meet to talk things over. When we met, he assured me that if he were indeed selected for the position, as far as he was concerned the past was the past. If I agreed, he was sure that we could work well together. I suspected that there was something not completely sincere in his words, but I told him that his approach sounded great and I would do everything to support him.

When he came on board, our relationship at first went well. However, soon we were fighting again. For one reason, when Big Al wanted something, he wanted it right away, whether this was possible or not. He resented being told that a law or regulation prohibited him from getting what he wanted; he was interested only in results—damn the rules. Also, he had a bias against civilians, particularly females, who had never served in uniform. These two traits of his combined to create a volatile working atmosphere, which almost resulted in physical confrontations.

Before long my work days became as upsetting as they had been under Wild Bill. Adding to the distance Big Al created between us, he constantly pointed to the eagles on his collar and claimed that I had no respect for the rank and that, moreover, I never could since I had not served the country as he had. Here was a man who had never seen combat or been placed in danger. As a matter of fact, his entire career included only one overseas assignment. Additionally, although he was in charge of the Army Reserve Military Intelligence, he had only recently become military intelligence qualified. When I thought about all the dangerous missions I had undertaken in the service of my country, it was almost more than I could stand to listen to Big Al's harangues. But I was in no position to disclose national secrets simply to soothe my battered ego.

Like Wild Bill before him, Big Al gave me a substandard annual performance appraisal and, like Wild Bill, he was told by the command civilian executive officer that it was not acceptable. Being told that he could not do something he wanted to do made him furious. Yet he rewrote my performance appraisal and nominated me for an award.

Big Al's two-year run came to an end, but not before the cruelest irony was laid on me. In the Army Reserve, when a colonel on the primary staff retires, he is generally awarded the Legion of Merit, one of the highest of military decorations. Although the award is signed by the commanding general, its actual nomination and justification is written by the deputy who has served under him. Thus, as his deputy, it fell to me to recommend Big Al. I had kept quiet about so much over the years that I decided I would continue my silence and do what was expected. My glowing—and false—narrative earned him that which he most assuredly did not deserve.

The next few directors of intelligence were the exact opposite of whom I had unfortunately grown accustomed. Working once again became a joy, and I resolved that I would stop my heavy drinking.

As 2002 approached, I found that stopping myself from drinking was no longer possible. I was a chronic alcoholic. As I learned later, alcoholism is the compulsive consumption of and dependence on alcohol. It is progressive and pathological. I certainly qualified. I was at the point where if I did not have a good amount of alcohol in at least twelve-hour intervals, I would feel sick. I hated everything about alcohol—the taste, the effects, the hangovers—but I found myself unable to push it away. I told myself I would never take another drink, and before I had finished the thought I was downing another one. I drank a liter of 100-proof vodka a day and made sure I had an uninterrupted supply. I hid bottles all over the house. I bought the vodka, poured it into empty liter-sized bottles that had held water, and stashed them where I was sure nobody but I would ever look. To complete the deception, I stored one bottle of regular vodka openly with the rest of our household liquor, pouring only a little bit into a glass each night. This is what I let my wife see; this is what I wanted her to believe.

At about that time, my new boss, Col. Larry Hamara,

put me in charge of setting up and providing personnel support to the counterintelligence and human intelligence (HUMINT) operations for the detainee facility at the Guantanamo Bay Naval Base in Cuba. Before I could do that, I felt that I needed to go to Guantanamo and see the entire detainee facility in operation. So on December 5, 2002, Colonel Hamara, our command sergeant major, and I requisitioned a UC 35A Cessna Citation, one of the seven-passenger corporate jets the USARC maintained, and flew from Dobbins Air Base to Cuba.

Although at one time the detainee detention facilities at Guantanamo Bay had up to ten camps, by January 2002 Camp X-Ray was the only camp left on the northern side of Guantanamo. This was where the ranking Taliban and al Qaeda personnel were held starting after the American conflict with Afghanistan.

U.S. Southern Command (SOUTHCOM) was put in charge of the whole operation and it in turn activated Joint Task Force 160 (JTF-160) to deal with the detainees. Their primary mission was the care of captured enemy combatants. They established JTF-170 to handle the interrogation operations in support of what was named Operation Enduring Freedom (OEF). The camp quickly reached capacity, which forced the government to suspend flights with new detainees on January 24, 2002, when the population reached 158 prisoners. At Camp X-Ray, the detainees were kept in temporary 8' x 8' cells consisting of wire mesh. Housed one to a cell, they slept on mattresses on a concrete floor, Afghani style. The flights in were reinstated, and by March 27, the detainee count was up to three hundred men from thirty-three different countries. Construction was ongoing to handle the ever-growing numbers of prisoners, and on April 28 and 29, the entire population was transferred to the new facilities named Camp Delta. The security needed to watch over these three hundred men required an American force of more than 850 personnel coming from each of the five services.

Even considering the fact that the prisoners were kept in those 8′ x 8′ wire cages that looked a lot like dog kennels, they were treated humanely. They ate well, were given access to regular showers, were allowed their normal prayer sessions throughout the day as prescribed by the Muslim faith, and could consult with a Muslim chaplain whenever they needed. Red Cross personnel were constantly on site, making sure everything met international prisoner treatment conventions. American personnel were in constant fear of violating human rights regulations and so they went out of their way to treat the detainees well. One thing these prisoners did not have was any indication of what would become of them. The government had decided to treat them as illegal combatants rather than prisoners of war, which would have granted them certain rights, such as legal representation, under the Geneva Conventions. For all they knew, they would be kept there for the rest of their lives.

As I walked down the aisle between two rows of these cells, I was struck by the total lack of privacy. Everything a detainee did was visible at all times. The men's ages ran the gamut from teenagers to one detainee who was reportedly more than 100 years old. The guards had named him "old dead Bob" because he never moved and said nothing. I went to the unit that held the most violent of the prisoners. As I passed by one cell, the occupant called out, "Hey Rambo, give me the key. Give me the key." Most of the other prisoners were simply reading from their Korans.

When it was time for a detainee to be interrogated, his hands and feet were shackled so that he could move with only small steps. The prisoner was then led to the interrogation rooms escorted by two military policemen, one at each arm. The interrogation rooms were quite small. The prisoner was led in and told to sit on a chair with an iron eye bolt anchored in the ground in front of his chair. His shackles were padlocked to this bolt. The interrogator sat directly across from the detainee with his back to a wall that had a one way mirror in it through which the interrogation was witnessed. I was able to watch many of these interrogations this way. Although I do not speak any of the Arabic languages, each of the interrogations I witnessed seemed to be good natured. The prisoners smiled and had no trouble rambling on and on. One of the interrogators even gave his subject a McDonald's cheeseburger.

The assumption that all American personnel at the camp had to remember was that these men—no matter how young, old, docile, quiet, religious, or passive they might seem—were seasoned combatants who were hardened by life in a harsh environment as well as by years of tribal fighting long before the Americans appeared in Afghanistan. If given the opportunity, I had no doubt that any one of them was capable and willing to kill any American by whatever means was at hand. They were alert and cognizant of everything that went on around them. As an illustration, military intelligence had discovered an elaborate code consisting of tapping on the metal posts at the edges of their cells, developed by the detainees to pass news throughout the camp.

I packed my usual bottle of vodka for the trip to Cuba. Every evening I went to my room in the transient officer's quarters and drank while the others in my party went to dinner. Singer Jimmy Buffett was on the installation to give a free concert to the troops the following night, and it was rumored that his band would be practicing that evening. Yet even given the opportunity for a free Buffett concert, I preferred to stay in my room and drink. I was also pleased to find out that the Army and Air Force Exchange System (AAFES) had a Class VI store— the Army's equivalent of a liquor store—where alcohol was sold at outrageously cheap prices. There might not have been much for the service people to do at Guantanamo, but they could still buy good, cheap liquor.

The next day, December 6, proved to be much more interesting than the first. I was taken to see one prisoner who had been separated from the rest because of his rank and importance. Detainee 063, Mohammed al-Qahtani, was kept in a part of the camp that was no longer used and was held in a small wooden building that had once been used as a housing unit for guards. The house was surrounded by guards day and night and, except for some very short periods of sleep, this prisoner was interrogated around the clock.

Al-Qahtani was a Saudi believed to be the "twentieth hijacker," the man supposed to be the fifth terrorist on United Airlines flight 93 that was slated to hit the White House on 9/11 but ended up crashing into a field in Pennsylvania. Al-Qahtani had missed the flight when he was denied entry to the United States at the Orlando airport. He had been shipped to Guantanamo after being captured while trying to escape from the Afghani battle of Tora Bora. This was one prisoner I was sure that the Red Cross did not know about.

The United States government was positive that Al-Qahtani had information about what went into planning the 9/11 attacks, but he was not cooperating. He said mostly nothing at all, but when he did speak or answer any questions he used evasive maneuvers most probably learned at an al Qaeda training camp. Because of his reticence, sixteen "special interrogation techniques" had been approved by Secretary of Defense Donald Rumsfeld on December 2 for use on Al-Qahtani. These special techniques included depriving him of sleep, forcing him to stand for extended periods without rest, denying him the use of a toilet, shaving his beard, dripping water on his head, pouring water on him when he refused to drink on order, and forcing him to listen to loud, sexually suggestive American music. He was, after a regimen of intense isolation, sleep deprivation, and ceaseless psychological assault, on a fast track to becoming a physical and emotional wreck.

On December 7, a twenty-four-hour break in the interrogation was called to pump a massive amount of

fluids into him since Al Qahtani was losing consciousness because of severe dehydration. While some might
view the interrogation of al-Qahtani as a violation of the
prisoner's rights, I saw it as completely necessary to obtain information that could possibly preclude another
attack like the ones the United States suffered on 9/11.

After completing my observations at Guantanamo,
I returned to Atlanta where my disease continued to eat
away at me. By now my whole day revolved around pro-
curing vodka. Drinking a bottle a day, I was afraid that
the local liquor store would somehow alert my wife, so I
came up with a schedule for buying it. One day I drove
to the package store just outside of the gate at Fort
McPherson where I worked. The next day I drove a couple
of miles farther into the city of College Park. The day
after I drove to the store in East Point. There were three
liquor stores in Peachtree City I rotated between as well
as the package store off the highway where I exited for
home after work.

I stopped doing anything at all after work except
get drunk or plan to get drunk. My wife mentioned events
she was interested in attending and I told her that I was
a) too tired, b) feeling sick, c) not interested, or d) too
busy. I gave any excuse so that I could stay at home. Of
course I was more than happy for her to go wherever she
wanted. If she weren't around, I could drink openly and
not have to rely on the one-drink ruse.

Whereas at work I finally had decent bosses, now it
was the alcohol that made my job agonizing. After drinking a liter of supercharged vodka the night before, staying awake on the job became harder and harder. Occasionally I shook because too many hours had passed since
my last drink. But I always had the perfect excuse. I was,
after all, a diabetic, and I blamed any problems that I
exhibited on complications with diabetes. I then started
adding pills to my alcoholic mix, again—anything I could
find—either over-the-counter or prescription. Finally, I

stopped going to work altogether. I laid on the couch, sick to my stomach, and waited for an opportunity to drink more vodka when there was nobody around to watch. I even stopped going to bed at night so that I could take a drink every time I woke up throughout the night. My wife called my office and told them how sick I was, and everybody assumed it was because of complications from diabetes. The fact of the matter was that being diabetic increased the risk to my health that the heavy drinking was posing.

One night, I did go up to our bedroom and passed out on the bed. After a couple of hours I woke up craving more alcohol. With the intention of walking to the stairs, I rose and blacked out, fell down, and banged my head on the nightstand next to my bed. I survived that fall only to become progressively worse with my consumption. I became completely incoherent. I no longer knew where I was or what I was doing most of the time.

Then, on February 1, 2004, my wife came home to find a neighbor of ours in the house. I had called him incoherently, asking for help. My wife put me in the car, along with my son who was thirteen years old and could not be left alone in the house, and drove me to the hospital; the neighbor followed close behind. Knowing that the doctors would immediately recognize the problem as substance abuse, I tried to jump out of the moving car, much to the horror of my son who was in the back seat. But somehow, my wife got me to the hospital.

As I expected, the hospital staff knew right away what was wrong with me. As I waited in one of the examination rooms, I saw the walls pulsating, as if there were thousands of ants crawling all over them. I remember my sister-in-law, Joyce, and my sister Sharon being there, but I have no idea of what I said or did. It was decided that I needed to spend a few days in a detoxification unit where I would also receive some psychiatric observation and counseling. On February 2, I checked into a facility run by the Southern Regional Medical Center. After a few days of minimal counseling, I managed to convince the attending psychiatrist that I was stable enough to go home, although I did have to agree to outpatient counseling.

I thought that I had hit bottom and that there was no place to go but up. I was wrong. As soon as I returned home, I started drinking again. I had managed to hide so many bottles of vodka that there was an ample supply at hand. My wife set me up on the living room couch with a large jug to vomit in whenever I felt sick. The problem was that I felt sick constantly. More often than not, I just sat on the toilet with diarrhea while I vomited into a container. I was dying and knew it—and I didn't care. I called my son over and told him that I wouldn't be with him much longer—an unspeakably horrible thing to do to a thirteen-year-old boy, but my mind was so far gone that I really didn't think about anything except finally finding an end to my misery. My body was not far behind my mind as I could no longer keep even a spoonful of soup down. I didn't have the strength left to take more than a few steps at a time and soon didn't even bother getting dressed anymore. I was ready for it all to end.

CHAPTER 22

THE FINAL PLUNGE

My final plunge into oblivion came late during the night of February 15, 2004. I went to bed drunk, as usual, and immediately passed out. At some point I rose and headed toward the stairway to go downstairs for a drink of orange soda—at least that is what I told myself, although the trip usually resulted in more vodka. As I reached the top stair, a feeling of intense dizziness overtook me. The last thing I remember was saying, "Oh my God, no!" and seeing the stairs rushing up to meet my face as I fell forward.

I have no recollection of what happened next, but through the stories of doctors, my wife, and other family members, I can piece it together. I went down the twelve stairs hard, apparently without attempting to break the fall; it is clear that I was unconscious before I hit the bottom. I made quite a bit of noise, which brought my wife and brother, whom she had summoned to Atlanta from his home in Chesterton, Indiana, because of my deteriorating condition. They found me crumpled and bloody and called 911. The paramedics arrived shortly after 4:00 A.M. and assessed my condition as too serious to be handled by the local hospital. Instead, I was transported to the Atlanta Medical Center, which had a superior trauma unit.

After tests, X-rays, and an MRI, the doctor evaluating me determined that I had broken six ribs and numerous bones in my face. Worse, I was seriously addicted to alcohol and my body would have to detoxify. (I have been told numerous times that in a way I was lucky that I drifted in and out of consciousness over the next few weeks in the intensive care unit because that way I did not experience the full hell of detoxification.) A short time after being admitted, my lungs filled with fluid and threatened to fail. Emergency surgery was performed, but life was still touch and go.

Whereas I was certainly physically out of touch, I remember distinctly the gyrations that my mind was going through. I had many dreams, or visions, during this time that covered a wide variety of scenarios, and they all had one common thread—my death. I relived every mission I had, going all the way back to my first kills in Afghanistan, but this time things were different in that I failed and died each time. In some of these dreams, I was killed by my intended targets. In others, I was seriously wounded but ended up killing myself rather than say something forbidden. And since I was wounded and held by the enemy, there was no convenient way to bring about my own death, so I resorted to intensely lengthy and painful methods.

The one that was probably the worst was the final dream I remember having before I regained consciousness. In that particular dream, I ripped my own veins out of my arms and legs and slowly bled to death. I clearly "felt" each inch of vein being stripped from my body and suffered through it as if it were actually happening. Unlike normal nightmares, I could not wake up from this extended death scene. When I had finally managed to die, I was put into a coffin for shipment back to the United States. But death did not bring the desired relief because although I was physically dead, my mind continued to function within my body. I was not able to move or speak, locked in a pitch black coffin, but perfectly aware of what was happening around me. I heard the drone of the airplane engines and felt the jostling as my coffin was moved from one place to another. Additionally, during the whole trip, I heard the conversations of those around my coffin. I was condemned to spend eternity locked within myself—a horrible place to be.

While I was going through these mental tortures, my body was going through its own physical hell. A week after being admitted, the doctors determined that I had also fractured my right wrist, so more surgery was needed to put that back together. According to the doctors, I repeatedly tried to leave the hospital and thrashed around violently, trying to tear the intravenous tubes out of my arm, and escape from my room. They resorted to restraints on my hands and feet to keep me from harming myself or anybody else. And, according to hospital staff, I screamed nonstop for help. When I was no longer able to scream, I whimpered softly.

There were times when I did open my eyes and interact, to some extent, with those around me. But even though my eyes were open and I was trying to speak, I was clearly not in control of anything I was seeing or saying. I remember seeing people from my office who seemed to be moonlighting in the hospital as janitors and administrative staff. Erroneously, I concluded that they too had been patients at one time or another and were not able to pay their bills; hence they were forced to work instead. I also "recognized" one of my nurses as a lieutenant colonel from Fort McPherson and addressed her as such. The staff humored me, which only led credence to what I thought I was seeing.

Eventually I regained my senses and then had to face the reality of what had happened to me. In many ways, confronting what I had done was worse than the dreadful extended dream state in which I had been living. That was the first time I admitted to myself that I was an alcoholic. There was no hiding that fact anymore. As this was the second time I had fallen while in a drunken stupor, the staff psychiatrist suggested that my fall down the stairs was actually a suicide attempt. In my weakened state of mind, I agreed that it was possible. I knew in my own heart, however, that had I wanted to kill myself quickly, I would have certainly chosen a more reliable method than throwing myself down twelve heavily carpeted stairs. Yet the psychiatrist was correct with his idea: What else could I call my relentless drinking of vodka if not suicidal?

With the return of full consciousness also came the realization of how much damage my body had suffered. I had changed from a 235-pound, rock-hard power lifter to a 180-pound shell of withered, flabby skin. All of my muscle tone was gone. I no longer had the strength even to roll over in bed or raise my head off of the pillow. Like a newborn baby, I was totally helpless. But unlike a baby, I knew deep and total humiliation.

Physical humiliation was one half. The prospect of having to face my family was the other. Had I been able to run away and hide I surely would have done so. My wife came to the hospital regularly and I could hardly bear the look of sadness in her face. Yes, she knew that I drank, and that I drank too much, but she had had no idea exactly how much I consumed. She had covered for me with friends and with my job for much too long, and the strain had taken its toll on her.

I would not have blamed her one iota if she had decided to divorce me. Facing my son and daughter was also unbearable. I could not undo what I now realized I had done to them. I wondered whether I would be able to explain myself and whether they would accept my explanations and apologies. I was sure that I had lost them all, and I knew that I deserved it.

Another concern was over my employment. I held the Top Secret clearance with sensitive compartmented information access, which was necessary to do my job. If I lost the Top Secret, I would also lose my job, and then what would I do to handle the bills, especially the ones that were growing geometrically the longer I stayed in the hospital? Alcoholism was certainly grounds for losing that special trust that came with that clearance. The Department of Defense regulation covering the personnel security program (DOD 5200.2-R) lists as a disqualifying factor, the "habitual or episodic consumption of alcohol to the point of impairment or intoxication."

I had become seriously drunk every night for the past fifteen years. I was always able to lie about my drinking before, but there was no way I could explain away what had happened to me this time. I was visited by the command chaplain and a trusted friend from the office named Leon. Although I could be wrong (and I have certainly not asked them), as far as I knew they were convinced that I had simply fallen down the stairs while going for a drink of water.

On March 15, after one month in intensive care (and a hospital bill already totaling $302,000, *not* including the various doctors' costs), it was decided that I would be moved to a ward for people with psychological disorders for further observation and evaluation while I continued to heal. That decision was obviously made because of the suspicions that I had attempted to kill myself. I needed an oxygen tank to breathe properly, suffered intense pain from the broken wrist and ribs, and was unable to walk more than a few steps before total fatigue set in, but the surroundings were a bit cheerier. Patients attended daily group sessions with a counselor where we played word games to help the professional assess our conditions. The staff psychiatrist who had decided to send me to this ward came by to talk to me a couple of times, but each talk lasted only a few minutes, and I was beginning to wonder on what she was basing her diagnosis or treatment.

After a week on this ward, I began to move somewhat better. Soon, I didn't need the oxygen anymore, and I was able to get out of my bed without help, but the movement remained time consuming and painful. I lengthened my walks up and down the hallway, taking short, shuffling steps close to the wall in case I became dizzy. I was able to shower and shave again but with my right arm in a cast. I learned to use my left hand, including to feed myself, and more often than not, much of my food ended up on the floor next to my bed.

My wife and son continued to visit regularly and brought me high protein supplements to help me regain my strength. Their visits were emotionally painful as I was still not able to face what I had put them through. My wife wanted to talk about our relationship and how we would tackle the future. Although I knew that she deserved some answers, I was in no mental or emotional state to provide them. Additionally, the unspoken understanding that she could walk out on our marriage at any time and nobody would blame her added to the strain. I found it difficult to look her in the eye.

Then one day, the staff psychiatrist decided that it was time for me to leave the ward. I was elated at the news until she told me that she was not releasing me to go home. She was referring me to a substance abuse treatment center—news that initially crushed my remaining self-esteem. I had been in intensive care, a psychiatric ward, and now would be transferred to a substance abuse clinic. She was clear that I had no choice in the matter, yet after thinking about it for a while, I had to agree that I really needed further help. A facilitator on the ward assisted my wife with gaining approval from our health insurance carrier to have me admitted to Anchor Hospital, a part of the famous Talbott Recovery Center, located fairly close to our home.

When I heard the phrase "substance abuse clinic," I imagined myself sharing space with blithering addicts and other assorted mental cases. But despite my apprehension, it was clear that this was a necessary step before I would be able to return to the outside world. On March 25, after ten days in the psychiatric ward (and an additional $23,000 tacked on to my hospital bill), I was taken to Anchor by ambulance—a requirement to ensure that I would actually show up there. After going through the in-processing procedures, I was taken to my new home for the next twenty-eight days, Ward D.

I was shocked and amazed as I entered Ward D. What I saw was a clean, airy common area surrounded by patients' rooms. All ten people on the ward had private rooms and bathrooms. The patients wore regular clothes rather than hospital gowns. I hadn't walked a dozen steps into the ward before a patient named Louis introduced himself and welcomed me aboard. His greeting caught me off guard as he said,

"Hi. My name is Louis, vodka and benzos. What's your drug?"

Others also welcomed me and in the process told me for what they were being treated. I had expected everybody to be very private about their own addictions and too embarrassed to let anybody know their failings.

The backgrounds of the other patients astounded me. My vision of a typical alcoholic was one of a human wreck swilling cheap booze out of a paper bag while living under a bridge deep in the heart of the city. These people were all professionals. The Ward D patients consisted of three doctors, a dentist, a couple of housewives (one of whom was the wife of a member of Congress), a lawyer, a pilot for a major airline, a major contractor, and a student. All but one had completed college and a number of them held advanced degrees. I had been denigrating myself for having fallen so far, but I soon understood that mine was not a unique story.

Next, I learned the routine on the ward. Most of every day was dedicated to group counseling sessions with my ward mates. A few times a week, we attended lectures, along with the rest of the patients on the other wards, given by prominent doctors. Every evening we were required to attend an Alcoholic Anonymous (AA), Narcotics Anonymous (NA), or spiritual meeting. During the day and evening we had free time when we watched television, read, studied, walked, or socialized with the other patients. This experience felt a lot like college, without the Frisbees, booze, and drugs.

There was an even bigger shock when I met the people who were entrusted with my care and rehabilitation. The head counselor for Ward D was a lady with a master's degree in counseling who was also a recovering alcoholic and addict with fourteen years of sobriety. Along with alcohol, she had battled recreational, prescription, and hard drugs and had sunk to some appallingly low depths to feed her habits. As a matter of fact, many of the doctors on the staff had gone through recovery for a variety of substance abuse issues. Patients were not treated based on their textbook studies; they had experienced hell as I had, some even worse, and had returned to lives as productive people.

I met with the psychiatrist who had been assigned my case on a daily basis. I found out that along with suffering from alcoholism, a disease in and of itself, I was also clinically depressed and had been for quite some time. He started me on a regimen of non-addictive mood stabilizers. Ironically, until then I had viewed people who took drugs for depression as weak individuals who couldn't deal with life. The fact that I had self-medicated for such a long period was okay as far as I was concerned and not a sign of weakness because I did it for "fun." Unfortunately, the fun had escalated so far out of hand that if I saw a pill I took it, even without knowing what it was. Nobody's medicine cabinet was safe from me.

Days passed and I learned the structured rules on how group sessions were conducted. Everyone present was required to speak during every session. The counselor announced the topic and then each person took a turn to respond. Whenever we spoke, we identified ourselves by name followed by "I am an alcoholic," or "I am an addict," or, in some cases like mine, both. We were also required to announce our sobriety date, what AA refers to as a person's birthday. Considering I was starting life over again, the term birthday was very appropriate. Far from being the humiliating experience one might expect, it was actually quite liberating to be able to openly admit and face the addiction. Once my problem was defined, it becomes easier to formulate a solution to it.

The first task I was given as "homework" was also the first step of the AA twelve-step program: I needed to admit that I had become powerless over alcohol and, as a result, my life had become unmanageable. (I find it ironic that what brought me to this twelve-step program was actually falling down the twelve steps in my house.) Admitting my dependence was easy; it had become painfully obvious. But in writing out my answers to the various questions involved in this step I found that I was not willing to be totally honest with my counselor, my doctor, or the group.

I knew my actions throughout my life led me to who I was, and I was more than willing to admit those things to myself. At the same time, I felt bound by the restrictions placed upon me by my Top Secret security clearance and the secret life I had led, and I used that to create an emotional safe haven for myself. Whenever I didn't want to admit something to the group (or to myself) I cited the security clearance issue and retreated into myself. Nonetheless, I became more at ease with the group and the sessions.

Along with total honesty, there was another aspect of the rehabilitation process that was problematic for me. The twelve-step program makes constant reference to "your higher power." This higher power "as you understand it," is not necessarily any traditional concept of God, but rather a presence having a guiding role in one's life and thoughts—a presence to which one can totally surrender one's life. This was a tough one for me. The devout Catholic child I had been decades ago had long since come to the conclusion that Catholicism's particular God didn't care about me; from then on I acted on the belief that I was the only God I needed in my life. I made my own decisions and I controlled my own life. Clearly, I was not working out as a self-appointed God.

One evening, the patients in my ward were driven to an AA meeting on the other side of Atlanta. When we returned, I walked by the nurse's station, and the nurse on duty said,

"Roland, you had a call. Your mother called and asked about you and how you were doing. I told her that you were doing well, but that you were out and would not be back until much later. She just asked me to tell you that she called."

The rest of the group noticed that I stiffened as I asked, "My mother called? Are you sure you got the message straight?"

"Yes," she answered, "It sounded like an older lady, kind of weak or far away, with a German accent. She was clear. She said, 'this is Roland's mother.'"

It was then that I told the nurse that my mother had died exactly one year earlier. The color drained out of her face and she started shaking. Everybody else stood there in silence.

I won't pretend to understand or know what that phone call meant. There were only a few people who knew where I was, and all but one of them were close family members. None of them would have been capable of playing such a cruel and tasteless joke. Two things were clear to me in this episode. One is that the nurse swears that she talked to a dead woman (she quit shortly thereafter). The other is that I got the message.

While I was working on putting down on paper what impact my drinking might have had on my family, friends, and work, the counselor called my wife and asked her and my kids to write impact letters to me. In these letters, they were to describe what life with me was like when I was drinking and what it did to them from their perspective. Then, during one counseling session some days later, I read to the group my perspective on what my home life had become, after which the letters from home—which I was not permitted to see—were read to me in the group's presence. I wrote what I thought was a thorough examination and then waited to hear what my family had to say.

I was devastated. Their pain and suffering went so much deeper than I ever imagined. Here is what my son Damien, thirteen years old at that time, had to say to me:

Dear Dad,

I would like to begin by saying that no matter what I say in this letter, know that I still love you from the bottom of my heart. You mean the whole world to me, my best friend. I really would much rather talk to you in person. I know that this letter may hurt your feelings a bit, but I am only writing this to make us a better family. However, I have to write this, so I will give you some of the things that upset me.

I was told that after I made you promise on the phone that things would be different, Mom told me that you told your doctor that this whole ordeal has affected me more than you thought. That led me to the conclusion that you didn't remember very much of what you did while being "sick."

For a whole year, your sickness flickered on and off. Those were times when I felt that I did not have a father. All I ever saw of you was when your sugar got low and we had to shove cookies in your mouth to keep you alive, and when I heard you throwing up in the bathroom. I hated to look at you. It made me sick. When you came downstairs (which is where I was because I didn't want to be upstairs in the bonus room alone. I'll get to that in a moment) I would hide behind the couch if I was sitting there so that I didn't have to see you. I cried so much. I missed my daddy. But I also noticed that the "real you" bubbled back to the surface when you saw me. That gave me hope. At the times when you came back to normal, I always was so happy because I thought that things were back to normal. I was wrong. Mom and I would hear you throw up again, and the cycle started over. I thought it was from diabetes. When I found out that you were doing this to yourself with alcohol, I became furious. I didn't like coming home, even though it is my only refuge. I was sad when it came time for winter break. I didn't want to be stuck home for two whole weeks.

Now let me get to the reason I didn't like to be upstairs alone. One night while you were sick in bed, I was watching TV in the bonus room. You came in to talk to me. You started to cry. You told me that you had to tell me something, and it was very hard to tell me. You told me you were dying. And I believed you. You took me into your room to talk some more. "Just remember, I was your dad." You told me to take care of Mom. You said it wouldn't be fair to just die without saying goodbye. I respected that then, but now looking back on it, it just steams me up. You told me that Mom was still young and to be accepting when she re-marries.

One day, Mom and I came home from K Mart to see you and our friend from next door in our kitchen talking. That is when we drove you to Riverwood in Southern Region Hospital. You took off your seatbelt in the car. Mom could tell you were getting ready to jump. I was crying and yelled, "Dad, no! Please, don't go! You're my best friend and I love you so much!" You then started to cry and said, "You had a best friend." That hurt me so badly. Waiting for you to be admitted to Southern Regional, I stood outside shivering and crying. I hugged you for as long as I could. Walking from the car to the actual building, you said you loved us. Mom started to sob.

These are some of the things that upset me. I will talk to you further when you get home. Just know that I still love you so much. Also, I want you to know that most of the angry feelings I had are relinquished. I now understand that your alcoholism is a disease and you were addicted. I am not at all angry or upset with you, only with what you were. I am looking forward to having you home.

> Your son, best friend, and
> racquetball partner,
> Damien C. Haas

My wife's and daughter's letters were much the same, even though I know that my wife softened what she had to say quite a bit. And they all had the same effect on me; they tore at my heart. They also made me realize how far gone I had been by the time I took that fall—so far gone that I no longer had any idea of what I was saying or doing.

I now threw myself into rehabilitation full bore, with one exception. Although I tried to evaluate myself and my actions with total honesty, I could not bring myself to openly discuss my deepest feelings with the group or medical staff. No matter how good my intentions were, over forty years of barely speaking to anybody on anything more than a superficial level was something that I could not change in a few short weeks.

This was also true in my relationship with my wife. While she had been shocked at the extent of my drinking, now that I was in recovery she wanted some assurances from me. First, she wanted to know if I still loved her and if I wanted to continue in the marriage. Second, she wanted me to promise that I would become more communicative across the board, in other words, no more sneaking—and no more secrets. I was clear that I definitely wanted our marriage to continue if she would have me. I also promised that I would *try* to communicate more, but I could not promise any overnight results. She had always suspected that there was more to what I did for a living than met the eye, but she had no concept of just how much more. To reveal to her my entire history would have probably been too much of a shock for her to weather.

My rehabilitation was going well—so well that my insurance carrier felt that it was time for me to go home. I, on the other hand, wasn't ready to leave; actually, I was terrified at the thought of leaving. I wanted to go home, but as much as I had resisted psychological treatment at first, I had come to understand that if I didn't address certain root problems, I would be right back to feeding my addictions. The Anchor psychiatrist in charge of my case intervened with my insurance carrier on my behalf and succeeded in extending my stay for three additional short terms, which would bring my stay at Anchor up to a total of twenty-eight days.

On April 22, I left the treatment center and faced the real world for the first time in more than two months. I hadn't drunk any alcohol or taken any drugs in sixty-five days. This was the longest I had gone without altering my consciousness in the last twenty-eight years.

CHAPTER 23

BACK TO LIFE

As I look back, there are a number of things that have become clear to me. First, the state of intelligence operations in the United States today is inadequate and ineffective, and for several reasons. Many of our allies are unwilling to share information with the United States anymore. Their justification for this is that we have proven ourselves unable to keep secrets. Their assessment is absolutely true. The media in this country appear more interested in breaking a story than in protecting national security. The mistaken belief that the American public has a right to know everything that its government undertakes has trumped common sense security concerns.

This inability to keep secrets extends to the leadership of both the government and to a lesser extent, the military. Whereas the president, vice president, and other ranking members of our government and military need to know about any and all operations, they do not need to know the identities of covert operatives involved or the details of the operations. There was absolutely no need for Vice President Dick Cheney to know that Valerie Plame was a covert agent. There was even less reason for him to have talked about her position with his Chief of Staff Lewis "Scooter" Libby. Libby testified that Cheney told him about Plame "in an off sort of curiosity sort of fashion." Cheney trivialized how serious his offhanded comments were, when in fact they could be a matter of life or death. Plame's actual profession had supposedly become more or less an "open secret," yet those two men were responsible both for verifying a rumor and lending it credibility. In doing that, they allowed national security to be breached. The prime reason I myself have managed to stay alive and functioning in this field is that I never, ever told anybody anything about what I did. I didn't hint or allude to it at any time during the thirty years that I was active. The only one person who knew was "Phil," a succession of men who served as my contact. I trusted Phil to keep my identity secret and they lived up to that promise. As far as I know, nobody else connected my name with any operation. At the same time, I did not know the identities of any other people doing the same kinds of things that I was doing. This was not a club where people got together to swap stories and tips.

In his play *Hamlet*, William Shakespeare said, "there are more things in heaven and earth, Horatio, than are dreamt of in your philosophy." Hamlet's point is that talking ghosts and murdering brothers might exist outside of the understanding of normal men, but that these things can and do occur in the real world. Along those same lines, people really do kill each other (with their government's tacit approval) and things are seldom what they seem. Sometimes a covert operator is the man or woman next door, the people nobody would believe capable of such things who are the most successful. For those who struggle to believe this reality, they can find astounding evidence contained in the Rosenholz files.

In the course of my thirty years in intelligence operations, I have had to kill eighteen people. I don't make that statement lightly or say it as a source of pride; it had to be done and I was the one selected to do it. For those of you who have kept count throughout these pages, the numbers will not add up as I have discussed only eleven of them. There are good reasons why I have not dealt with the other seven here, not the least of which is my continued freedom.

Some will take issue with me describing what I have done as intelligence operations. They will, instead, call me an assassin or a common murderer. I can't argue with labels or a person's point of view, but I can say that what I have done is no different than what a soldier in a tank or a pilot in an F-14 does. A pilot drops a bomb that hits a target thousands of feet below the airplane. A sailor offshore pushes a button to launch a missile that will destroy a building and everybody in it. They are rewarded with medals and a hero's homecoming, something I see as justified and well earned; after all, they have done their duty.

Yet many soldiers, pilots, or sailors have not met and looked at each and every person they killed. When I said that I have killed eighteen people, I did not qualify the statement with, "I think," or "around." I know the exact number because I was with them when they drew their last breaths. I directly witnessed the results of my actions. Right or wrong, I was put in the position of doing what only God should do, and I have to live with those moments for the rest of my life. And beyond the fact that these were bad people, they were probably also brothers, sisters, fathers, mothers. Perhaps they were respected within their own milieus. I did not have the luxury of considering those things before I acted and so I can not allow myself to suffer for retrospective considerations now. To me, they were only objectives—necessary if distasteful tasks to be completed.

Maybe those who cannot see my actions as comparable to a soldier's will see them along the lines of a tradition I saw depicted in a movie recently. The Sin Eater is about men destined by ancient religious custom to eat a meal on the coffin of the person who has just died, thereby both symbolically and literally consuming his sins and ensuring the deceased's entry into heaven rather than hell. The problem was that the sin eater was consequently saddled with the very sins he had consumed and thus condemned himself to hell. I killed killers—bad people who would have gone on to kill many others one way or another. I removed these people from society when nobody else could or would; I have, in essence, eaten the sins they represented.

I have come to realize how wonderful it is to be sober. I have maintained that sobriety for two years now, a milestone that I celebrated with my AA home group who presented me with a bronze medallion to mark the event. My sobriety date is every bit as important to me, and even more so, than my actual birthday. I did not choose to be born, but it was a gift. I do choose to be sober, and that sobriety is also a gift. I cherish them both.

Although sobriety has been wonderful, it has not always been easy. On more than one occasion, especially right after I celebrated my first year, I went into a liquor store and bought a bottle of Smirnov Blue vodka. Then I poured it out without so much as taking a sniff. I have carried the bottle to the car and then seen the faces of my family and their pride in what I have become. I also have seen the faces of my friends in my home group and imagine what they would say to me to help get me over this hurdle. I don't know how to explain what is going on other than that I am grateful when that last drop leaves the bottle and disappears into the ground, down the sink, or anywhere other than into me.

I have real friends now in the people I have come to know through Alcoholics Anonymous. Whatever else we might be, we are all alcoholics who sincerely care about helping each other maintain sobriety. Unfortunately, I have not taken full advantage of what they have to offer. I have an AA sponsor whom I am supposed to call frequently, but I don't. What would I talk about? What kind of understanding should I expect? It would be an unfair burden to put on another person. But still, the gift that my friends give me on a daily basis, just by being there and by sharing their own stories, is well beyond any monetary value.

When I go to bed now I fall asleep after meditating, not medicating, and reflecting over the events of the day. I actually have dreams and remember them when I wake up. I hear the sounds of the night—the wind, the rain, the creaks of the house. It is a great change from passing out (mentally, if not physically) on the couch and wondering the next morning how I ever made it too bed. Now, I am tired because of the labors of the day, not because I am exhausted by the ravages of drugs or booze, and for that I am grateful.

I recently got my first speeding ticket in thirty-eight years of driving. Two years ago I would have been terrified seeing flashing blue lights in the rearview mirror, knowing that an arrest for DUI was imminent. While I was never afraid of getting killed, I was terrified of being identified as an alcoholic. With all the times I drove a car drunk or stoned, I am lucky that I never killed anybody accidentally.

I now also have a large portion of my physical health back. Although I cannot change the fact that I am a diabetic and an alcoholic, both of which have taken some tolls which I cannot reverse, those are two diseases I can, with help, control from this point on. I find that I have suffered some significant nerve damage. My eyesight has diminished significantly as has my hearing. But I am also on course for bench pressing 400 pounds again—not bad for a guy my age who couldn't lift 10 pounds over his head when he was released from the hospital a couple of years ago. Six miles on a treadmill is like a walk in the park; I barely break a sweat. I can swim in the ocean and know which way is up. There were times I would have had to think about that.

There are, however, some things that I will never fully recover, the biggest of which is with my mind. The memory I was once so proud of now skips and leaves blanks. I remember some events with excruciating detail—recipes from Pakistan, facts and figures about troop concentrations around the Iron Curtain—and then there's a skip and I forget a colleague's name. I can't seem to remember my two kids' exact birthdays. I haven't read or spoken Russian in more than a dozen years, and even though I taught Russian refresher courses to military intelligence linguists through the University of Maryland in Fulda, I find that knowledge and ability are all but gone.

And along with sobriety and clarity there are still, despite my equivocations and statements to the contrary, occasional periods when I feel heart-rending guilt. There are no post-traumatic stress disorder groups for people like me, no VFW clubs to join where I and others like me can swap stories about the old days. Luckily, there are a couple of medications that treat depression, which even a person like me, prone to substance abuse, can take. Those pills have become a part of my cost of staying alive.

Perhaps I am most grateful for finally having put all of these events in writing. It has been an incredibly cathartic experience and has allowed me to look at myself from a distance. In doing so, I haven't always liked what I saw, but at least I have been able to confront it and come to grips with it.

The Roland Haas who was born fifty-four years ago, who was a scared and abused little kid, and who went off to college dreaming of becoming a Marine, doesn't exist anymore. He has long ago entered the past tense. With any luck, the same will happen to the Roland Haas who recently finished his thirty-plus-year stint as a spook and substance abuser. The only fitting place for him is also the past tense; I hope he can find some peace there. I also sincerely hope that the present Roland Haas does much better.

Glossary

AA	Alcoholics Anonymous
AAFES	Army and Air Force Exchange Service
ADCSINT	Assistant Deputy Chief of Staff for Intelligence
AOR	Area of Responsibility
ARISC	Army Reserve Intelligence Support Center
ARNG	Army Reserve National Guard
BDE	Brigade
BLUF	Bottom Line Up Front
BN	Battalion
CCF	Central Clearance Facility
CFE	Treaty on Conventional Forces Europe
CI	Counterintelligence
CIA	Central Intelligence Agency
CINCUSAREUR	Commander in Chief, U.S. Army Europe
CNO	Chief of Naval Operations
CPO	Chief Petty Officer
CPO	Civilian Personnel Office
CTW	Command Transition to War
DCSINT	Deputy Chief of Staff for Intelligence
DDR	Deutsche Demokratische Republik (East Germany)

261

DET	Detachment
DIA	Defense Intelligence Agency
DIV	Division
DM	Deutsch Marks
DOD	Department of Defense
EO	Executive Order
EUCOM	European Command
FBI	Federal Bureau of Investigation
FRG	Federal Republic of Germany
GRU	*Glavnoye Razvedyvatelnoye Upravlenie*, Russian military intelligence service
GSFG	Group Soviet Forces Germany
GSG9	*Grenz Schutz Gruppe*, elite German federal border police unit
HAHO	High Altitude High Opening
HALO	High Altitude Low Opening
HAPPS	High Altitude Precision Parachute System
JAC	Joint Analysis Center
JRIP	Joint Reserve Intelligence Program
JTF	Joint Task Force
KGB	*Komitet Gosudarstvennoy Bezopasnosti*, Russian committee for state security
LOM	Legion of Merit
MFF	Military Freefall
MI	Military Intelligence
MOS	Military Occupational Specialty
MOSSAD	*ha-Mossad le-Modiin ule-Tafkidim Meyuhadim*, Israeli institute for intelligence and special operations
NATO	North Atlantic Treaty Organization
NCO	Noncommissioned Officer
NCOIC	Noncommissioned Officer in Charge
NEO	Noncombatant Evacuation Order

NGIC	National Ground Intelligence Center
NIT	National Invitational Tournament
NROTC	Naval Reserve Officers Training Corp
NSA	National Security Agency
NSFO	Naval Special Fuel Oil
NSW	Naval Special Warfare
NVA	*National Volks Armee*, East German National People's Army
OEF	Operation Enduring Freedom
ONI	Office of Naval Intelligence
OPLAN	Operations Plan
OSIA	On Site Inspection Agency
OSS	Office of Strategic Service
PLF	Parachute Landing Fall
POI	Plan of Instruction
PR	Pakistani Rupees
QSL	Radio transmission Q Code, meaning "I confirm contact with you"
RAF	(British) Royal Air Force
RAF	Red Army Faction
RC	Reserve Component
SAVAK	*Sazemanoe Ettelaat va Amniyet-e Keshvar*, Iranian organization for intelligence and national security
SBI	Special Background Investigation
SCI	Special Compartmented Information
SCIF	Special Compartmented Information Facility
SEAL	U.S. Navy Sea Air and Land Forces
SF	Special Forces
SFC	Sergeant First Class
SHIN BET	*Sherat ha-Bitachon ha-Klali*, Israeli military intelligence division

SOL	Shit out of luck
SOUTHCOM	U.S. Southern Command
SPETZNAZ	*Voiska Spetzialnovo Naznacheniya*, Russian special purpose unit (Special Forces)
SPO	Security, Plans and Operations Office
STASI	*Ministerium fuer Staatssicherheit*, East German security police
TDY	Temporary Duty
TK	Talent Keyhole (SCI Designation)
TP-AJAX	CIA and British joint operation, 1953
TS	Top Secret
USAR	U.S. Army Reserve
USARC	U.S. Army Reserve Command
USAREUR	U.S. Army, Europe
USMC	U.S. Marine Corps
USPF	U.S. Powerlifting Federation
VFW	Veterans of Foreign Wars
WSI	Water Safety Instructor
WTA	Wildflecken Training Area
XO	Executive Officer
YMCA	Young Men's Christian Association

About the Author

Roland Haas served many years as a CIA deep clandestine operative. He has also taught English composition as well as German, Russian, and English literature. Presently he is assistant deputy chief of staff and command senior intelligence officer of the U.S. Army Reserve Command. With his wife, Marilyn, and children, Annemarie and Damien, he lives in Peachtree, Georgia.